Locus of Control in Personality

E. Jerry Phares

Kansas State University

General Learning Press
250 James Street
Morristown, New Jersey 07960

Manufactured in the United States of America

Published simultaneously in Canada

Library of Congress Catalog Card Number 75–18260

ISBN 0–382–25073–7

Preface

An astonishing phenomenon in personality research in recent years has been the explosion of research on the concept of internal versus external control of reinforcement, or locus of control. The volume of research published has been remarkable, as one can see from a casual scanning of the references in this book.

A significant portion of the research is probably explained by the availability of the Rotter Internal-External Control Scale. Such scales always tempt people to produce large numbers of correlations. But beyond that, the notion of locus of control seems to have sprung alive just as this nation entered a long, agonizing period of scrutiny, self-doubt, internal division, and alienation. In short, locus of control has not just been a "measurable" concept in psychology; it has also articulated with current social concerns and problems.

The purpose of this book is threefold: (1) to provide some insight into the origins of the locus of control concept; (2) to discuss locus of control systematically as a theoretical concept within the framework of social learning theory of personality; and (3) to provide up-to-date coverage of the research that has been carried out. While several brief reviews have appeared over the years, few have been able to devote sufficient space to include history, theory, and current status.

Several people and organizations contributed to the completion of this book. Acknowledgment is made to Julian Rotter, whose social learning theory and point of view quite obviously enhanced whatever virtues this book may have. I am also deeply indebted to the National Science Foundation, whose grant support over the years (including GS-112, GS-1034, GS-2405, and GS-32265X) assisted in much of my own research reported herein and also in the writing of the book itself. Acknowledgment should also go to Kansas State University, whose atmosphere encourages a part-time administrator like myself to write such a book. The assistance of my family was also invaluable in ways that they little realize. I am also appreciative of the contribution of those graduate students who have worked with me over the years, in particular, William L. Davis, Elaine Ritchie Davis, Kenneth G. Wilson, and James T. Lamiell. Finally, I wish to thank Marilyn Whitaker, whose patience, promptness, and fine effort substantially facilitated the production of the manuscript.

Thanks go also the the American Psychological Association, Duke University Press, and the Society for Research in Child Development, for allowing material to be reprinted or adapted.

E.J.P.

Contents

I

Overview:
The Case of Karl S.

What happens when an individual develops a pervasive belief that no control can be exercised over the outcomes that follow behavior? Suppose that person feels that personal achievements, failures, victories, and shortcomings all stem from the capricious or unfathomable hand of fate or luck. Contrast this person with one who is convinced that such outcomes are the direct product of one's own efforts (or lack of them) or personal attributes. Will there be a difference in the behavior and overall life-styles of two such divergent individuals? Much evidence has been accumulating that suggests that when a person perceives rewards and punishments as being contingent upon personal actions, behavior is quite different than it is when such reinforcements seem to occur independently of efforts and characteristics. Let us consider an example.

The Case of Karl S.

Karl S. (not his real name) was an unmarried man about 23 years old. He was seen as a psychotherapy patient by the author in 1954 in a Veterans Administration Mental Hygiene Clinic. A variety of diagnostic tests were administered and several interviews were conducted to collect background information and to identify the nature of his problem. As therapy moved along, it became evident that Karl's problem was not of the common variety. That is, he did not evince the usual anxiety and neurotic complaints or symptoms, recognition and treatment of which make up part of the foundation of modern psychotherapy, and which strongly influenced therapeutic approaches in the 1950s. It did not seem possible to view Karl as a person in whom unconscious forces were striving to erupt into consciousness, thereby creating a variety of neurotic defenses. He was unhappy and distressed, but not in the classic neurotic sense.

As it developed, the essential basis for his discomfort appeared to be that he commanded only a limited repertoire of social behaviors; he possessed almost no interpersonal skills at all. Except for his relationship with his mother, his social contacts were virtually nil. Thus, in the important need areas he was not achieving significant satisfactions, and his expectations for achieving such satisfactions were quite low. So limited were his skills and understanding that he had not initially sought out psychotherapy as a potential solution to his problems. Psychotherapy contacts began as the result of a VA Claims Officer's recommendation.

With some general social learning principles in mind, the goal became an increase in Karl's expectations for achieving gratifications in two general need areas: the social-sexual area and the education-employment area. Psychotherapy was regarded less as an uncovering process than as a process by which I sought to educate the patient in specific ways of seeking and finding gratification in these two need areas. To make a long story short, therapy became an attempt to teach the patient how to find a job, keep a job, talk to a girl, interest her, make dates, etc. This was a painfully slow process. Usually, specific recommendations were made to Karl, and in the next session he reported on his attempts to carry out these recommendations, which were discussed in great detail.

After months of this, a suspicion began to arise that the initial assumptions were somehow mistaken. Therapeutic efforts were predicated on the assumption that as Karl tried out various behaviors and witnessed their reinforcement, this would increase both his expectancy that these and similar behaviors would be successful in the future and his willingness to repeat them. For example, it was assumed that if Karl were successful in carrying on a conversation with a girl, this would be reinforcing and would likely occur again, thus leading to an upward spiral of effects. This seemed to be the path of a "tried and true" psychological principle.

After a while, however, it became obvious that very little progress was being made. Karl was trying out behaviors as recommended, and very often he was successful in his modest attempts. But these success experiences did not seem to affect his expectations for future success. It was as if Karl were determined to be a prime exception to modern learning theory. Most of us accept the elemental fact that the more often a rat is reinforced for running to the goal box, the more often he will run there when hungry. For Karl, reinforcement did not seem to have any implications for the future. It certainly did not enhance subsequent reinforcement-seeking behavior by raising his expectancy that the same behavior would lead to reinforcement again.

It gradually dawned on the clinician that Karl did not perceive any causal relationship between his behavior and the occurrence of rewards. He attributed such occurrences to luck or to other factors over which he had no control. Once the clinician realized this, Karl's behavior made more sense. Karl was not responding in defiance of learning theory; rather, he was asserting that our learning theory was inadequate. It appeared that reinforcement may "stamp in" behavior only when the causal link is perceived by the individual. The view that behaviors followed by reward tend to be repeated while behaviors not rewarded tend to disappear is just too simple.

On one occasion, after much therapeutic discussion and coaching, Karl applied for a job and got it. It became obvious following this incident, however, that his expectations for being similarly successful in the future had not changed one bit. Although pleased that he got the job, he regarded it as merely good fortune. He offered a variety of explanations: the employer was partial to veterans, he just happened to feel good that day, or he had not seen any other applicants. Karl was adamant in his unwillingness to accept the responsibility for his success. There were comparable episodes involving asking young women for dates.

After many such episodes of this kind, a pattern began to emerge. In nearly every instance Karl's verbalizations suggested that he regarded reinforcement as beyond his control. In short, he believed the outcomes of his behavior were controlled by external factors rather than by any aspects of himself or his behavior. This stimulated the thinking that was later formulated in terms of belief in an external or an internal locus of control (defined by Rotter [1966]), which is the subject of this book.

A particularly salient characteristic of Karl's was that he possessed very little information that was of use in achieving relevant goals, whether they were vocational, social, sexual, or educational. Furthermore, he made almost no attempts to seek information; he did not seem to care much one way or the other. He paid very little attention to the cues in his environment that would have enabled him to cope more effectively with the world. As will be seen, such behaviors (or lack of them) are prime correlates of an external belief system, that is, a belief that outcomes are the result of factors other than one's own behavior.

Although such behavior had been initially puzzling, the suspicion grew that Karl was using an external orientation and that enabled an understanding of his behavior. That is, if Karl did not believe that his behavior was the effective agent in achieving rewards, then it would make very little sense to him to expend great effort in acquiring information normally considered relevant to need satisfaction. He apparently felt that if a reward was going to occur, it would occur, so paying attention to environmental cues or seeking information would be a waste of energy.

Karl, with his external beliefs, seemed singularly susceptible to influence, particularly when he felt that the influence was coming from someone with status. This may account for the fact that it was relatively easy to induce Karl to initiate specific behaviors; he regarded psychotherapists as having high status. He could be induced to try out a new behavior only to realize later that nothing had changed following his successful utilization of that behavior.

Karl showed little if any concern with personal achievement. Matters of exccllence or high standards were of little moment. Had he been administered tests of need for achievement, it seems certain that he would have shown a response style devoid of the usual signs of need to achieve. As far as can be recalled, reaching a goal never led him to raise his level of aspiration for the next occasion. By the same token, he was not prone to delay gratifications in any premeditated fashion. Again, it was as if his external orientation prevented him from organizing his life, or planning, which requires a capacity to delay reinforcement. The picture of an achieving personality that successively increases its level of aspiration while maintaining the ability to delay immediate rewards in preference for long-term gains certainly did not fit Karl.

In limited contacts with Karl, the clinician observed a curious mixture of calmness and anxiety. On some occasions he seemed uneasy, as if he realized how ill-prepared he was to cope with a potentially overpowering world. On other occasions he was relaxed, as if to say, "I know things are beyond my control and that my efforts are not really very important, so, why should I get upset? Whatever will be, will be."

Very little was learned about the antecedents of Karl's presumed beliefs in external control. Childhood events, socioeconomic variables, and other factors were hardly touched on. Therapy efforts focused on immediate behavior changes and were directed toward rapid improvement. The practical necessity of this orientation was dictated by factors such as the length of time the therapist was available, which precluded much rummaging about in the past.

It has been intimated that Karl's external orientation was mediating a whole host of behaviors. It should follow that altering his external orientation in the direction of greater belief in internal control should have significantly facilitated the initiation of more "desirable" behavior. Contacts with Karl were not extensive enough to permit a systematic exploration of the possibilities of changing his external beliefs. Even now, one would be ill-prepared to set about doing this. While some changes were observed in Karl's behavior (including improved job performance and a subsequent marriage), the extent of changes in his belief system are not known.

Is the Internal-External Control Dimension a Useful One?

The developing notions about internal-external control that emerged from working with Karl immediately raised two very important questions.* First, is locus of control a useful concept by which we can characterize Karl? Is it an abstraction that helps generate predictions about a person's behavior in specified future situations? It does seem that locus of control is a useful notion for understanding Karl's behavior. The extent of its durable utility can only be judged by the results of the research that has been and will be carried out.

Second, were Karl's perceptions highly idiosyncratic, or are there significant numbers of people who can be similarly described in terms of the locus of control concept? We were beginning to develop hypotheses about a continuum that had at one extreme persons who feel they control the occurrence of reinforcements through their own behavior ("internals") and at the other extreme those who feel reinforcements occur independently of their actions ("externals"). Such a hypothesis is extremely provocative and has a multitude of implications.

In order to confront these questions we could have attempted to develop a valid personality instrument to measure internal-external differences. However, rather than search for persons to validate such

*Out of the work with Karl S. the first faint outlines of the locus of control concept emerged. This emergence was facilitated by Professor Julian B. Rotter, who provided the clinical supervision for the case. Such a case provided an opportunity for applying clinical encounters to the concepts of social learning theory (Rotter, 1954; Rotter, Chance, & Phares, 1972), which culminated in the internal-external locus of control concept. Hints of the concept had been suggested in earlier social learning theory research (Lasko, 1952; Worell, 1956).

an instrument, we attempted to elicit these two types of behavior from individuals (volunteer students) by exposing them to two different types of situations. In the first type, the situation is structured so that individuals perceive that they exert control over the reinforcements that follow their behavior. In the second type, the situation attempts to convey a clear perception that individuals do not have such control. Thus, we sought to create situational analogues of the extremes of our proposed continuum. If we could not demonstrate the hypothesized differences in behavior in highly structured situations with a great deal of stimulus saliency, however, it seemed highly unlikely that we would find them at a personality level.

We have suggested that perceived locus of control may be viewed as a somewhat narrow expectancy arising out of a specific situation or it may be viewed as a relatively stable characteristic that persons carry with them from situation to situation. It is important to recognize that while individuals' generalized beliefs about control affect their behavior, so does the structure of the specific situation. We shall return to this point many times throughout this book. For the moment, suffice it to say that behavior is determined both by the structure of the situation and by the beliefs or expectancies brought to the situation by the person, with the relative contribution of each varying from situation to situation in lawful ways. A complex theory of social behavior (as described in Chapter II) can provide a framework for determining the relative contributions of situational expectancies and personality variables.

The initial research (Phares, 1955) was basically a study of the consequences of inducing in subjects either the belief that they are or are not in control of the rewards that follow their behavior. An attempt was also made to develop an instrument that could assess individual differences in a generalized tendency to construe events in terms of personal control. These attempts were crude, but the results did provide a limited basis for postulating that, indeed, there are reliable and valid individual differences in such expectancies. The ensuing struggle to develop more sophisticated instruments has increased our understanding of the internal-external control (I-E) dimension.

Plan of the Book

Much of our understanding of Karl was subsequently reflected in future research associated with locus of control. Indeed, one can very nearly outline the organization of this book in a fashion that parallels our previous descriptions of Karl. One may recall, for example, that Karl was an individual who manifested little interest in mastering or controlling his environment. He neither possessed the knowledge nor did he make any concerted efforts to acquire or utilize information to achieve goals. In fact, he did not seem to care much about such things. At the same time, he was quite pliable and showed little resistance to influence, particularly when it emanated from prestige sources; in some ways he could be described as a conforming person. He exhibited little capacity to delay gratifications, and he was not achievement-oriented. He was often defensive and sometimes anxious. The origins of his external belief system were not systematically explored nor was much learned about specific techniques for altering his locus of control expectancies. In narrative form, then, this paragraph parallels the Table of Contents.

Chapter II provides a brief introduction to the theoretical framework from which we shall analyze the I-E research area. This is social learning theory (Rotter, 1954; Rotter, Chance, & Phares, 1972), a theory that has generated much of the I-E work. From the time the I-E Scale (Rotter, 1966) was published until the end of 1969, there were over three hundred studies (see Throop and MacDonald [1971]). Since that time, the volume of published I-E reports has been even greater, as reflected in some of the more recent reviews (Joe, 1971; Lefcourt, 1966a, 1972; Minton 1967; Phares 1973b).

Chapter III presents an analysis of situations that differ in the extent to which they lead to perceptions of personal control. Here, the focus is on situations rather than individuals.

Chapter IV is devoted to a description of the development of several measures of locus of control. The emphasis is on personality measures that allow us to differentiate individuals by the extent to which they have adopted a generalized belief corresponding to a point along the I-E dimension. While the I-E Scale is highlighted, other I-E measures, suitable for both children and adults, are also discussed. It is only through the construction of such measures that we can study the effects of various locus of control beliefs on behavior.

Much of the research in personality and social psychology today is problem-oriented. In Chapters V-VIII the reader can see the results of attempts to apply the notion of internal versus external control to some of these important current problems in psychology and sociology. Some of the topics and concerns are mastery and control over the environment, conformity and reactions to social influence, achievement needs, anxiety, adjustment, and defensiveness. These are some of the areas that were so compelling in the case of Karl S.

Chapters IX and X address some of the crucial questions psychology must consider even though complete answers are presently elusive: What are the antecedents of enduring beliefs in internal or external control (Chapter IX) and how can these beliefs be changed (Chapter X)?

The final chapter (XI) draws some conclusions, offers some speculations, and suggests a few directions for future research.

II

The Theoretical Framework: Social Learning Theory

All of us seek to account for and to explain both our own behavior and that of others. A large part of our behavior is composed of social interactions, and our achievement of satisfactions requires that we look to others. As society becomes increasingly complex, this interdependence or social aspect of life takes on increasing importance. Furthermore, as Western people have become successful in building their technology, their basic survival needs have been secured. This has enabled Western people to turn their attention to themselves; they have become the object of their own study.

There have been a host of ways proposed to understand and explain human behavior. These have ranged from the rich and insightful theories of Freud to the scientifically more rigorous stimulus-response approaches. The elusive quality of truth requires that the theories proposed to account for human behavior be regarded as alternatives. None is necessarily right or wrong. Utility, rather than truth, is the yardstick by which we must measure such a theory.

Social learning theory is one theory by which an attempt can be made to understand human social behavior and the sometimes bewildering array of conditions that affect it. It was social learning theory that guided therapy efforts in the case of Karl S. The concept of locus of control emerged from this theory, and we can fully understand locus of control only by examining this framework. Bear in mind, however, that while the locus of control concept arose from social learning theory, social learning theory itself ultimately underwent some modification as a result of our increased understanding of locus of control.

Human behavior is so complex that it cannot be explained through single concepts. The actions of Karl S. were not solely the product of locus of control. The strength of his desires, his self-confidence, his aspirations, and his fears all operated in concert to direct his life. Thus, while the importance of locus of control can hardly be overemphasized, it is not enough. A theory is required that will enable one to determine the manner in which I-E interacts with other variables to produce certain reactions. Social learning is such a theory. As we review the research on I-E, we shall find that much of social learning theory has demonstrated the importance of I-E in influencing a wide variety of behaviors. Much less work has been devoted to an analysis of the ways in which the effects of I-E are moderated or influenced by other factors. The amount and kind of effects that are attributable to locus of control depend upon its relationship to other variables in that situation. Social learning theory can help us assess that relationship.

There are at least three reasons (Rotter, 1954) why a theoretical framework is useful. First, new hypotheses, theories, or modes of ordering evidence may be realized. Second, we often need to evaluate ideas and research long before all the evidence is available, and a theory can assist us in making such judgments. Third, a theoretical analysis provides a way of resolving some of the contradictions and ambiguities that inevitably arise from the use of different procedures or from the lack of a theoretical orientation. Often the diverse spectrum of reported findings can be understood by attempting to fit such studies into a consistent theoretical schema.

The major goal of this chapter is a presentation of the basic concepts in social learning theory that the reader must know in order to understand the nature of locus of control. The theory's major assumptions regarding how best to approach the understanding of human social behavior will be presented. Then the basic concepts of the theory will be explained. A fuller explication of the theory may be found in Rotter (1954) and in Rotter, Chance, and Phares (1972).

Major Assumptions of Social Learning Theory

Every personality theory either explicitly or implicitly takes a position on how to view human nature and makes assumptions as to which concepts will be most useful in explaining human behavior. These assumptions are never tested directly nor are they ever really proved or disproved. Rather, when the hypotheses and ideas that have been derived from these assumptions are supported by research, then we have evidence for the *utility* of those assumptions. The following are the most important assumptions of social learning theory.

1. "The unit of investigation for the study of personality is the interaction of the individual and his meaningful environment" (Rotter, 1954, p. 85). To deal accurately with behavior, personal determinants and environmental determinants must be utilized. Traits, needs, habits alone are not sufficient; situational parameters must be examined. This theme will be seen throughout the book. It is important to add the qualification "meaningful" noted earlier. Individuals respond subjectively to their environment on the basis of their specific learning history or experience. The objective properties of stimuli are not enough; we must consider how people interpret them. This gives a somewhat phenomenological quality to the theory. At the same time, however, within a given culture, individuals share a great deal in the way of common experiences. Therefore, it is unnecessary to rely exclusively on subjective determinants of behavior, as do Rogers and other phenomenologists.

2. The emphasis of the theory is on learned social behavior. With this social focus, it is contended that unlearned, biological determinants are less important than they would be were the theory dealing with perception or sensation, for example. The area of human behavior with which one chooses to deal determines in large part what kinds of concepts will be useful. In the realm of social behavior, learned attitudes, values, and expectations seem more useful than instincts, hormones, and blood pressure.

3. There is unity to personality. Individuals' experiences—their interactions with their meaningful environment—though varied, are interrelated. The common thread is their personality with all its stable aspects. New experiences become tinged by the effects of accumulated knowledge from previous experiences. Therefore, though change is still possible through proper selection of new learning experiences, it is fair to say that as individuals grow older their behavior and personality take on increasing consistency.

4. Social learning theory emphasizes both general and specific determinants of behavior. It rejects the polarities inherent in the exclusive use of one or the other. For many years, work by personality theorists has been dominated by the view that the major determinants of human behavior reside in broad, general traits that are responsible for the presumed consistency in behavior across situations. Psycho-

dynamic and trait approaches have shared the limelight over the years. They have encouraged the view that dispositions have a strong tendency to outweigh situational variables as determinants of behavior. More recently there has been increasing attention devoted to the apparent inconsistencies in behavior across situations (Block, 1968; Mischel, 1968, 1969). It seems unfruitful to argue over the supremacy of either dispositions or specific situational determinants in this context, as social learning theory regards behavior as determined by *both* situation-specific factors and dispositional elements. From this vantage point, the argument devolves into an examination of the relative contributions of these sets of factors. Social learning theory provides one possible framework for conceptualizing the manner in which these relative contributions may vary.

Moss (1961) pointed out that not all subjects are equally responsive to the same situational cues; a situational variable may influence only the behavior of subjects who exhibit a particular personality characteristic. If we pool subjects and disregard personality differences, the role of the situation may be attenuated. By the same token, strong situational cues may neutralize the operation of personality variables. Moss contends the optimum approach would be to consider the two classes of variables both as separate and as combined determinants of behavior. This is consistent with the use of moderator variables as described by Kogan and Wallach (1964).

There is another aspect of the argument between "situational" and "dispositional" views. Quite dissimilar behaviors are often emitted by the same person, and these disparate behaviors are often regarded as manifestations of a more basic disposition. Inferring genotypes or dispositions from diverse behavioral signs is neither wrong nor impossible. It simply has not been demonstrated, after many studies, to be a productive approach. All too often such inferences turn out to be post hoc exercises in imagination. Within social learning theory it is possible to infer consistency in personality from different behaviors that occur across situations. To the extent that several behaviors are seen by individuals as leading to the same reward, those behaviors are functionally equivalent. For example, a politician may tell jokes, kiss babies, or smile broadly, all for the same purpose: to gain attention from voters and secure their ballots. The fact that smiling is selected on one occasion and joking on another does not rule out consistency in behavior; on both occasions the politician is acting within a behavior set that is believed will achieve voter attention. However, the crucial objective is to demonstrate empirically in advance that, for a given person, certain functional relationships among goals and behaviors have been established. To devise an explanation for differences *after* they have been exhibited is to generate essentially untestable hypotheses.

5. There is a purposeful quality to human behavior. Behavior may be said to be goal-directed in the sense that people strive to attain or to avoid certain aspects of their environment. This is the familiar notion that behavior is motivated. The positive and negative motivators can be determined by observing the "direction" of behavior. An event or stimulus is identified as a positive reinforcement if the person's behavior is directed toward the achievement of that goal. When individuals seek to avoid something, it is inferred that the goal is a negative one. This view embraces the principle of the *empirical law of effect.* Definitions of drive reduction in terms of physiological changes such as tissue alterations and the like are rejected in favor of a less restrictive view that considers the directional aspect of behavior.

6. Finally, "[t]he occurrence of a behavior of a person is determined not only by the nature or importance of goals or reinforcements but also by the person's anticipation or expectancy that these goals will occur" (Rotter, 1954, p. 102). Expectancies are regarded by social learning theorists as prime determinants of behavior; reinforcement *alone* does not explain behavior adequately. In other words, according to this theory, behavior is determined by the degree to which people *expect* that their behavior will lead to goals, as well as by reinforcement through goal achievement. The magnitude of a given expectancy will depend upon the people's previous experiences with certain behaviors and their outcomes. Successful past experience with a given behavior will lead one to expect that it will work in the future. Failure will decrease the individual's expectancy that the behavior will achieve a given goal. Expectancies for the outcomes of behaviors are learned, and they depend upon the degree of success or failure they have enjoyed in the past. Changes in expectancies can be brought about by introducing new experiences that alter previous patterns of success and failure.

Basic Concepts of Social Learning Theory

Social learning theory is a theory of how choices are made by individuals from the variety of potential behaviors available to them. Naturally, if only one behavior is possible, one does not have to be a psychologist to predict it. Usually, therefore, the task of prediction involves ordering the potential behaviors in some fashion to determine which is potentially the strongest and thus most likely to occur.

To determine which behavior has the strongest potential for occurrence, one must consider *expectancy, reinforcement value,* and the *psychological situation.* One might conveniently state the relationships among these variables as they are used to predict goal-directed behavior by the following formula:

$$BP_{x,s_1,R_a} = f(E_{x,R_a,s_1} \, \& \, RV_{a,s_1})$$

This formula is read, "The potential for behavior x to occur, in situation 1 in relation to reinforcement a, is a function of the expectancy of the occurrence of reinforcement a, following behavior x in situation 1, and the value of reinforcement a in situation 1" (Rotter, Chance, & Phares, 1972, p. 14). Put most generally, it is clearly demonstrable that a behavior potential is higher when expectancy and reinforcement value are both high, or when one is high and the other moderate, than when both are low. This "more or less" quality will have to suffice until the exact nature of the mathematical relationship is ascertained.

An example may clarify the foregoing. Imagine a male employee who must submit a departmental report to his boss tomorrow. Our goal is to predict his behavior tonight. Assume that he has three possibilities of actions open to him: he may work on the report, watch a football game on television, or call his girlfriend for a date. In examining these possibilities, it is found that

1. Although he has a very high expectancy that he can spend the evening watching television, he does not really care very much for either football team (low reinforcement).
2. While his heterosexual needs are pretty strong, he is certain that his girlfriend is studying for an important exam and will not go out (very low expectancy).
3. His desire to turn in a good report is quite strong because he knows that it will lead ultimately to a sizable raise.

In this instance it could be predicted that alternative 3 would occur since both reinforcement value and expectancy are high. In the other cases, either reinforcement value or expectancy is low.

Although social learning theory may seem complex in requiring that expectancies, reinforcement values, and the situation all be considered in making predictions about behavior, such complexity appears preferable to relying on a single variable such as a trait, habit, or other internal characteristic. An individual's behavior potential is far from being static; it changes as that person encounters new experiences that in turn lead to changes in his or her expectancies or in the values he or she ascribes to reinforcements.

REINFORCEMENT AND NEEDS

Before proceeding further, let us define our terms. A *reinforcement* is anything that has an effect on the occurrence, direction, or kind of behavior. Further, the *value* of a reinforcement for a person may be defined as "the degree of preference for any reinforcement to occur if the possibilities of their occurring were all equal" (Rotter, 1954, p. 107). Thus, reinforcement value is a relative term. The value of a reinforcement is determined by its strength relative to that of other anticipated reinforcements.

What determines the value of a reinforcement? This is determined by the value of those reinforcements with which it is associated and by the expectancy that those associated reinforcements will occur. The primary reinforcers—e.g., food and water—are perhaps the easiest to understand. Organisms always have a greater or lesser need for them, and their value as reinforcements depends on the organism's body requirements at the time. For example, the degree to which a rat will work at a task for a food reward depends largely on how "hungry" it is. If other reinforcements are simultaneously available to the rat (e.g., water, a compatible sex object), it will have to make choices, and presumably the frequencies of its choices over a period of time will reflect the relative values of reinforcements for the rat. Humans value a wide range of objects and events—not only food and water but also other objects that enable them to obtain items perceived as needs. For example, money acquires reinforcing properties because it allows the purchase of goods and services that have value for humans (e.g., food, clothes, prestige). On the other hand, criticism from loved ones regarding our desire for money might reduce its value slightly. When an individual behaves so as to obtain a certain reinforcer, it may be concluded that, at that moment, that reinforcer has a greater value than others the individual might have sought. To some extent the value of reinforcements can be raised or lowered by manipulating the outcomes with which they are associated (and the expectancies for those outcomes).

Needs develop originally from the learned consequences of biological or other built-in reinforcements. Thus, a child's need for the presence of others may have originated in the fact that others were present during the satisfaction of hunger, thirst, contact comfort, etc. A need is expressed by a collection of behaviors that have become functionally related—that is, they all lead to the same or similar reinforcements. How strong a given need may be depends upon the value of the goals toward which the need is directed and the overall expectancy of attaining them. Generally speaking, within social learning theory both reinforcement values and needs are inferred from the individual's behavior. When the focus of discussion is on the person, the term "need" is used; when the focus is on the environmental factors determining the direction of behavior, the term goal or reinforcement value is used. Thus, admiration by girls or peers may be environmental factors or reinforcements that generate competitive behavior in the male; in so behaving, he is expressing a need for recognition-status.

While there has been reluctance to establish an "official" list of needs (since no one is motivated by exactly the same pattern of goals), a list of *learned needs* that have widespread relevance has been suggested (see Rotter [1954], p. 132). They include Recognition-Status, Protection-Dependency, Dominance, Independence, Love and Affection, and Physical Comfort. In today's advanced society, it is probably the learned needs that are most prominent in affecting human social behavior—the focus of social learning theory. Once initial learning has occurred, cues in the environment seem to be more compelling influences on the direction of social behavior than are internal, cyclical states. Of course, one must remember that this may certainly not be true with subhuman species, human infants, or even adults under severe conditions of food or water deprivation, for example.

EXPECTANCY

Expectancy is the "probability held by the individual that a particular reinforcement will occur as a function of a specific behavior on his part in a specific situation or situations" (Rotter, 1954, p. 107). While generally expectancy is independent of the value of the reinforcement, there may be specific conditions in which a learned relationship exists between them. For example, in Western culture, people generally learn that highly valued achievement goals are difficult to attain, yet nothing demands that valued goals automatically create a low expectancy of occurrence. Expectancies are measured on an absolute scale, in contrast to reinforcement value, which implies preference and therefore relativity. It should be emphasized that expectancy is a *subjective* probability. It is determined not just by one's objective past history of reinforcement but also by expectancies generalized from other, related behavior-reinforcement sequences.

When individuals are in a relatively novel situation, *generalized expectancies* will be more important in determining their expectancy than will *specific expectancies* based on prior experience in that situation. When individuals have had a great deal of experience in a given situation, generalized expectancies will prove of little signficance while specific expectancies will be the primary determinants. To illustrate: suppose a college student who has never taken any work in chemistry is asked to state her expectancy for receiving an A on her first quiz in the course. Her statement might be determined by her overall experience in those science-related courses that she regards as similar. That is, she has no specific expectancies based on prior chemistry experience. However, if that same question were posed at the end of the chemistry course, her answer would be based almost entirely on her specific experience with chemistry quizzes and hardly at all on expectancies generalized from related courses.

THE SITUATION

Implicit in social learning theory is the view that the *psychological situation* is an extremely important determinant of behavior. This view is in sharp contrast to those positions that state that once the basic elements of personality are identified, reliable prediction follows. Although personality traits or dispositions are important, failure to take account of the psychological situation significantly reduces predictive efficiency. There can be no substitute for the careful analysis of situations in order to identify the cues that may directly affect the expectancies and reinforcement values for a given person. As noted earlier, there is similarity in behavior from situation to situation. In part, this is because a given individual may see several situations as similar even though they are objectively dissimilar. For example, a man may categorize both the bedroom and the playing field as occasions for the demonstration of masculinity and therefore be aggressive in both. Another individual might behave very aggressively on the playing field and be very timid in the bedroom because the latter arouses specific expectancies for failure. The crucial thing is to determine both the specific and the general effects on behavior that a given situation will have by the manner in which that situation affects expectancies and reinforcement values.

Descriptive categories for different situations would be useful; however, little research in this vein has been done. Rotter (1955) has made a preliminary effort by describing four methods of categorizing situations, but little in the way of implementation has occurred.

Broader Conceptions

Social learning theory was originally developed for the clinician. Typically, the clinician is less interested in predicting specific bits of behavior than he or she is in the prediction of classes of behavior. Thus, it is important to be able to predict, for a patient, that he or she will respond in a certain situation with physical aggression; of less concern is whether the patient will use the right or left hand, strike the victim's mouth or ear, etc. It may have occurred to the reader that the concepts thus far elaborated (behavior potential, expectancy, reinforcement value) are relevant to specific, molecular aspects of behavior. For convenience these broader conceptions may be expressed in the following formula:

$$NP = f (FM \& NV)$$

This is to be read, "The potentiality of occurrence of a set of behaviors that lead to the satisfaction of some need (need potential) is a function of the expectancies that these behaviors will lead to these reinforcements (freedom of movement) and the strength or value of these reinforcements (need value)" (Rotter, 1954, p. 110).

In the laboratory there is often an interest in a specific behavior whose occurrence is governed by expectancies and reinforcement value. More often, however, the personality psychologist is concerned with broad classes of behavior (need potential). For example, the need for love and affection may be composed of many separate reinforcements (praise, kissing, fondling, etc.). The mean value of those separate reinforcements is referred to as need value. Similarly, there is an expectancy for the occurrence of each of those individual reinforcements. The overall strength of those separate expectancies is freedom of movement. Thus, when it is said that individuals' need for love and affection is high it is meant that, on the average, they attach great value to those separate reinforcements of kissing, fondling, or words of endearment (the exact composition and strength of individual components of the need will vary from person to person, however). By the same token, if generally their expectancy for the attainment of these separate reinforcements is low, then it is said that their freedom of movement in the love and affection area is low.

DISCREPANCIES BETWEEN EXPECTANCIES AND NEEDS

Instances in which an individual possesses a strong need but a low expectancy of reinforcement (freedom of movement) may give rise to a variety of defensive or psychopathological behaviors. It is possible to think of anxiety as a low expectancy or low freedom of movement in a valued need area (Phares, 1972). The consequences of such low expectancies may include repression, avoidance behavior, depressions, and failures in learning. In some ways, a strong need and a low set of expectancies for its satisfaction may be thought of as a specific instance of maladjustment. However, it is important to note that maladjustment is essentially a value judgment that reflects the ethical position of the observer and is not based on scientific theory. Furthermore, many factors may contribute to maladjustment beyond a mere discrepancy between need and expectancy (Phares, 1972). Several of these notions, as they relate to locus of control, are discussed in Chapter VIII.

Generalized Expectancies and Problem Solving

Generalized expectancies in terms of a probability for success that has been generalized from past related situations have been mentioned. This implies the assumption that people categorize situations along a dimension of similarity of reinforcement. For example, individuals may categorize a situation as being similar to one in the past in which behaving aggressively led to success.

It is also an assumption of social learning theory that individuals categorize situations in other ways. Such categorization might be in terms of which concepts would be most useful in allowing them to cope with a given situation. For example, they may generalize expectancies for the success of certain problem-solving approaches. Expectancies for the success of various ways of viewing reality may emerge. People may develop a generalized expectancy that categorizing other people as threatening or greedy will best enable them to cope with others. Or they may learn to view the world as highly competitive and may adjust their behavior accordingly. The potential ways in which people may use such categories is limitless and renders the predictive task of the psychologist enormously complex.

In this context, generalized expectancies are akin to learning sets or higher-level learning skills: situations are rendered similar because the individuals see them as presenting similar problems to be solved. For example, the behavior of looking for alternative solutions (Schroder & Rotter, 1952) might be regarded as being dependent in part on a learned, generalized expectancy that problems can be solved by the technique of looking for alternative solutions. This would be independent of the reinforcement or needs involved in the given situation. To illustrate further, many social situations can be construed as involving the problem of whether to trust another person. This would involve problem-solving generalized expectancies for interpersonal trust (Rotter, 1967b; Hamsher, Geller, & Rotter, 1968).

A special and important example of such a generalized expectancy is the degree to which people believe in internal or external control of reinforcement—whether they believe that what happens to them is dependent upon their own behavior and is thus controllable by their actions or is contingent upon luck, powerful others, etc. It is the thesis of this book that locus of control constitutes a personality dimension that can be quantified and used in conjunction with other social learning theory variables to predict human social behavior. Therefore, as Levy

(1970) emphasized, expectancies can be construed as more than the narrow correlates of a subjective probability of occurrence of an event. An expectancy construct is flexible enough to be used as a generalized personality construct that describes individual differences in beliefs.

It was noted earlier that an individual's expectancy that a behavior will succeed in a specific situation is determined by the individual's specific experiences in that situation and by related experiences from situations he or she regards as similar. The introduction of problem-solving generalized expectancies requires that this statement be modified. The role of problem-solving generalized expectancies has been succinctly expressed by Rotter, Chance, and Phares (1972, p. 41) as follows:

$$E_{s_1} = f \frac{(E\,' \,\&\, GE_r \,\&\, GE_{ps_1} \,\&\, GE_{ps_2}, \cdots, GE_{ps_n})}{f\,(N_{s_1})}$$

This shorthand signifies that an expectancy in situation 1 is determined by the expectancy that a given reinforcement will occur based on previous experience in the same situation $(E\,')$, experiences generalized from other related situations (GE_r), and a variety of problem-solving generalized expectancies $(GE_{ps_1}, \cdots, GE_{ps_n})$ divided by some function of the number of experiences the individual has had in the specific situation (N_{s_1}).

The foregoing expression, then, systematically incorporates problem-solving expectancies, such as locus of control, into the overall formula for determining expectancies. The basic mode of calculating the likelihood that a given behavior will occur remains unchanged. According to social learning theory, then, both the value of the reinforcements toward which the behavior is directed and the expectancy that the behavior will lead to those reinforcements must be determined. This can be demonstrated through an illustration of how the social learning theory concepts of reinforcement value (or need), expectancy, and locus of control can be utilized in the prediction of a specific behavior.

AN EXPERIMENTAL ILLUSTRATION

Davis and Phares (1967) studied the effects of locus of control on information-seeking behavior. The issue involved was attitudes toward the Vietnam conflict. They found that internals sought significantly more information about a person whose attitudes they thought they would be trying to change later. When instructed that inducing attitude change was a matter of skill, internals were superior to externals in information-seeking. When instructions suggested that successfully changing another's attitudes was largely due to chance, no differences between internals and externals occurred. When neither skill nor chance instructions were provided (an ambiguous situation), internals again sought more information than externals. Of more interest here than the specific results obtained, however, is the manner in which this study may be conceptualized, thus highlighting the interplay of several social learning theory concepts.

Before their attempts to influence the other person, subjects were asked to jot down questions that they might wish to have answered about the other person. Presumably, the answers to these questions would facilitate their efforts to influence the person's opinions. Typical questions jotted down included the other person's attitude toward the war in Vietnam, his or her family background, and his or her intelligence level. Davis and Phares were interested in comparing the number of questions subjects indicated they wished answered prior to their influence attempts.

According to social learning theory, this behavior parameter (number of questions) should be determined by the value of the reinforcements for the subjects (what they attempted to gain by their attempts to influence the other person) and by the subjects' expectancy that asking questions of the experimenter would lead to those reinforcements. Since the focus of the study was locus of control, reinforcement value (or need) was ignored, although it was recognized that this would decrease the level of prediction possible. It was assumed that most subjects would want to influence the other person because it might bring reinforcements such as recognition (praise for success from either the experimenter or the other person), dominance (the awareness of having successfully manipulated someone), or affection (warm regard expressed by the experimenter through compliments). To the extent that some subjects were little motivated by such considerations, their information-seeking behavior would likely be reduced (some subjects' only motivation may have been to escape the situation and get back to their bridge game), and support for the hypothesis would be diminished. It seemed a safe assumption, however, based on knowledge of the subculture, that subjects would respond to at least one of the several classes of reinforcement available in the situation.

What are the determinants of the expectancy that asking questions will lead to those reinforcements possible in the situation? The first determinant concerns specific expectancies, i.e., how much previous experience the subjects have accumulated in the situation. If they have been in many very similar information-seeking experiments, their behavior potential of asking questions will be almost solely determined by their history of previous successes and failures in those situations. Of course, no person is ever in exactly the same situation twice, but that person may see situations as similar in specific ways. In this case it was unlikely that the subjects had ever been in a situation that was like the experimental conditions of the study; therefore, it was deemed that a specific expectancy would carry relatively little weight (i.e., for most subjects the value of specific expectancy would be close to zero).

The second factor to be considered is generalized expectancies for success transferred from other situations involving functionally related behaviors. In the present experiment, such a generalized expectancy was manipulated by providing different sets of instructions. One group of subjects was told that success in influencing others had been found to be almost exclusively a function of one's skill. A second group was instructed that the process was so complicated that the success of any one person in influencing another would have to be regarded as pure chance. A third group was given no instructions regarding the skill-chance nature of the activity—the so-called ambiguous condition.

It was expected that when subjects were instructed that success was determined by their own skill, they would generalize from their experience in related skill situations. Skill instructions would serve as a cue that there is direct connection between the amount of skilled effort exerted and the likelihood of the occurrence of reward. Thus, the accumulation of information about the other person would lead to a greater possibility of being successful in influencing the other person. In the skill situation it makes more sense to ask questions than it does in the chance condition, where there is no contingency between "influencing" behavior and the occurrence of reward.

The level of information-seeking behavior in any particular subject would be correlated with expectancies for success in such behaviors as based on generalizations from past performance in related situations. It may be that some subjects with a history of little success in related skill situations will show a low rate of emission of questions. In general, however, with the population used, the likelihood was that, overall, the rate of questions asked would be greater under skill than under chance conditions.

It is in the ambiguous condition that perceived locus of control as a *problem-solving* generalized expectancy can best be demonstrated. Presumably, the lack of explicit situational cues (instructions) allows the subjects to react in their own characteristic fashion—as an "internal" or an "external." Internally oriented subjects who feel they are in control of the reinforcements that occur could be expected to engage in greater information seeking than externally oriented subjects. On the other hand, the behavior of externals given skill instructions would be less external than it would be in an ambiguous situation. We can state generally: *the presence of explicit situational cues about the contingency between behavior and outcome should diminish the importance of a generalized expectancy for internal or external control.*

To complicate prediction further, one can argue that a generalized expectancy such as interpersonal trust also is important and may differentially affect responses to experimental instructions. Usually several classes of problem-solving generalized expectancies are called into play as people categorize situations in such a way that they may select those behaviors from their repertoire that seem to hold for them the highest possibility of success. Locus of control and interpersonal trust are just two examples of the many such categories.

The notion of perceived locus of control seems to work best in those situations that are not highly structured and that permit varying conceptualizations by individuals. It seldom contributes much to prediction in very highly structured tasks. Thus, no matter how "external" individuals may be, they still flip the light switch when they want more light. They do not say to themselves, "I want more light, but since the world is externally organized, it doesn't make any difference whether I flip the switch." Because they have been reinforced so many times in the past for flipping the switch, they will continue to do so regardless of whether they are predominantly "external" or "internal." In such a situation, knowledge of perceived locus of control contributes little to prediction.

Therefore, locus of control can be utilized effectively by integrating it with other theoretical concepts and applying the whole to prediction. The mindless reliance on I-E in every situation is a waste of time and seems to imply a simplistic view that behavior can be predicted with but one or two concepts. It is doubtful that many people would assert that social learning is the only theory that can incorporate locus of control. But to use locus of control without at least some larger behavioral theory or complex analysis of the overall situation is to invite a low level of prediction.

In conclusion, an analysis of the Davis and Phares study illustrates an approach to prediction that systematically incorporates locus of control with other social learning theory variables such as reinforcement value (or need value), specific expectancies, and two classes of generalized expectancies. This analysis also suggests how the situation acts as a set of cues to determine for the individual the values of these variables. This view of what is needed for predicting multidetermined behavior can serve as an effective brake against the overutilization of locus of control at the expense of the other theoretical concepts. With the use of this theory, a more balanced and less traitlike approach to the prediction of human social behavior is achieved.

Summary

This chapter is devoted to a brief exposition of the relevant assumptions and concepts of social learning theory. Its presumption is that human behavior is complexly determined by several variables, including reinforcement value (or need), expectancies, and the psychological situation. While locus of control is an important determinant of behavior, its effects are moderated by these other social learning theory concepts. Therefore, a fuller understanding of the potential behavioral effects of locus of control will result from an analysis of the manner in which it relates to these other concepts. In succeeding chapters, the reader will find that a great deal of I-E research has been carried out with little regard for its relationship to other variables. This probably limits the usefulness of that research. A theoretical orientation such as social learning theory can assist in the evaluation of such data before all the evidence is in, help resolve contradictions in that evidence, and enable us to formulate new research questions and ideas.

III

Locus of Control as a Situation-Specific Expectancy

Chapter II presented behavioral determinants as both situation-specific and also general. By the same token, belief in personal control (or lack of it) is both a general disposition that influences individuals' behavior across a wide range of situations and a rather specific belief that may apply to a limited number of situations. For example, while people may generally subscribe to the notion that they have only restricted control over their lives, they nevertheless may feel that in some specific situations they can exert much control.

This chapter reviews some of the investigations that deal with perceived locus of control as determined by the situation. For the time being, those studies of the situations that deal simultaneously with dispositional variables will be excluded. The central thesis of this chapter is that learning and performance in specific situations are different when subjects perceive that they control the contingency between behavior and reinforcement and when they perceive that they lack such control. Demonstration of this thesis will support the social learning theory view expressed earlier: Situational factors are very important and should not be ignored just because of the presumed operation of more "glamorous" dispositional variables.

Behavior in Skill versus Chance Situations

The following description of a study should detail a feeling for the kind of procedures used in this research area. Phares (1962) presented a list of 12 nonsense syllables to subjects to establish their perceptual thresholds. Subjects were then seated before a reaction-time panel, and electrodes were strapped to their fingers. Through the electrodes electric shock could be delivered at a level that each subject regarded as painful. Subjects were later told that on each of 10 trials, 12 nonsense syllables would be projected on the wall one at a time. The same syllables would appear each trial, but their order would be randomly varied from trial to trial. They were also told that 6 of the syllables would be accompanied by a 2-second shock when projected and 6 would not.

Subsequent instructions divided the subjects into two groups. One group (the *skill* group) was further instructed that they could terminate the shock each time by pressing an appropriate button on a control panel. Each syllable had its own control button, and if the subjects learned which button went with which syllable, they could press the button and stop the shock each time. Since the length of the shock received was dependent on the subjects' skill in figuring out which button was associated with which syllable, potentially the subjects were in at least partial control of the situation.

The second group's (the *chance* group) instructions were that if they pressed the correct button the shock would terminate but that the association between button and syllable would change on each trial. Terminating the shock therefore was purely a matter of guessing—no learning was possible. In this sense, the subjects did not have any control over their situation beyond the chance level.

All subjects were instructed to read each syllable aloud to ensure that they paid attention to the stimuli. The skill subjects were run first and then a chance subject was yoked to each skill subject. This was done to control for sex, number of "escapes," point of escape in the trial sequence, etc. In short, only the instructions differentiated the subjects in the two groups. Following this procedure, all subjects were returned to the tachistoscope, and their recognition thresholds again were taken for the 12 syllables. A control group also gave pre- and post-shock thresholds; in between, they merely viewed the 120 slides without any accompanying shock. Results indicated that, as predicted, perceptual threshold decrements were significantly greater under skill conditions than under chance conditions. This difference occurred on both shock and nonshock syllables.

The results of this study suggest that perceptual learning with behavior-reward sequences experienced under skill conditions is different from that under chance conditions. When people feel they control the situation, they are more likely to exhibit perceptual behavior that will enable them to cope with potentially threatening situations than are subjects who feel that chance or other uncontrollable forces determine whether their behavior will be successful. In short, there appears to be a direct relationship between extent of coping behavior and the expectancy that one's skill or ability is the crucial variable in achieving reinforcement.

This study lends credence to the notion that every behavior is not inevitably strengthened through reinforcement. If this were true, people might characteristically behave very much like superstitious pigeons. A behavior is likely to reoccur if it is reinforced in subjects who believe that there is a contingency between behavior and reinforcement in that situation. In the absence of such a belief, the behavior will be unlikely to occur again. Put in simple terms, behavior will be different under *skill* conditions than under *chance* conditions. Perceived locus of control as a determinant of behavior may be so obvious or so taken for granted that it has escaped the systematic investigation it deserves. One thing is clear, however; much of the research in learning to date has been conducted under the assumption that the subject feels in control of the situation. One wonders on how many occasions this assumption has been unfounded.

The following presentation of some research that is closely allied to social learning theory or the skill-chance classification of situations as well as related areas, such as reactions to controllable versus uncontrollable aversive stimulation, effects of lack of personal freedom on "reactance," and personal responsibility should affirm the important role played by the specific situation in developing expectancies for the success or failure of certain behaviors. Such studies also show in greater detail how such effects are achieved.

EFFECTS ON EXPECTANCIES

Following the experiences with Karl S., Phares (1957) carried out a study designed to test the general hypothesis that expectancies for success will differ under chance and skill conditions. This was intended to be a situational analogue of what we thought was a dispositional characteristic (generalized expectancy) in Karl S. Subjects were asked to match colors and lengths of lines. Some subjects were told the task was so difficult that success was largely a matter of chance or luck. Others were instructed that success was possible and had been found to be a function of the skill of the individual. Half of the skill subjects were given the line-matching task and the other half were given the color-matching task. Chance subjects were similarly treated. In this fashion we could avoid any possibility that subsequent differences in expectancy behavior might be construed as having been caused by the nature of the task rather than by the instructions. Both groups were partially reinforced (were told they were right or wrong) in a fixed order. The measure of expectancy used was the number of plastic chips the subjects were willing to bet on their chances of being correct on the succeeding trial.

Several findings are of interest here. First, increments and decrements in expectancy were greater under skill than under chance conditions. Second, the frequency of expectancy changes was greater in the skill situation. Third, there was a trend toward greater utilization of the "gambler's fallacy" under chance conditions. That is, the tendency for subjects to increase their expectancy following failure or decrease it after success (so-called unusual shifts) was greater under chance instructions than it was under skill instructions. Similar results have been reported by James (1957) and by Walls and Cox (1971).

The general explanation offered for the above results was that skill conditions provide a greater basis for generalizing from the past to the future than do chance conditions. When reinforcement is seen as being under one's own control, the past should have very direct implications for the future. On the other hand, chance perceptions encourage one to disregard the past and also to engage in conceptualizations such as the gambler's fallacy (e.g., "I've been wrong four times in a row. It's about time I was right!"). Therefore, skill situations can be construed as members of a class of situations that permit individuals to generalize from the past to the future. Other members of this class might be their relatively permanent characteristics (Rotter, 1966, p. 1), such as athletic ability, beauty, etc.

In a study by James and Rotter (1958), subjects performed an extrasensory perception (ESP) type task, with one group instructed that success in guessing was controlled by ESP skill and another group told that such guessing was totally a matter of luck. Half of each group were given partial reinforcement (50 percent correct guesses), and the other half, 100 percent reinforcement. Although the groups did not differ significantly at the end of their training trials, they did show differences in subsequent extinction of expectancies (stating an expectancy of 1 or 0 on a scale of 0 to 10 for three consecutive trials).

Under skill conditions, the trials to extinction were longer for the 100 percent reinforcement than for the 50 percent reinforcement conditions; under chance conditions, the reverse was true. The authors suggest that under chance conditions the extinction series was interpreted as a change in the situation by subjects in the 100 percent reinforcement condition (a disappearance of previous lucky guesses) but not by the 50 percent reinforcement subjects. For subjects with skill instructions, the 100 percent reinforcement subjects took longer to accept the idea that they were not succeeding. Stabler and Johnson (1970), using children as subjects, report similar results.

Subsequently, Fazio and Hendricks (1970) reported evidence suggesting that skill-instructed subjects manifest greater resistance to extinction than chance-instructed subjects. However, it is important to note that their response measure did not involve verbalized confidence levels but, rather, button pressing.

Holden and Rotter (1962) also utilized response measures for expectancies and extinction that were different from simple verbalized expectancies that had been used in several of the previously cited studies. Subjects were given small amounts of money to bet on each trial. Amount bet was the measure of expectancy. Extinction was defined as voluntarily quitting the experiment. Three groups were all given 50 percent partial reinforcement: one with skill instructions, one with chance instructions, and one without any explicit instructions. Using the previously noted ESP task, results indicated that subjects given chance instructions and those given no instructions showed significantly more trials to extinction than did the skill-instructed group.

CATEGORIZATION WITHOUT INSTRUCTIONS

In the work thus far reported, locus of control was manipulated by giving skill or chance instructions. Another approach is to select tasks that, on a cultural basis, are likely to be perceived as skilled or chance tasks.

The latter approach was utilized in a study by Rotter, Liverant, and Crowne (1961), in which the nature of the tasks themselves was varied rather than the instructions or statements by the experimenter. For the chance task, the previously noted ESP task (without skill instructions) was utilized. A hand steadiness task adapted from Sky (1950) was used for the skill condition. In general the results supported two basic hypotheses. First, under skill conditions, positive and negative reinforcements lead to greater changes in verbalized expectancies. Second, the extinction of expectancies under continuous negative reinforcement will reverse under chance and skill conditions, so that the 50 percent reinforcement group is more resistant to extinction than the 100 percent reinforcement group under chance conditions, and the 100 percent reinforcement group is more resistant to extinction than the 50 percent reinforcement group under skill conditions. This study supported both the earlier studies of Phares (1957) and James and Rotter (1958).

Rotter, Liverant, and Crowne (1961) felt that subjects would, in the normal course of events, categorize the hand steadiness task as a skilled activity and the ESP task as a chance activity. To study futher the question of how various conditions affect subjects' categorization of events as chance-controlled, Blackman (1962) used a task involving a series of randomly appearing lights in which the subject had to predict the occurrence of a red or a green light. It was found that the sequence length and the number of sequences affected the number of red responses in extinction and the expectancy associated with them. Taken in conjunction with work by Bennion (1961), as well as that of Rotter, Liverant, and Crowne (1961), this research suggests several things. When the percentage of positive reinforcement deviates significanly from 50 percent in a right-wrong task, subjects are more likely to see a sequence of reinforcement as *not* being chance-controlled. A similar perception is likely to result when the sequence of reinforcement seems to be patterned, when very long sequences of one or two alternative events occur, and when variability of performance is very low in tasks permitting graduated scores.

Considering the foregoing work on the skill-chance classification of situations, at least two implications seem apparent. The first is that whenever the subjects adopt the expectancy that they do not control the occurrence of reinforcement, they generalize less from the past and cannot use increasing experience on a task to develop better strategies or more accurate expectancies. Whether they are confronted with chance instructions, a task they have learned in the past is chance-controlled, or a highly variable or unpatterned performance, the results are the same: *They learn a great deal less, and this decrement in learning seems directly attributable to the effects on expectancy of a belief that, in a given situation, they do not control the relationship between behavior and reinforcement.*

The second implication was stated by Rotter (1966). Differences in learning and performance in skill and chance situations suggest that many findings on human learning could bear reexamination, since much of human learning data has been collected under conditions of experimenter control. For example, it is quite likely that many subjects really believe that the experimenter is maintaining surreptitious control over the tasks on which they are being asked to perform. As Rotter, Liverant, and Crowne (1961) have shown, such perceived experimenter control can lead to some rather startling reversals in our conclusions; in this case with respect to extinction as a function of partial reinforcement.

STABILITY VERSUS INTERNALITY

It has been argued by Weiner and his colleagues (Weiner, 1972; Weiner, Heckhausen, Meyer, & Cook, 1972; Frieze & Weiner, 1971) that skill-chance studies have confused locus of control and stability dimensions. According to Weiner, skill or ability situations are really stable conditions, while chance situations are unstable ones. Thus, Weiner contends that expectancy changes are caused not by locus of control considerations but by subjects' seeing skill situations as stable and the chance ones as unstable.

Since skill-chance research is not the central focus of the internal-external control area, a few general remarks will be made, rather than a discussion of Weiner's attempts to reanalyze the skill-chance research. Weiner somehow seems to have felt that social learning investigators equate the skill-chance dimension with internal-external control. Such is not the case at all. The early skill-chance research was designed to be a crude analogue of what evolved later into the broad personality dimension of locus of control.

As noted earlier, skill situations are part of a larger group of situations that encourage generalizations from the past while chance situations do not. As a result, expectancies, and thus behavior, are different in the two types of situations. Internal and external control are generalized beliefs that individuals have about whether they exert control over the occurrence of rewards or outside forces exert that control.

In his attempts to deal with issues of internal-external control, Weiner focused only upon skill-chance studies. Such studies involve very simple situational manipulations, and the behaviors are equally simple expectancy statements. The actual I-E literature (as we shall see in ensuing chapters) deals with a much broader class of behaviors in more complex situations (e.g., information seeking, conformity, persuasion, defensiveness, etc.). One should not assume that external subjects will always behave as if they were in a simple chance situation. This may be one reason why most studies do not produce expectancy change behavior in externals that is the same as that obtained from chance situations. Some externals may believe that the experimenter is manipulating things and may, therefore, exhibit expectancy changes that are quite stable and predictable.

In conclusion, it cannot be emphasized enough that Weiner's work has been carried out largely within the rather narrow limits of restricted laboratory achievement situations. The I-E literature is more diverse, deals with several needs other than achievement, and involves a much wider array of behaviors than attribution. Thus, it is difficult to assess the saliency of Weiner's attributional analysis of skill-chance studies as applied to locus of control. Just as the relationships that exists between expectancy and reinforcement value in achievement situations may be different from that in other need areas, so too attribution of outcomes to internal or external control factors may vary analogously.

Other Reactions to Perceived Lack of Control

In addition to the expectancy changes documented earlier, inability to control or predict outcomes can also mediate a variety of intrapersonal reactions, especially when the situation is highly aversive in nature. More research efforts are being devoted to this area at the present time, but much anecdotal material has existed for years. Personal lack of control coupled with malignant and inexplicable influence from others has been offered as an explanation for "voodoo" deaths (Richter, 1957). In Nazi concentration camps the prisoners' sense of personal helplessness and lack of control not only seemed to produce apathy and withdrawal, it often culminated in death, a death produced by something beyond sheer physical deprivation and cruelty (Bettelheim, 1960). The following experimental studies give some insight into the nature of the reactions and the stimuli that produce them.

D'Amato and Gumenik (1960) reported an experiment in which subjects showed a preference for predictable over unpredictable punishment. Pervin (1963) subsequently suggested that it was less anxiety-arousing for subjects to administer shock to themselves than for the experimenter to do it. These results also indicated that unpredictable shock was more stressful than predictable shock. Champion (1950), Corah and Boffa (1970), and Haggard (1943) all reported that when subjects believed they could terminate an electric shock, they showed less stress than when they thought they were incapable of terminating it. The work of Geer, Davison, and Gatchel (1970) indicates that perception of effective control, even when not correct, can reduce autonomic responding. Staub, Tursky, and Schwartz (1971) demonstrated that no-control subjects judged a less intense shock as uncomfortable and tolerated fewer shocks as compared to self-control subjects. These authors suggested that personal control and predictability can reduce the aversiveness of noxious stimulation. Geer and Maisel (1972) emphasized, however, that the obtained effects are determined by more than just predictability of shock. They feel that the ability of subjects to terminate an aversive stimulus tends to reduce the impact of that stimulus.

All of this work seems to be in general support of Lazarus' (1966) contention that individuals' perception of threat in potentially anxiety-arousing situations is mediated by their belief about their ability to exert control over that potential threat and their feelings of stress in an aversive situation are proportional to their expectations about personal control over the situational events.

Houston (1972) manipulated beliefs in personal control by telling some subjects they could avoid shock by not making mistakes on a task and telling others there was no way of avoiding shock. As expected, he found that subjects regarded threatening situations over which they had no control as being more anxiety-provoking than those in which they did exert some control; however, their physiological arousal was greater under self-control circumstances than under no-control conditions. Houston regarded this arousal as a function of the effort subjects exerted in their attempts to achieve such control.

A recent monograph by Glass and Singer (1972) presents evidence from a systematic series of studies on the effects of controllability and predictability of aversive events. Several of their studies revealed that predictable aversive and distractive events are significantly less disruptive in their effects on subjects' performance than are unpredictable distractions. The authors were especially interested in urban stress as it is affected by noise and other social variables.

The work presented thus far in this chapter suggests that subjects learn more, perform better, and are rendered less anxious when aversive stimuli are under their own control or else are predictable. In a review paper, Averill outlined three major types of personal control: (1) behavioral (direct action on the environment), (2) cognitive (the interpretation of events), and (3) decisional (having a choice among alternative courses of action) and states:

> Each type of control is related to stress in a complex fashion, sometimes increasing it, sometimes reducing it, and sometimes having no influence at all . . .the relationship of personal control to stress is primarily a function of the meaning of the control response for the individual. Stated differently, the stress-inducing or stress-reducing properties of personal control depend upon such factors as the nature of the response and the context in which it is embedded and not just upon its effectiveness in preventing or mitigating the impact of a potentially harmful stimulus. (Averill, 1973, p. 286)

Previous social learning theory work has suggested that inability to control or predict in situations prevents individuals from generalizing expectancies or experience from the past. Increasing experience, then, does not lead individuals to expect an increase in ability to cope with the situation. In aversive situations, this can be a particularly debilitating turn of events. Nothing in such a situation leads them to increase their expectancy for being able to deal successfully with events. As they maintain a low expectancy for being able to cope successfully with the situation (with successful coping regarded as having strong positive reinforcing qualties), their anxiety mounts.

As suggested in Chapter II, whenever there is a marked discrepancy between expectancies and needs, individuals are anxious. Thus, perceived lack of control or predictability becomes a cue that lowers the expectancy for achieving the positive reinforcement of avoiding or ameliorating the effects of the aversive events. Emotions and autonomic changes can serve as cues and, along with other situational cues, can affect learned behavior (Schachter, 1966; Lazarus, 1968). The effect is likely to be an impairment in learning and performance.

One might argue that the debilitating effects of anxiety do not really matter in such conditions. If learning is impaired, so what? When control is not exerted in the situation or predictability is not possible, learning is impossible anyway. Thus, other than on humane grounds, little concern should be registered. However, most situations are not completely unpredictable, chance-controlled, other-controlled, etc. Therefore, a perceived lack of control could result in a lower level of effectiveness than might otherwise be possible. In addition, in some instances, unpredictability may be only intermittent, and yet it may impose behavioral effects that extend beyond its own periodicity and thus may reduce each subject's performance below what it might be. Finally, if the individuals spend a substantial amount of time in no-control or unpredictable situations, they may develop a generalized belief in external control that could then extend beyond the confines of their current specific situation.

LACK OF FREEDOM, REACTANCE, AND COGNITIVE DISSONANCE

Another aspect of lack of control or unpredictability is reduction of one's "freedom." In fact, it often appears that goals that are threatened by a loss of freedom take on more value than they had before the threat, a phenomenon called *psychological reactance* (Brehm, 1966). Hammock and Brehm (1966) found that children who expected to be given a choice between candy bars and toys but were not, showed an increase in the value they assigned to the promised object. Children who did not expect to be given a choice showed no change in value.

Although lack of freedom and lack of control may seem to be overlapping constructs, they are not identical. For example, individuals could be in a totalitarian situation and yet realize that, at least up to a point, they retain control. And certainly, totalitarian or not, there would be a great deal of predictability in the situation. Only when a specific person or system both denies the individual freedom and also acts in a completely capricious fashion would there be a one-to-one relationship between lack of freedom and unpredictability. Indeed, if individuals can identify the source that has denied them freedom, they may show reactions other than simple stress—e.g., anger, retaliation, reactance. Weitz (1972) documented such reactions in describing his feelings during a 24-hour period as a patient.

Such affective reactions are also seen in work reported by deCharms (1968). Experiments demonstrated not only that feelings of freedom and choice can be experimentally manipulated but that such manipulation can produce positive reactions (e.g., liking of tasks, wish to continue working) if the subjects feel they are originators of action, and negative reactions if they feel they are pawns. In a student-teacher setting, group members tended to display more positive feelings toward a leader when they felt they were the origin of suggestions as opposed to situations in which they were treated as pawns. We will come across this "origin-pawn" variable again in Chapter X.

Another phenomenon touched by such notions as control, foreseeability, or predictability is *cognitive dissonance*. When individuals believe one thing but behave in a manner discrepant from this belief, an unpleasant feeling state of cognitive dissonance ensues (Festinger, 1957). Cooper (1971) argues that individuals must feel a personal responsibility in order to be subject to cognitive dissonance. Personal responsibility was defined in his experiment as a condition in which subjects were able to foresee the consequences of their choices and *voluntarily* chose to behave in ways discrepant from their beliefs. Cooper's subjects either were ordered to work with or chose to work with a partner who possessed certain negative personal qualities, which either were or were not foreseeable. As predicted, subjects who freely chose a partner and who knew about the negative traits ahead of time experienced dissonance, while the other subjects did not. Cooper's work suggests that personal responsibility in a specific situation will be reduced when the elements of foreseeability, predictability, and personal control are absent. Hence, less cognitive dissonance will be experienced in those circumstances.

Lack of Control at the Infrahuman Level

An important reason for psychologists' study of animal behavior is the insight it can provide into human behavior. Of course, the problems of generalizing here are enormous. The issue of anthropomorphizing inexorably creeps in when we begin to attribute expectancies or beliefs to animals. However, animal studies can be particularly valuable since they allow us to investigate the effects of experimenter control and aversiveness on behavior in a fashion that would be impossible with humans. As a result we may be able to pinpoint the salient component cues of such situations much more systematically than we can in human research.

One of the earliest studies in this connection was carried out by Mowrer and Viek (1948). It showed that in rats trained to escape shocks by performing an instrumental response, emotional reactions to an aversive shock were much less than in the case of matched control rats who could not control shocks through their own behavior. More recently, Seligman, Maier, and Solomon (1971), in a series of coordinated animal studies, reported results in support of the view that aversive events that are subject-controlled result in effects quite different from those stemming from uncontrollable conditions. In particular, less stress is engendered.

In a somewhat controversial study by Brady, Porter, Conrad, and Mason (1958), a so-called "executive" monkey could control shock to itself by pressing a bar. A control animal received the same shocks as the executive monkey but could not exert such control. Several of the executive monkeys died after several days in the apparatus, and all apparently suffered severe gastrointestinal damage. This result contradicts previous work at both human and infrahuman levels inasmuch as it usually is the no-control subject that experiences the greater stress. However, it is important to note that the executive monkey research has not always been replicated. Indeed, in some cases opposite trends have been produced.

To summarize, work with animals does provide additional demonstrations of the situational determinants of locus of control and thereby may increase our understanding of its role. Beyond this, it is difficult to know how the animal work adds to our knowledge of human behavior. In some ways, it seems that the human work has stimulated the animal research.

Summary

In this chapter we have examined locus of control as a situation-specific expectancy that is aroused by the nature of the cues in the situation rather than as a broad generalized belief. Whether the situation is one of skill or chance, predictable or unpredictable, controllable or noncontrollable, is very important. Learning and performance are affected, expectancies for future success are differentially aroused, self-reports of anxiety and autonomic arousal are influenced, and even cognitive dissonance and reactance may be affected.

The basic notion to be emphasized here is that if people construe outcomes of their behavior in certain specific situations as chance-determined, outside their personal control, or otherwise unpredictable, the stage is set for several important consequences. Most fundamental is the fact that the regularities of the past cannot be relied upon in the future. The effects on learning are considerable. Equally serious are the debilitating affective responses that may ensue. Such reactions are the understandable outgrowth of a perceived lack of control—an awareness that one's efforts to cope with the world are not effective.

Beyond their obvious direct significance, the foregoing results are important for two other reasons. First, such findings give us added confidence that what we have discovered in the nature of specific situations will also be found to operate at the personality level. For example, if most individuals tend to respond in no-control situations with heightened anxiety, then perhaps it can be demonstrated that people who chronically believe they lack control are anxious in a wide variety of situations. Futhermore, these situation-specific findings give us some hints about the manner in which generalized locus of control beliefs affect behavior.

The second reason is that the findings support our use of a theoretical orientation, specifically social learning theory. Based on this theory, we have construed control versus lack of control as both a situational variable and a personality variable and so have investigated both situational and personality characteristics of locus of control. Such an approach has not only been heuristic, it has also served as a further demonstration of the utility of proceeding from a theoretical base.

One final point. While the importance of the work cited in this chapter cannot be denied, we must remember that locus of control has been studied with a variety of methods. The different operational definitions may or may not be functionally equivalent. Lack of control, for example, may or may not be the same as instability, lack of freedom, unpredictability, or complexity. Their equivalence must be determined empirically. A working assumption from the beginning has been that such situations are similar only if subjects show similar amounts of generalization of experience from the past to the future. Should they turn out to differ in terms of the characteristic emotional reactions they produce, we must be careful not to lump them all together.

IV

The Measurement
of Individual
Differences
in Locus of Control
Beliefs

We have gained some insight into the clinical origin of the I-E variable, and we have discussed its role in the framework of a social learning theory of personality. In the preceding chapter we also examined some situational analogues of locus of control. Now we turn our attention to individual differences in generalized expectancy or belief in internal or external control. Personality, by definition, refers to relatively broad, stable differences among people and the interplay between these differences and specific situational variables. Our ultimate goal is to learn how a generalized personality variable such as locus of control relates to important human activities: Does it help us to predict social influence reactions? Efforts at mastery? Achievement needs? These are compelling questions, but before we can deal with them we must have a valid way of measuring locus of control expectancies. We need a measuring device that will allow us to sort out, with some certainty, those people who have differing beliefs about their overall ability to exert an influence on their world.

Phares (1955) made the first crude efforts to develop a scale to measure such individual differences. The instrument he used consisted of 13 skill items and 13 chance items presented in a Likert scale format.

The items for this scale were gleaned from a priori notions about the nature of skill-chance situations, from common sense, and from reworded items from authoritarianism scales. It was hoped that on this scale subjects who predominantly endorsed the internal (or skill) items would exhibit expectancy changes that were similar to those changes produced by skill instructions; a comparable opposite reaction was anticipated from subjects who chose the external (chance) items. This hope was not fulfilled, although some encouragement was provided by the fact that the predictions generated by the 13 "external" items approaced statistical significance. That is, subjects endorsing the external items tended to show more frequent unusual shifts in expectancy, a smaller magnitude of increments and decrements in expectancy, and less frequent shifts in either direction than did subjects whose scores were less external. As noted in Chapter III, such expectancy changes were also characteristic of subjects receiving chance instructions. Thus, Phares' results suggested it might be worthwhile to pursue the measurement of individual differences in locus of control beliefs or expectancies.

James (1957) followed up this early work by Phares by improving and revising the latter's scale. Like Phares, James predicted that subjects achieving external scores on his scale would tend to behave on an experimental task as if they were in a group receiving chance instructions, while an internal group's performance would parallel that produced by skill instructions. In the main, his hypotheses were substantiated. His scale has been used subsequently in several studies (e.g., Lipp, Kolstoe, James, & Randall, 1968).

Rotter Internal-External Control Scale

PRELIMINARY WORK

These primitive test construction efforts were followed by more systematic and extensive scale development work initiated by the late Shephard Liverant and his collaborators, J. B. Rotter and M. Seeman. Much of that work is detailed by Rotter (1966); other preliminary work is described by Rotter, Seeman, and Liverant (1962).

In order to develop a satisfactory measuring instrument, it is desirable to make explicit exactly what is being measured. Therefore, Rotter, Seeman, and Liverant (1962) distinguished among ideal, theoretical, and operational definitions of the I-E variable. An ideal definition refers to a verbal description of the I-E concept that is broad, general, and rich in surplus meaning. A theoretical definition states the antecedent conditions for I-E and the subsequent behaviors that are, in turn, mediated by I-E, and it relates I-E to other social learning theory concepts. Finally, the operational definition refers to the test or measure of I-E that is utilized.

In one sense, those sections of the first two chapters that describe the origin of I-E and also some of the related concepts from other theories (see Chapters V and VI) all represent material necessary for an ideal definition of locus of control. Chapters VI through X, together with the theoretical background in Chapter II, represent an approach toward a theoretical definition of locus of control. That is, those chapters describe how belief in an external or internal locus of control develops, what kinds of behaviors are produced by these beliefs once they have developed, and finally, how locus of control relates to other theoretical concepts within Rotter's social learning theory. In the present chapter, our focus is at the operational level—the construction of specific instruments to measure perceived locus of control.

Part of the ideal definition that guided much of the early work on the development of an I-E scale and still succinctly describes the I-E variable is the following:

> When a reinforcement is perceived by the subject as following some action of his own but not being entirely contingent upon his action, then, in our culture, it is typically perceived as the result of luck, chance, fate, as under the control of powerful others, or as unpredictable because of the great complexity of the forces surrounding him . . .we have labeled this a belief in *external control*. If the person perceives that the event is contingent upon his own behavior or his own relatively permanent characteristics, we have termed this a belief in *internal control*. (Rotter, 1966, p. 1)

Very early, Rotter and his colleagues decided to try to construct an I-E scale that would capitalize on the functional relationships among various goals, or reinforcements. That is, it was recognized that for any given individual, behaviors based upon locus of control beliefs would be more highly related within a given need area than across different needs. An individual may well behave in a predominantly internal fashion when dealing with academic goals but be significantly more external in his behavior when love and affection goals are involved. The utility of devising relatively independent need categories had been demonstrated earlier by Liverant (1958) in his work on the measurement of recognition and love and affection. As applied to I-E, this simply means that prediction ought to be enhanced when we measure perceived locus of control separately in different life areas. Such a strategy should be superior to that of using a single I-E score that must perforce be used in many different predictive situations. We shall return to this point later. For now we may just note that the idea of multidimensional I-E scales has been around almost as long as the I-E concept.

Therefore, Liverant, Rotter, and Seeman set about developing an

I-E scale that would contain items from several areas—academic recognition, social recognition, love and affection, dominance, social-political events, and general life philosophy. The earliest version of the scale contained 100 forced-choice items selected from the many that were written. One item in each pair dealt with an external belief and the other with an internal belief. Efforts were made to control for social desirability. This early scale was submitted to an item analysis and a factor analysis. On the basis of this work, Liverant reduced the 100 items to a 60-item version. Several things conspired to weaken the utility of this 60-item scale. An item analysis revealed that the subscales were not generating independent predictions. Achievement items correlated highly with social desirability measures and correlations between some of the subscales were about as high as the internal consistency of individual subscales. As a result, efforts to pursue the subscale approach were abandoned.

From this point on, Liverant, Rotter, and Crowne collaborated on a refinement of the 60-item scale into a 23-item version that subsequently became known as the Rotter Internal-External Control Scale (often referred to as the I-E Scale). The basis for selecting items included two considerations: (1) internal consistency, and (2) validity data from two studies (Seeman & Evans, 1962; Rotter, Liverant, & Crowne, 1961). The Seeman and Evans study (described in Chapter V) indicated that among tubercular patients "internals" attempted to be more controlling of their environment than did "externals." The Rotter, Liverant, and Crowne study (see Chapter III) measured individual differences in trials to extinction. Items were retained for the final 23-item version if they were appropriately predictive of (1) efforts to control one's environment in the hospital, and (2) trials to extinction on an experimental task. Some changes in wording of items were also involved at this stage. In addition, items that manifested a high correlation with the Marlowe-Crowne Social Desirability Scale (M-C SDS) were eliminated, as were items in which one alternative was endorsed more than 85 percent of the time. Finally, items that did not correlate significantly with other items or that showed a near-zero correlation with both validational criteria were excluded.

In an attempt to disguise at least partially the purpose of the test, 6 filler items were subsequently added. Thus, the final version of the scale consisted of 23 I-E items and 6 filler items. This 29-item version, reproduced in Appendix A, is the one used in the vast majority of I-E research, as will be evident in subsequent chapters.

SCALE CHARACTERISTICS
An Additive Scale   Rotter (1966) described the I-E Scale as an

additive scale. That is, the items represent an attempt to sample I-E beliefs across a range of situations, such as interpersonal situations, school, government, work, and politics. Because it samples a variety of areas, the scale can more nearly lay claim to being a measure of *generalized* expectancy. If all the items clustered in one area, such as work, the scale would probably predict quite well to work situations but rather poorly to many other situations. Although the attempt to develop subscales representative of several need areas was abandoned, the additive nature of the scale was retained. Thus, we have a scale that potentially will predict moderately well across a number of situations. If our goals were solely the prediction of behavior in one situation or one very homogeneous class of situations, then it would be advantageous to develop a scale with all items essentially directed to that situation rather than a general, additive-type scale.

Internal Consistency   It is probably the additive nature of the test that resulted in the moderate but rather uniform set of internal consistency estimates reported by Rotter (1966). These estimates ranged from .65 to .79. As Rotter suggests, the noncomparability of the items in an additive scale of this type makes it difficult to achieve high estimates of internal consistency.

Test-Retest Reliability   In general, the test-retest reliability for the test appears adequate. Rotter (1966) reported reliabilities for several samples that vary from .49 to .83, depending upon the time interval and the sample involved. These numbers are close to the .48 to .84 reported by Hersch and Scheibe (1967). Similarly, Harrow and Ferrante (1969) reported a reliability figure of .75 for psychiatric patients over a six-week time span. Kiehlbauch (1967) found reliability coefficients of .75, .39, and .26 in reformatory samples over three-, six-, and nine-month intervals. In general, from a psychometric point of view, test-retest reliability of the scale appears adequate. Some additional aspects of reliability are discussed in Chapter X.

Social Desirability   Rotter (1966) reported that correlations between the I-E Scale and the M-C SDS ranged from $-.07$ to $-.35$ and cited occasional substantial correlations between I-E scores and social desirability. It is important to remember that such correlations are not independent of the situation or conditions under which the testing is carried out. Under some circumstances it may be to the individual's advantage to place himself or herself in a favorable light, and his or her answers to a questionnaire may be correspondingly affected. As with any behavior, making marks on a questionnaire is not independent of situational influences.

Other investigators who have studied responses to the I-E Scale and the M-C SDS generally have not obtained significant correlations (e.g., Strickland [1965], Tolor [1967], and Tolor and Jalowiec [1968]). Feather (1967b) found a significant correlation of − .42 for females but no significant correlation for males. Altrocchi, Palmer, Hellman, and Davis (1968) reported a significant correlation of − .34 for males but nothing of significance for females. Lefcourt and Wine (1969) found correlations similar to the foregoing.

Cone (1971) compared I-E Scale scores and Edwards Social Desirability Scale scores in groups of Army mental health clinic outpatients and stockade prisoners, VA Hospital alcoholics, and disadvantaged youth. There were significant correlations, particularly in the two Army groups. Cone concluded that the I-E Scale is susceptible to the influence of social desirability. He did not, however, discuss situational testing conditions, which may have influenced the data.

Another approach to the assessment of social desirability is to have subjects rate the I-E items for social desirability. Bernhardson (1968) used this approach and derived a social desirability index that correlated .82 with I-E Scale scores. Hjelle (1971), in a similar series of studies, reached the conclusion that the I-E Scale may not be free of contamination from social desirability. Joe (1972) reported data to indicate that 13 of the internal alternatives on the I-E Scale were judged by subjects as significantly more socially desirable than the corresponding external statements. These data are similar to what Hjelle found (although Hjelle's data are subject to interpretation).

Taken as a group, the aforementioned studies suggest that while the I-E Scale is probably not entirely free from the effects of social desirability, it would be incorrect to conclude that the scale is seriously impaired. We can, conclude that at least a portion of the variance associated with the I-E Scale is attributable to social desirability. The exact amount will probably vary depending upon the reinforcements that subjects see available from the specific testing conditions. As contrasted with independent measures of social desirability (such as M-C SDS), item-by-item analyses or judgments of the social desirability of I-E items or item pairs probably over estimate the effects of social desirability on the I-E Scale.

Intelligence   Rotter (1966) concluded that correlations between intelligence measures and I-E Scale scores are negligible or at best low. Hersch and Scheibe's (1967) data tend to corroborate this conclusion. They reported correlations from − .07 to .17 (not significant) for three different measures of intellectual ability. Kiehlbauch (1967) was unable to find a correlation between intelligence and I-E Scale scores in a reformatory sample. It certainly does not appear defensible to explain I-E Scale scores as being a function of intelligence even though an occasional study may report a modest correlation between internality and an intellectual measure (Powell & Centa, 1972).

Sex Differences   There does not appear to be any simple way of summarizing sex differences on the I-E Scale. Many studies do not report separate means for males and females. A wide majority of studies does not find significant differences in I-E scores between men and women. Occasionally, however, a study will report sex differences (Feather, 1967b and 1968). It is clear that sex often moderates the relationship between I-E Scale scores and other behaviors. For example, internality often is related to a variety of achievement behaviors in males but not in females (see Chapter VII). Similarly, the notion of defensive externality seems to work better for males than females. Because of greater cultural pressures for success, males seemingly have a greater need to protect themselves against failure by recourse to external attributions (see Chapter VIII).

Consistent with these observations are the data of several other studies. These studies used the Intellectual Achievement Responsibility Questionnaire (described more fully later in this chapter) to measure I-E in children in intellectual-academic settings. It also provides sub-scores based on I-E beliefs for both success and failure. At any rate, frequent differences in scores between boys and girls (particularly on the failure items) are found on this scale. Again, it is possible that such sex differences are mediated by differential cultural roles commonly assigned to boys and girls.

Platt, Pomeranz, Eisenman, and DeLisser (1970) reported a variety of differences in adjustment and personality dimensions for internals and externals—particularly when scores for females are analyzed separately from those of males. They suggest that the moderating effects of sex may be due to the greater socialization undergone by females as contrasted to the greater responsiveness of males to situational considerations.

Ethnic and Social Class Differences   We can probably safely assert that variations in I-E Scale scores are related to differences in access to power or to the presence of social barriers to group mobility (see Chapter IX for more discussion of this topic). Most of the evidence indicates that blacks and individuals from lower socioeconomic groups are relatively more external in their beliefs. Such evidence of racial differences was noted by Rotter (1966) and has been supported by others (Battle & Rotter, 1963; Lefcourt & Ladwig, 1965, 1966; Lessing,

1969; Scott & Phelan, 1969; Shaw & Uhl, 1971; Strickland, 1972; Zytkoskee, Strickland, & Watson, 1971). Gruen and Ottinger (1969) noted the greater internality in middle-class children as compared to those of the lower class. In cross-cultural work, Hsieh, Shybut, and Lotsof (1969) found that Anglo-Americans are more internal than either American-born Chinese or Chinese born in Hong Kong. Jessor, Graves, Hanson and Jessor (1968) studied a tri-ethnic community and observed greater internal scores for Anglos as compared to Spanish and American Indian groups. Cross-cultural differences among groups from the United States, Denmark, West Germany, and Japan have been studied by Schneider and Parsons (1970) and by Parsons, Schneider, and Hansen (1970).

As we shall see in Chapter IX, such group differences are particularly important, not just because they may ultimately mediate group differences in certain kinds of behavior but also because of their implications with respect to the antecedents of I-E beliefs.

Mean Levels of I-E Scale Scores   It is very difficult to summarize the vast I-E literature and then present a "typical" I-E Scale score. Such scores vary significantly from study to study, from population to population, and from one point in time to another. Most often the I-E Scale is scored in the external direction (the higher the score, the more external the belief). In Rotter's original 1966 monograph, mean scores ranging from 5.48 to 10.00 were reported. Such wide variations may present interpretational problems, but they also illustrate the point that one figure cannot meaningfully reflect the wide variations in populations and testing conditions. We have already noted social class and ethnic differences. There could be geographic differences as well, although these may reflect the operation of factors such as differential population crowding and ethnicity.

At first I-E Scale means were clearly skewed in the internal direction. Especially in college populations, means tended to be about 7.50 to 8.50. Over the years, these means have characteristically moved in the external direction at least two to four points, depending upon the specific conditions and populations. For example, Schneider (1971) reported mean I-E Scale means for University of Oklahoma students that range from 7.42 in 1966 to 10.38 in 1970. Some of the possible explanations for such shifts are examined in Chapter X.

GENERALITY AND MULTIDIMENSIONALITY OF THE I-E SCALE
Generality   Like any other behavioral variable, I-E does not possess complete generality. By this we mean that its effects on behavior

are not uniform and invariant across all situations. As a generalized expectancy locus of control is regarded as affecting a wide range of human behavior. It will, however, affect some more than others, and different individuals will manifest differing patterns of effects.

Individuals may show a series of specific or circumscribed beliefs about locus of control, each of which applies more to certain situations than to others. Taken together, these locus of control beliefs may average out to a high level of internal control. However, just because those individuals show a mean level of internality that is high does not mean we can infer that they are high in internality in every situation. In certain specific situations, their beliefs may be quite external.

What a general measure of locus of control allows us to do is describe each individual's "average" locus of control attributes over many situations. But we should remember that the wider the range of situations, the less predictive the concept will be. Therefore, I-E may do a good job of predicting people's behavior in general but miss rather badly in any specific situation. Whether we can tolerate such misses depends upon our purposes.

If our only purpose is to predict sociopolitical behavior, let us say, then it would be sensible to construct an I-E scale whose items pertained solely to sociopolitical events. If we wish only to deal with school success, then the items should be directed entirely to school situations.

If our purpose is broader, however, such a strategy would be inappropriate. To use this strategy to construct a general measure would necessitate developing many I-E scales, each pitched to a highly specific situation (or at most a class of situations). Instead, we need a scale that has some generality. If we opt for such a strategy we must recognize the potential predictive shortcomings that are associated. Further, if we go for more generality than specificity, the scale must be validated as a general measure, which means relating I-E to many types of situations.

The latter probably best describes the I-E Scale. We know that it predicts moderately well in a wide range of situations, especially those that involve personal mastery or coping efforts. However, we are beginning to discover that its success is variable in sociopolitical situations, depending upon a number of factors (e.g., race, age, nature of the "cause") that are just beginning to be identified.

There are many good reasons for conceptualizing personality at least in part in terms of broad dispositions and having appropriate scales for their measurement. One is simply the fact that clinicians, as well as other psychologists, *must* deal with the behavior of people in circumstances which are unknown to the clinician. That is, they must predict (or guess) what patients are likely to do without knowing completely the exact nature of each situation the patients will find themselves in. Experimental psychologists, on the other hand, usually predict behavior in highly controlled laboratory situations and know a great deal about the nature of the stimuli and their impact. Obviously, in these highly contrived and structured situations, the observed differences in behavior are going to be rather modest. If one does research in one or the other of these settings long enough, it is easy to understand how one might begin to overlook the contributions of either situation-specific factors or personality factors.

Clinicians can seldom deal with such highly structured, unambiguous situations. They may be asked, for example, "If John Smith is discharged from the hospital, how will he do?" In short, clinicians may be asked to consider the effects of many situations, not just one. And clinicians seldom have the luxury of knowing specifically in what situation(s) the patients will find themselves five years hence. The lack of information regarding the nature of specific situations may force us to rely more heavily than we would like on general personality factors.

Multidimensionality   Evidence is being presented that the I-E Scale is not unidimensional in character but multidimensional—that is, there may be several components to I-E. For example, externality may refer to a belief that "powerful others" control the world or to a belief in fate or to a feeling that the world is so complex that comprehension and thus control are impossible. Such a multidimensional aspect is apparent in Rotter's (1966) original definition of I-E. It was implied in Chapter III that expectancies stemming from lack of freedom, experimenter control, complexity, etc, although often considered equivalent expressions, may not be empirically similar but may lead to dissimilar behaviors on occasion.

Furthermore, as we commented earlier in this chapter, the I-E Scale is an additive one, a scale that samples locus of control beliefs in a variety of situations. Such a scale, by its nature, is multidimensional. This is consistent with the original intent of the developers of the I-E Scale to produce a scale that would tap locus of control beliefs in several different need areas. While the I-E Scale offers the opportunity for multidimensionality, this opportunity is tempered by the relatively few (23) items that comprise the scale.

Rotter (1966) commented that several factor analyses of the I-E Scale were carried out during the early development of the scale. Although he did not deal with the issue in detail, he suggested that one general factor and several additional factors, involving only a few items and rather little associated variance, were isolated. He did not feel the additional factors were sufficiently reliable to indicate clearcut subscales within the I-E Scale. Franklin (1963) reported similar results. One should recognize that factor-analyzing the I-E Scale into two or more factors is one thing and demonstrating the differential predictive utility of these separate factors is something else. At the present time, there is evidence for the existence of separate factors, but there is much less evidence that demonstrates their predictive utility. Repeated demonstrations of the multifactor character of the I-E Scale are not useful unless evidence can be adduced that these separate factors generate empirically separate predictions. And so far we have little evidence that they do.

Indeed, one can hope that new mulitdimensional scales will be developed for I-E (or that present scales will be studied further for their multidimensionality). Perhaps the wisest strategy is to develop several measures of I-E—some broad, others rather specific to situations of particular interest or relevance, and others somewhere in between. No test can be all things for all purposes. Of course, as we noted earlier, Liverant, Rotter, Seeman, and Crowne (Rotter, 1966) refined the early crude I-E scales into the current I-E Scale. They hoped to broaden the early scales by developing subscales which would measure I-E separately in several different life areas such as achievement, affection, and socio-political affairs. By doing so they anticipated being able to derive subscores that could reveal I-E profiles in several life areas. They were not successful in developing such scales that were capable of yielding separate predictions. As a result, they fell back on the present 23-item version.

It is perhaps a tribute to the robustness of the I-E Scale—a robustness that reveals itself in the remarkably large number of behaviors that have been related to scores on the 23-item version—that when a particlar area, such as sociopolitical activity, seems inconsistent with the Scale, the multidimensional qualities get close scrutiny.

But, as noted before, the multidimensionality is inherent in social learning theory. An individual's perceived locus of control is composed of many separate expectancies that relate to many diverse life areas, or needs, and an overall I-E Scale *score* is based on items that sample a variety of these areas. Of course, having a scale with only 23 items has probably limited our ability to derive separate factors. With more items, there is more flexibility; for example, success versus failure events; personal control versus system control; sociopolitical events versus personal achievement, etc. The question is not whether to develop subscales, but rather, how far to go in that direction and how specific to make the life areas. The latter decision is not theoretical but practical;

it depends entirely upon what we wish to predict and what level of prediction is considered satisfactory.

At this point it may be useful to summarize some of the research on the dimensionality of the I-E Scale. Mirels (1970) factor-analyzed the 23 I-E Scale item responses of 159 college males and 157 college females. The Varimax rotation pointed to two factors each for males and females, accounting for 10.9 and 8.6 percent of the variance in males and 12.1 and 6.7 percent, respectively, in the females. Mirels described these two factors as (1) a belief concerning felt mastery over the course of one's life (Factor I), and (2) a belief concerning the extent to which the individual citizen is capable of having an impact on political institutions (Factor II). A subsequent study by Abrahamson, Schulderman, and Schulderman (1973) closely matched Mirels' findings.

Schneider and Parsons (1970), reanalyzing data from an earlier study, suggested that five categories can be reliably established from I-E Scale scores. These are general luck or fate, respect, politics, academics and leadership, and success. They report small positive intercorrelations among these five scales, which they interpret to indicate the multi-dimensionality of the I-E Scale.

Gurin, Gurin, Lao, and Beattie (1969) factor-analyzed the responses of black students and found evidence for two separate factors. The first factor (items phrased in the first person) relates to personal control—the control that one can exert in his own life. The second factor (third-person items) seems more akin to ideological or general beliefs—beliefs about how much control most people in our society possess. Lao (1970) subsequently employed these distinctions in a study of the relationship between subscale scores and several measures of competency in black college students. While these two studies go beyond the simple demonstration that there may be several factors underlying the I-E Scale, they are not directly comparable since they used modified procedures and items. In these cases it was assumed that there are several distinctions in control beliefs that can be made, and then special items were constructed to demonstrate such distinctions. For example, Lao's data came from a scale consisting of an extended version of the I-E Scale (excluding two items), three items from the Personal Efficacy Scale, and 14 items written specifically for situations with racial implications.

Generalizing from the aforementioned work, Abramowitz (1973) compared scores on the Kerpelman Political Activity Scale and three different I-E measures (the first was a total I-E score based on all 23 items; the other two represented Mirels' Factors I and II). Using college modest, was significant. This study, then, not only supports he multidimensionality view of the I-E Scale but also provides some prethe political items but not by the personal control items. The correlation between Mirels' Factor II scores and the Kerpelman scores, although modest, was significant. This study, then, not only supports the multidimensionality view of the I-E Scale but also provides some preliminary evidence of the predictive utility of distinct clusters within the I-E Scale.

Collins (1974) asserted that an individual may achieve an external score on the I-E Scale by subscribing to any of four views: (1) the world is difficult, (2) the world is unjust, (3) the world is governed by luck, or (4) the world is politically unresponsive. Collins administered the I-E Scale in a Likert agree-disagree format. This resulted in 46 alternatives. He also constructed 42 new items to provide an "it depends on the situation" alternative. This entire 88-item scale was administered to 300 undergraduates. Rotation of four factors resulted in four distinguishable and relatively orthogonal scales.

The study by Reid and Ware (1973) offers evidence for three components of I-E based on a multiple regression technique they utilized. However, as in the Lao (1970) and Gurin, Gurin, Lao, and Beattie (1969) work, it is important to note that they constructed a special I-E scale for their purposes. It is important to distinguish between those studies that find evidence of multidimensionality in the I-E Scale itself and those that, based on assumptions from previous research, build *special* scales to measure I-E. Obviously, if one constructs a scale so that it reflects several dimensions, it is not surprising to find evidence for such dimensions. Such studies are important since they do demonstrate the possibility of conceptualizing I-E along several different lines, however.

Several studies by Levenson (1973a, 1973b, 1973c) followed a similar theme. Levenson constructed three new scales (Internal, Powerful Others, and Chance) in order to isolate components of I-E that should lead to enhanced prediction. Her rationale is simply that people who believe the world is unordered should logically be expected to behave differently from those who feel that powerful others are in control. Such appears to be the case in many situations. The three scales have been used to study certain behaviors in psychiatric patients (Levenson, 1973c) and parental antecedents of I-E beliefs (Levenson, 1973b).

Let us try to summarize the research on the multidimensionality of I-E and also place it in perspective. First, while there is some commonality in the conclusions of various authors regarding the dimensionality of I-E, there is much disagreement. Some find two factors, some three, and others five or more. Much of this disagreement probably lies in the various methods of factor analysis used. Another difficulty stems from population characteristics. As will be noted in Chapter V, college students may make distinctions among several control beliefs because they are so sensitized to issues of politics, government, discrimination, etc. Younger or less sophisticated groups might not be sensitized and thus might show evidence of a different factor structure. Still another problem is the varying definitions of what should be designated as a significant factor loading.

Second, as we noted in passing, some studies merely factor-analyze I-E Scale scores while others create new or modified I-E scales and then carry out their factor analysis. While the latter strategy may be heuristic, it is important to recognize that one is no longer dealing with the I-E Scale. In effect, a new scale has been built, which may or may not be valid. In short, specially constructed I-E scales may be factor-analyzed into several subscales, but such a scale cannot lay claim to the construct validity data that support the Rotter I-E Scale.

Third, as noted earlier, it is important to distinguish between those studies that merely factor-analyze and those that also show that there is some utility in isolating such factors. In the final analysis it must be shown that by distinguishing several components of locus of control an enhancement in prediction is achieved. Several instances of this enhanced prediction were noted, and more may follow. At the same time, the recent modifications of the I-E Scale may be further studied so that their construct validity can better be determined.

A PASSING OBSERVATION

The I-E Scale is a very short instrument. In some ways, its psychometric qualities appear unimpressive. Solid evidence of psychometric strength is important in convincing people that they should begin using a new scale. But, after eight years and scores of studies, simple psychometric issues pale. Now we know what the scale measures or does not measure. The reader will find in subsequent chapters that there is a tremendous volume of solid validity data for the I-E Scale.

Psychometrics is a tool; it is not an end or goal unto itself. Certainly we hope that superior versions of the I-E Scale will emerge in the future. Let us hope that the issue of construct validity will not get lost in the process. The validity of the instrument and its relationship to a coherent theory of personality is crucial. Bersoff (1973) stated the following:

> Test developers, it seems, have lost sight of their original purpose—to gather samples of behavior that can be used to differentiate individuals— and instead have subjected their tests to more and more elaborate

statistical manipulation, at the same time stressing temporal economy and ease of administration and interpretation. (p. 893)

As Wesman (1968) asserted, "Efficiency is certainly desirable—but *validity* is *crucial.* How tests were constructed is interesting and even germane; how they *work* is the critical issue" (p. 272).

Other Measures of I-E

With the tremendous interest that researchers have shown in such topics as alienation and locus of control in recent years, it was inevitable that additional instruments would be developed to measure I-E. This is good. We may hope that over time, investigators can learn from experience with the I-E Scale and build better, more predictive scales.

A variety of measures designed to tap I-E and related attitudes in adolescents and adults has appeared. The measure, developed by Dean (1961) to measure powerlessness, normlessness, and social isolation, has its origins in the sociological concept of alienation. Harrison's (1968) View of the Environment Scale bears some relationship to I-E in that it deals with people's belief in their ability to control the environment. A personal control scale has been described by Lessing (1969) and seems related to locus of control. In several studies, specific measures of locus of control have been constructed for specific purposes (Dissinger, 1968; Graves, 1961; Gurin, Gurin, Lao, & Beattie, 1969; Jessor, Graves, Hanson, & Jessor, 1968; Lao, 1970). Another recently developed scale has been studied by Powell and Vega (1972).

Dies (1968) has provided another approach. He developed a projective measure of perceived locus of control. He administered the I-E Scale to 40 female psychiatric nursing students. Using a median split, he classified these subjects as internal or external. Then subjects wrote stories in response to seven standard TAT cards. Ratings of locus of control were made on a five-point scale according to a detailed manual. The internal subjects produced significantly more stories reflecting a belief in personal control than did the external group. However, two of the cards generated most of the significance obtained. In a similar approach Adams-Webber (1969) compared scores on a story completion test with scores derived from the I-E Scale. He found that the tendency to view moral sanctions as directly contingent upon immoral behavior was significantly related to belief in internal control.

The foregoing measures offer interesting alternatives to the traditional I-E Scale. It is difficult to assess these instruments since in most cases little research, especially of a construct validity nature, is offered. In several instances, the I-E Scale is used as the criterion, and the value of the new instrument is gauged by how closely it agrees with the I-E Scale. If one is not careful, such a method will simply produce a "junior" I-E Scale that adds little to the predictive enterprise.

THE NOWICKI-DUKE SCALE

Nowicki and Duke (1974) have produced a scale of 40 yes-no items that they feel is suitable for both college and noncollege adult samples. Their efforts to develop such a scale stemmed from what they regarded as several weaknesses in the I-E Scale. First, several studies have found evidence of the effects of social desirability on I-E Scale scores. Second, they feel the I-E Scale confounds personal, social, political, and ideological causation. Third, they believe that the I-E Scale is difficult to read. This, along with its forced-choice format, makes it, they assert, inappropriate for noncollege populations.

Nowicki and Duke sampled nearly 800 subjects in 12 separate studies. The correlation between the I-E Scale and the Nowicki-Duke Scale for Adults (ANS-IE) is .68. This suggests that the two scales overlap but do not measure exactly the same thing. Such a moderate relationship is desirable, since a high correlation would mean that the ANS-IE Scale is essentially identical to the I-E Scale. A low correlation would raise questions as to exactly what the new scale measures, in view of the number of validity studies already supporting the I-E Scale.

The ANS-IE Scale measures achievement behavior. It is not related to either social desirability or intelligence. Further, it appears easier to read and understand than the I-E Scale. Finally, it manifests suitable reliability. All in all, this scale shows considerable promise. Whether the test characteristics reported by Nowicki and Duke will hold up in future studies we do not know. It is too early to know the full utility of this scale. Its validity must be reliably established over a range of studies and populations. Until then comparisons with the I-E Scale are premature.

INTELLECTUAL ACHIEVEMENT RESPONSIBILITY QUESTIONNAIRE

The I-E measures discussed thus far were developed mainly for adult populations. The Intellectual Achievement Responsibility Questionnaire (IAR) was developed by Crandall, Katkovsky, and Crandall and is probably, at the present time, the most frequently used measure of I-E in children.

The IAR has several unique features. Crandall, Katkovsky, and Crandall (1965) were not convinced that I-E operates uniformly over a wide range of motivational areas. Therefore, they chose to measure locus of control solely in intellectual achievement situations. Developed in the context of a larger program of research on achievement, the IAR attempts to assess children's beliefs in reinforcement responsibility exclusively in intellectual-academic achievement situations. Another characteristic of the IAR is its focus on measurement of locus of control beliefs in situations that involve children with significant others— their parents, teachers, or peers. Luck, impersonal social factors, or fate are passed by with the emphasis on perception of control by significant others in the environment.

Another important feature of the IAR involves the decision to sample an equal number of positive and negative events. Crandall, Katkovsky, and Crandall felt that the forces leading children to assume credit for causing positive outcomes might be quite different from those causing the taking of blame for unpleasant outcomes. Thus, the IAR yields three scores. There is the total I (internal or self responsibility score) and also subscores for beliefs in internal responsibility for successes $(I+)$ and for failures $(I-)$. It may be fair to state that this scale was the first to systematically employ subscales in the measurement of I-E. A variety of measures now employ the subscale approach (either for success versus failure or in other ways), but the IAR scale was the first to demonstrate the feasibility of doing so.

The IAR is reproduced in Appendix B. It is composed of 34 forced-choice items. Since the authors found that children of average intelligence in the first two elementary grades had difficulty in responding to the IAR, only children in the third grade and above were included in the standardization sample. For children below the sixth grade, the authors recommended an oral form of presentation to ensure proper understanding of the items.

The sample consisted of 923 elementary and high school students. In general, distributions were skewed in the internal direction for all age groups and both sexes. Test-retest correlations over two months were .69 for total I, .66 for $I+$, and .74 for $I-$ for children in grades three, four, and five. Ninth-grade students produced similar correlations (.65, .47, and .69). Split-half reliabilities were .54 $(I+)$ and .57 $(I-)$. For older children, the correlations were .60 for both $I+$ and $I-$. In general, correlations between IAR subscores and a measure of social desirability lead to the conclusion that social desirability accounts for relatively little of the variance in IAR scores.

In subsequent chapters, particularly Chapter VII, relationships between a variety of criterion behaviors and IAR scores will be noted. That work supports the construct validity of the IAR and is consistent with the evidence reported by Crandall, Katkovsky, and Crandall. Different results for the $I+$ and $I-$ subscales are sometimes reported, thus reinforcing the wisdom of developing separate subscales for successes and failures.

Crandall, Katkovsky, and Crandall (1965) observed the following: "In general, the IAR has predicted best to young girls' standardized achievement-test performances and to those for older boys. It has predicted better to young boys' intellectual activities in free play than to those of young girls. Its most consistent prediction has been to report-card grades" (p. 108).

Although the IAR may be in need of further refinement, its basic utility seems to have been established and marks it as perhaps the most serviceable measure of locus of control beliefs in children in the relatively specific areas of intellectual-academic achievement.

Other Measures of I-E in Children

A variety of children's I-E measures have been developed in addition to the IAR, several of them quite recently. The earliest of these scales, the Children's Locus of Control Scale, was constructed by Bialer (1961) based on previous work by Phares (1955) and James (1957). It is a 23-item questionnaire with yes-no alternatives and was first developed for use with populations of normal and mentally retarded children. Typically, the items are read to each child. An alternative form of the scale was used by Gozali and Bialer (1968). Both versions were developed in the context of a research program on mental deficiency.

Battle and Rotter (1963) constructed the Children's Picture Test of Internal-External Control. This is a projective device consisting of six cartoons somewhat similar in conceptualization to the Rosenzweig Picture Frustration Study. Children state "what they would say" if they were in the situation depicted by the cartoon. The cartoon situations involve the attribution of responsibility. Scores on the Battle and Rotter measure (scored in the external direction) correlated significantly ($-.42$) with the Bialer measure (scored in the internal direction). Some of the correlates of the Battle and Rotter measure are reported in Chapter IX.

NOWICKI-STRICKLAND LOCUS OF CONTROL SCALE FOR CHILDREN

Nowicki and Strickland (1973) have provided evidence of reliability and validity for a measure of generalized expectancy for control in children. It is a paper-and-pencil measure containing 40 yes-no questions. The items describe reinforcement in a variety of areas, such as affiliation, achievement, and dependency. Results are reported for boys and girls in grades three through twelve. Starting with a pool of over 100 items, the authors reduced this to 40, based on comments from teachers and children and item analyses. The standardization sample included over 1,000 subjects, who were mostly white elementary and high school students in four communities.

Split-half correlations ranged from .63 to .81. Test-retest reliabilities over six-week periods were from .63 for third graders to .71 for tenth-graders. No evidence of significant social desirability effects were adduced. Internal locus of control belief seemed to relate to higher occupational level in parents and to higher achievement scores in boys (but not girls). For several different samples, correlations between the Nowicki-Strickland Scale for Children (CNS-IE) and other locus of control measures were significant: .31 and .51 with I+ scale of the IAR, .41 with the Bialer scale, and .61 and .38 with the I-E Scale.

Nowicki and Strickland reported that several other studies have found significant correlations between the CNS-IE and grade-point averages (but not intelligence) and also between internality and reading and math achievement scores. (The latter relationship was noted for males but not for females.) Other reported evidence of construct validity involves popularity, ability to delay gratification, and prejudice. Nowicki (1973) presented evidence concerning the factor structure of the CNS-IE and suggested factors that may be sex-related at different age levels. This may explain previously obtained inconsistencies in predicting female behavior at several age levels. A new measure of locus of control for preschool children and children up to 9 years of age is currently being developed (Wilson, Duke, & Nowicki, 1972).

STEPHENS-DELYS REINFORCEMENT CONTINGENCY INTERVIEW

Stephens and Delys (1973) felt that conventional measures of locus of control in children were too cognitively demanding for preschool children. Even oral presentation of items results in problems, since the very young children with short attention spans and limited capacity for understanding often agree with the last-read alternative. Forty questions were developed, half dealing with positive reinforcement and half with negative reinforcement. This permits the derivation of success-failure subscores as was done with the IAR. The questions present situations involving one of five sources of reinforcement: self, peers, mothers, fathers, and teachers. Presentation of the questions was quite flexible and allowed for rewording and repetition in order to enhance the likelihood of communication and understanding. Subjects (black and Head Start program students) gave free, verbal responses to questions such as, "What makes you smile?" Good internal consistency and test-retest reliability were reported. Intercorrelations among the IAR, CNS-IE, and the Stephens-Delys Reinforcement Contingency Interview were low, suggesting that each may be tapping a different aspect of locus of control. Behavior correlates and age and socio-economic differences suggest promising evidence of construct validity.

STANFORD PRESCHOOL I-E SCALE

Mischel, Zeiss, and Zeiss (1974) published preliminary evidence of the utility of a preschool I-E measure, the Stanford Preschool I-E Scale (SPIES). The scale is composed of 14 forced-choice questions, each describing either a positive or a negative event in the child's life. Thus, in the format pioneered by Crandall, Katkovsky, and Crandall (1965), scores for both positive and negative outcomes can be obtained. The SPIES is administered orally and individually to each child and the questions are roughly equivalent to the Stephens-Delys technique. As in the Stephens-Delys Reinforcement Contingency Interview, the examiner's approach is flexible and depends somewhat on the specific circumstances encountered with a given child. The SPIES was designed to be used primarily with children between the ages of 3 and 6.

While the split-half reliabilities for the positive $(I+)$ and negative $(I-)$ subscales were only .14 and .20, respectively, Mischel, Zeiss, and Zeiss feel this is desirable inasmuch as the scale items sample a diverse universe of situations. This raises interesting psychometric questions that could be better answered if there were more than 14 items so that some built-in redundancy might exist. Test-retest reliability over a mean seven-month interval was substantial, especially when 4-year-olds were removed from the sample.

Evidence for validity revolves around behavioral measures of delay of gratification under several conditions of working and waiting. As predicted by Mischel, Zeiss, and Zeiss, $I+$ scores were found to be related to persistence in three separate conditions in which an instrumental behavior would lead to a positive outcome. $I-$ scores correlated with persistance when instrumental behavior could prevent the occurrence of an unpleasant outcome. The same type of situation, structured so that instrumental behavior could not affect the outcome, resulted in a negative correlation between persistence and $I-$ scores.

While it is much too early to evaluate intelligently the utility or construct validity of scales such as the SPIES, CNS-IE, Stephens-Delys Reinforcement Contingency Interview, the Battle and Rotter measures, or the Bialer measures, they all show encouraging pre-liminary results. Further, with the exception of the latter two, they incorporate subscale approaches, and they not only permit finer measurement but also extend this measurement down to young children. This may ultimately provide added insight into the mode of growth and differentiation of locus of control beliefs.

Summary

In this chapter we have provided a brief overview of some of the instruments designed to measure locus of control beliefs. These instruments include objective tests and projective tests. Some are designed for children while others are suitable for adults. Some are read by subjects while others use an interview format. We have come a long way since the first crude skill-chance instrument (Phares, 1955).

However, the I-E Scale (Rotter, 1966) remains the most-used test to assess individual differences in locus of control beliefs. As a result, the major focus of this chapter is on the I-E Scale. While this scale is less than perfect, and it may even contain several important limitations, it probably is still the most serviceable instrument for adult populations. Some of the newer scales are bidding fair to remedy its imperfections. However, we must bear in mind that even with its defects, the I-E Scale has demonstrated its utility over a wide range of predictive situations. So much research has been carried out with the scale that it is very much a known quantity as compared to more recent versions.

The issues of generality and multidimensionality (particularly as they apply to the I-E Scale) were discussed. Generality was dealt with largely in terms of predictive goals. Particularly emphasized was the idea that the degree of generality that accrues to scores on an I-E measure depends upon how well it predicts in the situation(s) one is interested in. A broadly derived score may predict moderately well to a range of situations but poorly to any specific situation. Likewise, a narrow score may predict well to one class of situations but poorly to others.

A multidimensional aspect of locus of control has always been inherent in the social learning theory framework. Yet only rather recently have concerted attempts been made to exploit the possibilities. With, perhaps, the exception of the IAR, attempts to incorporate multidimensionality into new scale construction await systematic evaluation. Such efforts should increase the utility of the I-E concept. Efforts to factor the I-E Scale into two or more subscales are of great interest and potential utility. But as yet, there exist more demonstrations that factors or subscales can be isolated than hard evidence that these factors have predictive utility.

Much of the work reported in the chapters that follow was carried out using the I-E Scale (or, to a lesser extent, the IAR). Thus, in a very real sense, these chapters present the evidence for the construct validity of the I-E Scale as well as illuminating the nature of I-E.

V

Locus of Control as a Determinant of Mastery over the Environment

The best single indicator of the validity of the I-E Scale would undoubtedly be evidence showing that internals are more active, alert, or directive in attempting to control and manipulate their environments than are externals. Since locus of control refers to expectancies for control over one's surroundings, a higher level of coping and activity would be anticipated from internals. To obtain important positive outcomes and avoid negative ones, internals should, over a range of situations, show more active controlling efforts. While there are important exceptions to this statement that will be discussed later, the foregoing hypothesis is the one most consistently verified in a wide variety of experimental studies, surveys, and life situations.

Preliminary Evidence of Greater Mastery Efforts by Internals

Recognizing the fundamental importance of the hypothesis just stated, Seeman and Evans (1962), in one of the earliest studies in this area, focused on the relationship between locus of control and the knowledge and information-seeking behavior of patients in a tuberculosis hospital. They employed an early 12-item version of the I-E

Scale to select 43 internal-external pairs of white male patients (each pair being matched for occupational status, education, and ward placement). Physicians and nurses were asked questions similar to these:

1. How good is this patient's understanding of the details of his own illness (diagnosis, prognosis, and progress)?
2. How good is the patient's understanding of the nature of tuberculosis in general (its causes, cure, and preventions)?

In addition, patients were interviewed regarding their satisfaction with the information provided by the professional staff and were asked questions similar to the following:

1. When you receive a new treatment, medication, or test, does someone explain it to you in advance?
2. Do you think you are informed enough about your illness and how you are getting along?

Seeman and Evans found, as they had anticipated, that internals knew more about their condition, were more inquisitive with physicians and nurses about tuberculosis and about their own situation, and indicated less satisfaction with the amount of information they were getting from hospital personnel. Relatively speaking, internals attempted to gain a greater degree of control over their life situation than did externals.

In the same vein, Seeman (1963) also studied the social learning of inmates in a federal reformatory. The scale used to assess locus of control was a 40-item variant of the current I-E Scale. Consistent with the Seeman and Evans results, he found that internals were more knowledgeable about the manner in which the reformatory was run, were more familiar with parole regulations, and more cognizant of long-range economic facts that potentially could affect their future after release from the reformatory. The inmates had all been exposed to such information in an incidental fashion. Further, intelligence level was controlled. Again it appeared that more externally oriented individuals do not acquire the kind of information that would better enable them to cope with the world in an effective way.

It has been repeatedly demonstrated (see Chapter III) that when individuals are in a specific situation that contains substantial cues that they are not in control, their learning, or acquisition of knowledge, is significantly reduced. The Seeman study suggests that a low generalized expectancy for personal control also contributes to reduced acquisition of information. This is so because belief in an external locus of control (like specific external cues in a situation) is accompanied by a low expectancy that one's own efforts will have an impact; therefore information acquisition is not seen as a productive enterprise.

Another study by Seeman (1967) lends credence to the notion that the poor learning exhibited by persons with an external control orientation is relatively specific to situations that are particularly germane to issues of control and not to every single aspect of individuals' lives. Seeman hypothesized that individuals high in powerlessness (external orientation) will possess inferior knowledge in control-relevant areas of their experience. Using Swedish students, it was found that external (or "alienated") belief systems accompanied poor knowledge about nuclear events, but that so-called alienated and nonalienated students did not differ in their knowledge of general cultural information. In a different setting, Seeman (1966) found that male workers in Sweden who felt powerless also showed a relative lack of political knowledge (even with education, social class, and income controlled). This work not only extends and replicates that done in the United States but again suggests the predictive limits of the relationship between locus of control and information acquisition.

The Seeman studies appear clear in their message that internals are more knowledgeable, at least in terms of personally relevant information, then are externals. Such knowledge is essential if individuals are to seek to exert an effect on their surroundings. But how is such information acquired? Certainly it does not simply appear in the repertoire of internals. What is it specifically that internals do or feel that makes them learn or retain information better? To understand these differential behaviors we must push our inquiry further.

Some Cognitive Bases for Control

The most logical place to look for the basis of internals' superior learning is in the area of cognitive performance. If internals and externals differ in the amount or kind of information they acquire, they probably also differ in the very specific behaviors they use to achieve that information. Davis and Phares (1967), in a study described in detail in Chapter II, reasoned that if internals do possess a stronger generalized expectancy that reinforcements will be contingent upon their own behavior, they should more actively seek relevant information so that they can be better prepared to deal effectively with their world. The reader may recall that their results indicated, as anticipated, that internals requested significantly more information than did externals. Therefore, it may be fair to state that, consistent with Seeman's (1963, 1967) work, internals possess a higher level of knowledge, at least in part because they more actively seek to acquire such knowledge.

Williams and Stack (1972), using a different experimental task, showed that, among black subjects, internals more actively seek information (via asking questions) than externals, as was the case with Davis and Phares' predominantly white subjects. Also of interest is their finding that externals behave either externally or internally depending upon the specific nature of the situation.

All of the studies mentioned in this chapter suggest that internals and externals differ not only in attentiveness to and recall of material that is immediately present in the environment (as Seeman's work particularly indicates) but also in terms of how actively they seek additional relevant information. Partly because there was some question about the adequacy of Seeman's (1963) learning measure (which equated externals and internals for initial learning), and partly to demonstrate that internals are superior not only in acquisition and recall but also in *utilization* of information, Phares (1968) carried out a study in which subjects were led to believe they were in a computer simulation study designed to determine the marriage suitability of several men and women. Their task was to organize information provided about the individuals and decide who should marry whom. Both amount of information available and degree of learning of that information were controlled. Nevertheless, internals made significantly more effective use of the information than did externals.

One might describe the behavior of internals as alert and sensitive. The internal seems to be eager to seek out cues and to manipulate the situation so as to be better able to achieve certain outcomes. For example, several studies involving locus of control and verbal conditioning or awareness of reinforcement contingencies point to greater sensitivity on the part of internals (although some of this can also be construed as resistance to social influence, which is discussed in Chapter VI). Work by Getter (1966), Rothschild and Horowitz (1970), and Ude and Vogler (1969) suggests this greater perceptual sensitivity on the part of internals. In the Ude and Vogler study, as a case in point, awareness of reinforcement contingencies was the variable under study, and it was found that internals became aware of such contingencies substantially more rapidly than did externals.

Another method of studying cognitive activity in internals and externals is exemplified in the work by Lefcourt and his colleagues. Lefcourt and Wine (1969) had subjects interview other persons, one that avoided eye contact with the subject and one that behaved in a more typical social fashion. A specific finding was that internals looked at the person who avoided eye contact more often than they looked at the conventional person and looked at the person who avoided eye contact more often than did external subjects. Likewise, internals made more observations of both persons than did externals. Lefcourt and

Wine concluded, therefore, that when there are uncertainties in the situation, internals will be more likely to pay attention to potentially relevant cues than will externals.

In another study, Lefcourt (1967) placed subjects in a level of aspiration situation in which they performed a motor skill task (pushing a steel ball with a wooden stick). Subjects differed in the instructions they received regarding what reinforcements were available—some received high-cue instructions and others low-cue instructions. The internals' behavior did not differ in the two conditions. Externals showed greater variability. Lefcourt speculated that externals do not adequately search for reinforcement properties or that they fail to maintain the kind of cognitive awareness that might facilitate cognitive categorizing of situations so as to better attain reinforcement.

Using a similar task, Lefcourt, Lewis, and Silverman (1968) noted that attention-related responses in their subjects varied as a function of both locus of control and the skill-chance nature of the situation. When internals viewed the task as skill-determined, they exhibited less inattentiveness and reported more thoughts relevant to the task and fewer task-irrelevant thoughts than did internals who believed the task was chance-oriented. Similar differences among externals were much less pronounced.

The foregoing work supports the conclusion that internals are superior in cognitive processing. More recent work by DuCette and Wolk (1973) strengthens this conclusion. DuCette and Wolk used a simple problem-solving task for which a nonverbal cue from the experimenter suggested the solution to the problem. Internals took significantly fewer trials to discover the rule. In addition, when the same task was presented without the experimenters' having been instructed to emit the nonverbal cues (and with the task described to subjects as an ESP task) similar differences occurred; that is, internals were more often correct in what was essentially a chance game. It seems likely that internals were reacting to highly covert cues from the experimenters over the trial series. Thus, the study of DuCette and Wolk seems to have demonstrated several things: (1) internals are better at using their experience on a task to improve their perception of performance or test data; (2) internals are more accurate in remembering successes when feedback is provided; (3) internals can more quickly deduce an invariant rule from an ambiguous situation and use this rule to solve a problem.

Additional evidence for this cognitive and performance superiority of internals has also been adduced by Wolk and DuCette (1974). They presented verbal material to subjects to be scanned for errors. They found that internals were superior to externals on a measure of incidental learning (retention of the content of the material). The internals were also superior in intentional performance (actually finding errors). It should be noted that when the task was either ambiguous or very difficult, internals were even more superior on both finding errors and incidental learning. Once again, the role of the situation intrudes and suggests that the applicability of personality variables is particularly evident in unstructured situations.

Of course, much of the preceding work was carried out under laboratory conditions. As Pines and Julian (1972) pointed out, at least two classes of variables can influence any obtained performance differences in these kinds of situations. The first is what might be called the informational demands of the task. The second could be described as the social demands of the situation. We have already seen considerable evidence that internals are superior to externals in their responsiveness to informational requirements. In Chapter VI we shall see that externals seem to be more conforming, more susceptible to influence, and more sensitive to social demands.

College women participated in an experiment by Pines and Julian that varied locus of control, task difficulty, and social evaluation. As anticipated, internals were more attuned to the task difficulty and the consequent pressure it exerted for information processing, while externals were more affected by the social demand characteristics of the situation. This led Pines and Julian to suggest that performance differences between internals and externals are not completely explicable in terms of belief in one's control over outcomes. Rather, internals and externals may adopt different strategies in the pursuit of valued goals. Internals may pursue goals by paying more careful attention to the nature of the task while externals are more likely to rely upon behaviors oriented toward the social agent in the situation. Additional work by Pines (1973) supports this conclusion.

Additional Evidence on Personal Effectiveness

The cognitive functioning of internals should enhance their personal effectiveness as compared to externals. And it apparently does. Phares, Ritchie, and Davis (1968) created a condition of threat by having groups of internals and externals respond to a series of personality tests. The subjects (college students) were subsequently presented with interpretations of their personalities that were rather negative, along with some positive feedback. For example, they might be told, "At times, sexual thoughts become a problem and make you doubt your maturity." After having had an opportunity to digest their personality profiles, subjects were administered the following question-naire.

> I would be interested in
> (a) Receiving a copy of a brochure listing several sources of library material dealing with techniques of achieving better mental health.
> (b) Attending a lecture by a psychiatrist on techniques of achieving better mental health.
> (c) Attending a small group discussion to talk about common problems of college students in dealing with the stresses of college life.
> (d) Making an appointment with a clinical psychologist to discuss in greater depth the meaning and implications of my test results.
> (e) I would not be interested in any of the foregoing.
> (Phares, Ritchie, and Davis, 1968, p. 404).

Internals showed a significantly greater willingness to take overt remedial action to correct presumed personal shortcomings when presented the opportunity to do so. Whether one terms it action taking, confronting, or mastery, internals seem to be more disposed toward behavior that will enhance their personal efficacy, even in the sense of rectifying inadequacies.

Phares (1965) took a different approach in studying the differential effectiveness of internals and externals. The focus was on the social influence aspects of a personal interaction. On the assumption that internals have a greater belief in personal control, it was predicted that internals would be able to exert more influence upon others than would a similar group of externals. To test this general hypothesis, internal and external experimenters were used in an attempt to change female subjects' previously expressed attitudes regarding a variety of campus issues (such as required class attendance, role of sororities and fraternities, college athletics, and student parking). In a rather stringent set of procedures, experimenters were required to read from a standard prepared script in their attempts to influence subjects. As expected, internal experimenters were able to induce significantly greater attitude change than were external experimenters. Control subjects, who merely filled out an attitude questionnaire a second time with no attempted influence, exhibited changes equal to those of subjects paired with external experimenters.

While these results are striking because they were induced under rather restricted conditions, it is not clear how the superior influence on the part of internals was conveyed. That is, were the voice tones, gestures, facial expressions, or posture different for the two groups of experimenters? Some of the experimenter bias research suggests the importance of visual cues. Of course, it is important to recognize also that the subjects' attitudes in this experiment were of moderate intensity. It is not clear that similar results would obtain if subjects held very strong attitudes about volatile issues.

In a related study of expectancy effects, Felton (1971) demonstrated that internal experimenters were more effective with all their subjects in eliciting the expected data than were external experimenters. Maximum bias effects were obtained from internal experimenters working with external subjects under high-ambiguity conditions. Doctor (1971) tried to demonstrate the greater effectiveness of internal experimenters in producing responses from subjects in a Taffel verbal conditioning paradigm. He could find no evidence that the locus of control of the experimenter affects subjects' performance in verbal conditioning. While his results run counter to those obtained by both Phares (1965) and McFall (1967), as he indicates, it is important to note that there is a considerable difference between saying "Good" to a subject's verbal production and trying to influence a person by reading from a long prepared script.

Hersch and Scheibe (1967) found that internals describe themselves as more active, striving, achieving, powerful, independent, and effective. This is quite obviously what we would expect. In addition, Hersch and Scheibe examined effectiveness ratings on three samples of members of the Connecticut Service Corps (for the years 1964, 1965, and 1966). These effectiveness ratings were based on the combined ratings of peers and supervisors. For both 1964 and 1965 internal Service Corps members were rated as significantly more effective than external members. Inexplicably, the 1966 correlation between locus of control and effectiveness was not significantly different from zero.

Also, consistent with the foregoing is one of the findings in a study by Tseng (1970). Drawing from a sample of vocational rehabilitation clients, it was demonstrated that internal clients, as a group, showed significantly higher instructors' ratings of job proficiency and personal qualities than did external clients.

Brown and Strickland (1972) approached this question in a different fashion, relying on neither self-characterization nor effectiveness ratings of others. For their study they selected internal and external college students who were listed in their college yearbook with activity summaries. This provides a very nice nonreactive, archival measure of involvement in activities—an expected correlate of internality. Even with intelligence controlled in this study, several interesting findings emerged. In the case of males, internals significantly more often turned out to be office-holders on campus and also had significantly higher grade-point averages than externals. This is particularly impressive inasmuch as the college population utilized was quite homogeneous in other respects. Lack of comparable findings in females is consistent with most results, which tend to show relationships between locus of control and various achievement behaviors. The reasons probably reside in the cultural meanings associated with achievement and sex roles. Even though this study could find no relationship between locus of control and sheer number of activities participated in, the obtained findings nonetheless offer support for the generalization that internality does indeed lead to behaviors calculated to achieve a greater power over one's environment. Surely holding office portends a greater potential for influence or power than simple participation in activities.

The only time sex differences were implicated in the relationship between locus of control and effectiveness or participation was in the case of achievement behaviors; a relationship was obtained for males but not for females. In a very interesting reversal of these results, Ryckman, Martens, Rodda, and Sherman (1972) found a significant relationship between locus of control and commitment to social action; but only in the case of females. More specifically, they found that internal college women expressed a greater commitment to Women's Liberation activities than did similar external women. As might be expected, in the case of men there was not a significant relationship. The most likely interpretation of these results is that the males in the sample attached much less value to such liberation activities or goals than did the females; for males, the whole issue was, relatively speaking, not relevant enough to allow for the differential operation of locus of control.

Indirectly, such a study supports social learning theory. That is, the role of locus of control is usually mediated by other variables, such as need value and expectancies for success. The more sophisticated approach to prediction is one that considers each time the interplay of needs, expectancies for success, generalized problem-solving expectancies, and the nature of the situation.

Control of Self

We have discussed at length the relatively greater control that internals exert over their environment. Perhaps related to internals' feelings that they can control the environment is the feeling that they can control themselves. For example, Straits and Sechrest (1963) noted that nonsmokers were significantly more internal than smokers. James, Woodruff, and Werner (1965) replicated the finding of Straits and

Sechrest. In addition, they noted that in the case of male smokers, those who, following the Surgeon General's Report on the Hazards of Smoking, quit smoking and did not return within a given period of time were more internal than those who believed the report but did not quit smoking. For females, the difference was not significant. It should be noted, however, that Lichtenstein and Keutzer (1967) could not corroborate these relationships between locus of control and smoking.

Obviously, there are many complex determinants of smoking, with sex differences being one. Perhaps women are more influenced by a concern over gaining weight if they quit smoking. Further, while the results for males are statistically significant, the relationships are modest, which suggests that much of the variance must be accounted for by other variables. Nonetheless, the data provide further evidence that even alone (without systematic consideration of values, needs, other expectancies, or prior learning history) locus of control can differentiate among samples to a statistically significant degree.

Control over one's own behavior can be extended to include birth control techniques (Lundy, 1972; MacDonald, 1970). MacDonald showed that in single female college students (who were quite similar in degree of sexual experience) there was a significant relationship between locus of control and birth control practices. Thus, 62 percent of the internals reported practicing some form of contraception while only 37 percent of the externals did so. In the case of married females, the data were in the same direction but failed to reach significance.

Again, locus of control accounts for only a small portion of the variance even though the results are statistically significant. The wonder is that any results based only on locus of control can reach significance given the great number of variables affecting contraceptive usage. Phares and Wilson (1972a) studied the attitudes toward and the use of birth control techniques on the part of three groups of females: (1) girls confined to a girls' industrial school (GIS), (2) married females residing in university sponsored housing, and (3) both married and unmarried college women attending home economics classes. This research indicated several things. First, the GIS girls were more externally oriented than the samples of college women. Second, the GIS girls, although they reported a great deal of sexual activity, tended to disdain the use of contraceptives. All the college groups reported an extremely high percentage of use of contraceptives. However, within each group, I-E was not related to the use of contraceptives. The variability within each group on both locus of control and reported use of birth control techniques was extremely small.

Qualitatively, it was observed that the GIS girls placed very little value on family planning, they had a lower confidence level that family planning methods would work for them, they attached relatively little value to contraception, and they generally showed less aversion to having a child at that point in their lives. Further, their spontaneous comments provided a rich source of evidence about their lack of information, distortion of information, and superstition regarding contraceptive techniques and devices. It should be noted that the college and GIS samples also differed a great deal with respect to age, socioeconomic status, and education.

Despite all the complications and potential qualifiers, both the smoking and birth control studies strongly suggest that an internal orientation provides a greater potential for exercising the kind of personal or self control that will, in the long run, lead to more positive or valued outcomes. Such differential behavior is further evidence of the superior planning ability of internals, an ability that pays off in greater benefits over the long haul. Finally, such data are consistent with research (discussed later) that demonstrates the internal's greater capacity to delay gratification in the service of greater long-term gain.

Risk Taking

The research on risk taking generally seems contradictory (Joe, 1971). A major reason for this may be, as Rotter (1966) pointed out early, simply that much of this kind of research is carried out in highly structured, achievement-oriented situations. Such highly structured situations, coupled with the narrow range of locus of control beliefs tapped in most of the populations used, tend to suppress the operation of personality differences in locus of control to an appreciable extent.

Liverant and Scodel (1960), using a dice-throwing task, studied preferences for bets. The more internally oriented of their subjects seemed to prefer intermediate probability bets or extremely safe bets over so-called long shots. They also tended to bet more on safe as compared to high-risk outcomes than did the more externally oriented subjects. The locus of control measure used was an early 60-item version of the I-E Scale. Overall, the results support the idea that internals will be more cautious in their control efforts while externals will engage in riskier behavior. This interpretation is reinforced by a study in which internals were found to prefer choices with a high probability of success while externals were drawn toward choices with a low probability of success (Julian, Lichtman, and Ryckman, 1968).

On the other hand, some investigators have predicted greater risk-taking for internals inasmuch as they should be better able to know and circumvent the odds (Strickland, Lewicki, and Katz, 1966).

Baron (1968) provided data that are somewhat consistent with this interpretation.

Lefcourt (1965) replicated the Liverant and Scodel study using a population of both blacks and whites. He expected that blacks would be less external than whites in a chance situation since such a situation should not elicit as much defensiveness or failure avoidance. Blacks chose fewer low-probability bets and were generally less risky in their behavior than whites. Lefcourt's interpretation is that these results were obtained because blacks do not believe that achievement in self-evaluative, skill-demanding tasks is controllable. Rather, they presumably believe that success in externally controlled situations is at least obtainable as contrasted with those situations involving achievement, in which goals will be denied regardless of effort.

Locus of Control as a Motive

As we noted in Chapter II, behavior is determined not just by expectancies but also by the value of the goals toward which the individual's behavior is oriented. Most of the behaviors described in this chapter (information seeking, learning, utilization of knowledge, level of aspiration) have been successfully predicted through recourse to differential I-E scores. More specifically, groups of people are observed to differ in their performance of certain behaviors. Because they also differ in what are regarded as expectancies for personal efficacy or control, it is often assumed that these expectancies account for the bulk of the variance. However, what about potential differences in reinforcement value? Maybe internals try harder than externals due to differences in the *value* they ascribe to certain outcomes. Is it not possible, then, that there are associated motivational differences between internals and externals?

THEORETICAL FORMULATIONS

The Power Motive   Most of the research discussed so far, as well as that which is reviewed in subsequent chapters, suggests the greater effectiveness of internals. Stated otherwise, internals seem to enjoy a greater potential for power. If we define power as Minton (1967) does, in terms of "the ability to cause environmental change so as to obtain an intended effect" (p. 229), then we are discussing an aspect of internality. Therefore, before examining some of the evidence that is directed specifically toward establishing some of the motivational properties of locus of control, let us review briefly a few motivational conceptions that are related to power as an I-E concept.

Angyal (1941) posited *autonomy* as a drive that impels people toward need satisfaction through manipulation of and influence over the environment. The individual seeks to master the world, although he is governed at the same time by a propensity to subjugate himself to his environment. Rank (1945) offered a similar point of view. The individual strives to be powerful and independent and yet, at the same time, fears achieving that toward which he strives. The views of Angyal and Rank are difficult to assess. Their work has not led to much experimental research; indeed, their vague concepts do not lend themselves to research.

Sullivan (1947) discussed a *power motive* that propels individuals into any activity where there is an accomplishment or a satisfaction of needs. Failure to fulfill this motive leads to a negative effect on the growth and structure of the adult personality. A *power drive,* on the other hand, is a compensatory striving resulting from the frustration of the need to be capable. This often leads to behavior designed to dominate and subjugate others. Sullivan's notions, also, do not permit the quantification that will lead to tests of the utility of these concepts.

Adler (see Ansbacher and Ansbacher [1956]) felt that people discover they are inferior in one way or another, physically, psychically, or socially, and seek to compensate for these weaknesses through training and effort. Strivings for power and influence are seen as outgrowths of feelings of inferiority. To become powerful is to deny one's inadequacies by overcoming them. Horney (1942), similarly, felt that individuals may experience anxiety, which leads them to learn to cope with such anxiety. Attaining power is one method of coping. Both Horney and Adler regard mastery, control, power, striving for superiority, etc., as compensations for felt inadequacies.

The concept of *competence* also bears on our notion of internal control: "... visual exploration, grasping, crawling, and walking, attention and perception, language and thinking, exploring novel objects and places, manipulating the surroundings, and producing effective changes in the environment ... these behaviors all have a common biological significance: they all form part of the process whereby the animal or child learns to interact effectively with his environment... competence ..." (White, 1959, p. 329). In White's view, man emerges as someone with a need to know, to experience meaning, and to manipulate and control the environment.

Several of the concepts of power that are based on thematic apperception tests evince a potential relationship to locus of control. Veroff (1957) used methods adapted from the study of achievement motives; in judging power imagery from stories given by subjects in response to pictures, he uses the following criteria.

1. There is some statement of affect surrounding the maintenance or attainment of the control of the means of influencing a person....
2. There is a definite statement about someone doing something about maintaining or attaining the control of the means of influencing another person....
3. ...[There is] a statement of an interpersonal relationship which in its execution is culturally defined as one in which there is a superior person having control of the means of influencing another one who is subordinate. (Veroff, 1958, pp. 220, 222, 225)

The foregoing criteria for power viewed as a value seem to bear a clear relationship to an internal locus of control. Veroff and Veroff (1972) more recently have argued that the need to control or influence others is not a positive goal but (à la Adler) a compensatory thing designed to overcome feelings of inadequacy or powerlessness. However, McClelland, Davis, Kalin, and Wanner (1972), in accounting for drinking behavior, assert that power is experienced in a positive fashion. Thus drinking is not seen as compensatory but as a way of accentuating power feelings. Veroff (1957) seems to view power in the relatively narrow sense of interpersonal influence or control. Winter, however, states, "Under some conditions, the power motive leads to drinking, sex, vicarious powerful experiences, and having prestigeful possessions" (1972 p. 177). Still, in his most recent work, Winter (1973) seems to place the power motive largely in the interpersonal influence area. Certainly, in the case of locus of control, its effects go considerably beyond the narrow confines of interpersonal influence.

A Social Learning Theory View of Power   Based on the interaction of genetic and learning history factors, all people have a repertoire of potential behaviors at their disposal. It follows that the exercise of power is limited by people's behavior repertoires. However, even if a given power behavior is a part of individuals' repertoires, there is no guarantee that the behavior will occur. Its occurrence is mediated by the variables discussed earlier in this book: expectancies, reinforcement values, and the character of the specific situation. Thus, the exercise of power in the service of a particular outcome is determined by the same variables as any other behavior.

Viewed in this fashion, power has several aspects (Phares, 1973a). First, power may be viewed as a series of potential behaviors. Second, power can be analyzed from the vantage point of goals, needs, or motivation; that is, how important to the individual is the satisfaction of power needs? This view of power has been traditionally and historically the primary focus of psychoanalytic writers such as Adler (1927), Horney (1942), and May (1972). While this has been one of the dominant modes of approaching the study of power, its predictive utility has yet to be convincingly demonstrated.

Power can also be viewed as a set of expectancies. To oversimplify, power can be understood as a kind of confidence or a belief in the efficacy of one's efforts. This view of power suggests that it be regarded as a subjective probability. Further, locus of control as a generalized set of beliefs is likewise an integral part of power and, as suggested in Chapter II, contributes to the subjective probability. Of course, each occasion for the utilization of power involves a situation composed of cues that can significantly affect the magnitude of needs, expectancies, and generalized expectancies and thereby determine, in part, the occurrence of a given power behavior.

If individuals possess a general set of beliefs that they are not the effective agent in controlling the occurrence of rewards in their lives, then it is hard to understand how they could be expected to engage in actions calculated to attain power or influence over their environment. Therefore, if the individuals are going to make an effort to exercise such power, then a belief in the internal locus of control would appear to be a prerequisite. At the same time, however, an internal set of expectancies about the nature of control, while necessary, is not sufficient. People must also be motivated to achieve a given reward toward which their mastery efforts will be directed. And they must be reasonably confident of the success of their efforts.

EXPERIMENTAL EVIDENCE FOR LOCUS OF CONTROL AS A MOTIVE

Rotter and Mulry (1965) explored experimentally the possibility that locus of control not only can be regarded as being a generalized expectancy but also as having motivational properties. They reasoned that if subjects regard certain outcomes as very important, they will take longer in the decision-making process than if they place relatively little value on the outcomes. Furthermore, social learning theory research had shown that when expectancy for attainment is held constant while value of outcome varies, decision time for choosing one of a closely matched pair of possible reinforcements increases with the value of the outcome. As Rotter and Mulry state:

> . . .it seems logical that an individual who felt that what happened to him depended on his own skills would place higher value on demonstration of skill (since it indicated a promise for future rewards) than would a person who felt that reinforcements were arbitrarily dispensed independently of his own actions. The latter individual might, on the other hand, regard "luck" as a personal although unstable attribute and would have greater concern with whether or not he was a lucky or

unlucky person. Increased value in turn would lead to longer decision time in both cases. Since the discrimination was very difficult the person with more involvement in being correct would spend more time comparing the alternatives. (p. 599)

Rotter and Mulry used a difficult perceptual matching task and instructed half the subjects that correct matching was a matter of luck. The remaining subjects were given skill instructions. Results indicated a significant interaction between internal versus external control and skill versus chance instructions. That is, as hypothesized, internals took longer with skill instructions and externals with chance instructions (although most of the difference was contributed by internals in the skill condition).

Phares and Wilson (1971) pursued the question of whether Rotter and Mulry's results would apply to interpersonal attraction responses as well as task preferences. They found that internals showed greater evidence of attraction to an internally oriented stranger than they did to an external stranger. Also, internals showed a greater attraction to the internal stranger than did externals. Contrary to expectation, externals did not show a greater attraction toward an external stranger. What is striking about these results is that they are nearly identical in form to the decision-time results of Rotter and Mulry. In both studies, the lion's share of the difference is due to the internals while the externals do not show significant differences. While such results do not prove the existence of a motivational component of locus of control, they are consistent with such a notion.

Julian and Katz (1968) have also dealt with the motivational dimensions of locus of control. Their general hypothesis was that internals value self-determined rewards more than externals under skill conditions while the converse is true for externals under chance determined conditions. Subjects competed with partners in a laboratory task to earn points. In one study, internals did indeed prefer to rely upon themselves more than did externals (even when their opponents were seen as more competent). A second study was subsequently carried out in which groups receiving chance instructions were added. Here, internals and externals employed similar choice strategies under both skill and chance conditions. While the failure of the second study to show skill-chance differences as in the Rotter and Mulry study raises some questions regarding the interaction between skill-chance and internal-external locus of control, the evidence suggests there are probably motivational differences between internals and externals. At the very least, it is possible that expressed preference for internal control implies a *need* or desire to predict and control outcomes and to rely upon oneself.

It is also interesting to observe that the previously cited study by Lefcourt, Lewis, and Silverman (1968), using a level of aspiration task, found differences in decision time between internals and externals. Internals took more time to decide upon their subsequent expectancy statement on trials when they perceived the task as based on their skill; externals took more time when they believed the task to be a function of chance factors. These results are entirely consistent with the Rotter and Mulry data.

In a departure from the preceding methods, Watson and Baumal (1967) looked for incongruities between expectancies for personal control and situational opportunities for that control as evidence for the motivational properties of locus of control. Watson and Baumal found that internals tended to make a greater number of errors during a practice period prior to performing on a task that was structured as chance-determined. However, externals were more error-prone when practicing for a task that apparently involved skill. Watson and Baumal account for these results by asserting that anxiety is engendered by performance tasks that are incongruent with subjects' generalized expectancies regarding the locus of control of reinforcement.

A series of studies by Ryckman and colleagues also illustrates the motivational nature of I-E (Ryckman & Rodda, 1971; Ryckman, Stone, & Elam, 1971; Ryckman, Rodda, & Stone, 1971). In the last two studies, groups of internals and externals were strongly criticized by two experimenters while participating in a dart-throwing task. In general, internals showed greater concern (anxiety) than externals under skill conditions while externals exhibited greater concern under chance conditions. Being concerned (made anxious) by the criticism was taken as an indicant of motivation. These results are highly congruent with those reported thus far. However, it is important to note that in the Ryckman studies, sex of subjects significantly affected the obtained interactions between chance versus skill conditions and internal versus external control. For example, in one study it was the females who showed the predicted results while in the other study it was the males who gave the expected results.

While there are some inconsistencies in the foregoing research, its general thrust seems to support the notion that there are motivational correlates of locus of control. In general, internals manifest greater concern and attach more importance to success in skill or other self-reliant situations while externals are prone to be more motivated by chance or luck situations. If this is the case, then the differential behavior of internals and externals is based not only on their different generalized expectancies regarding the locus of control of outcomes but also on differences in motivation or needs. Just as social learning theory is both a cognitive and a motivational theory, so does locus of control seem to have both cognitive and motivational aspects.

Rotter and Mulry (1965) suggested that another manifestation of the motivational properties of locus of control might be found in the differential activity preferences of internals and externals. In short, perhaps internals tend to prefer tasks or activities in which they can demonstrate skill while externals prefer chance or luck situations.

Schneider (1968) tested this hypothesis by asking college students to express their preferences for skill versus chance activities in a forced-choice format. As anticipated, males exhibited the expected relationship between locus of control and activity preference. In the case of females, however, no such relationship was obtained. This sex difference, coupled with the failure of Berzins, Ross, and Cohen (1970) to find a significant relationship in male hospitalized drug addicts, raises questions both about the generality and stability of Schneider's correlation.

Of course, many variables can potentially affect activity preferences. We have already noted the sex variable, which may imply a masculine-feminine dimension of activities. Another variable is familiarity; activities may be chosen in a preference situation at least in part because they are familiar. Another possible variable is the active-passive nature of the activity. Schneider (1972), in two systematic studies that incorporated all of these considerations, once more examined the relationship between locus of control and activity preference. In the first study, the magnitude of the relationship between skill-chance preferences and locus of control varied as a function of sex of the subject and masculinity or femininity of the skill items. However, the active-passive nature of the activities appeared to confound the relationship. Therefore, a second study separated the skill-chance, masculine-feminine, and active-passive dimensions. Only the correlations with skill-chance reached significance, but this significance was of a lower order than in previous studies.

Additional variables that might be considered in future research are (1) the extent to which subjects really expect to have to perform the activities under study and (2) subjects' expectancies for being successful on those activities. Later discussions show that externals are generally more anxious (have lower expectancies for success than internals) and behave more defensively than internals. Thus, differential expectancies for success on certain activities could affect preferences. For this reason, it would be advisable, when measuring preferences, to control for expectancies for success. Otherwise, it could be assumed that both internals and externals really prefer to succeed on skill-achievement tasks, but since externals have lower expectancies for success, they choose chance tasks in order to avoid expected failure. Likewise, leading subjects to believe they really will have to engage in certain activities may significantly alter their preferences (particularly by neutralizing wishful thinking or boastful preferences).

The work reviewed in this chapter, taken in aggregate, highlights some important differences in the performance of internals and externals. A capsule description might be that internals are more cognitively active. They exhibit better learning and acquisition of material, they more actively seek information, they show a superior utilization of information or data once it is acquired, they are more attentive, alert, and sensitive than are externals, and they seem to be more concerned with the informational demands of situations than with any presumed social demands. There is also gradually accumulating some evidence suggesting that internals are more highly motivated to perform well in situations that allow them to exercise skill, control, or self-reliance. Combining the cognitive and motivational aspects of locus of control, we may expect that internals will be in a superior position to exert control and power over their environment.

Summary

The most basic characteristic of internal individuals appears to be their greater efforts at coping with or attaining mastery over their environments. This is the most elemental deduction that could be made from the nature of the I-E variable. Fortunately, this deduction has received widespread support from experiments with many different populations in a variety of situations. The hypothesis finds support through studies of tubercular patients, reformatory inmates, Swedish students, American and Canadian college students, among others. It is confirmed in the field as well as in the psychological laboratory.

To a great extent, the superior mastery and coping of internals seems to be accomplished through their superior cognitive processing activities. They seem to acquire more information, make more attempts at acquiring it, are better at retaining it, are less satisfied with the amount of information they possess, are better at utilizing information and devising rules to process it, and generally pay more attention to relevant cues in the situation.

Just as internals are more effective in controlling their world, they also appear to exhibit greater self-control as well. This is surely to be expected. The absence of self-discipline would make consistently successful control over the environment difficult. In a similar vein, at least some evidence suggests that internals are more likely to be cautious and to engage in less risky behaviors.

Social learning theory teaches us that the determinants of behavior will include not only expectancies of occurrence of rewards but also the values the person places on those rewards. Construing power, for example, as a motivational state has received extensive support throughout the psychological literature. Several investigators have pursued locus of control as a motivator, not just as a set of generalized expectancies. The general hypothesis has been that internals will prefer to attain skill-achievement outcomes or will attach greater value to them while externals will prefer chance activities or goals. The data supports the notion of locus of control as a motivational state. However, not enough systematic research has yet been done to substantiate the possibility that preferences for chance-related activities or outcomes are really defensive in nature and reflect, on the part of externals, a lowered confidence in their own ability to attain skill-related goals.

This chapter has depicted the coping-mastery characteristics of internals as compared to externals. It has also provided an extensive array of validation studies on the I-E Scale. That is, scores on the I-E Scale successfully predict the kinds of behavior we expect given the nature of the locus of control concept.

VI

Locus of Control in the Social Context

Chapter V offers clear evidence that internals are more active than externals in attempting to control their environments. Their behavior appears to be mediated by their belief in the efficacy of their own efforts and perhaps by a desire or need to remain in control.

It is but a short step from this conclusion to the hypothesis, first, that internals will resist the efforts of others to manipulate them through persuasion or other forms of influence. Obviously, to accept such influence without due regard to the validity of its content would be to abrogate one's own control. For example, to accept a persuasive message without analyzing the content would be tantamount to giving control to another person. This should not be a particularly congenial stance for an internal to take. Not that an internal will never conform to the dictates of another agency or person. Rather, such acceptance probably will be deliberate rather than reflexive and will be based on a more careful analysis of the potential positive and negative reinforcements likely to flow from such conformity.

Second, it might be expected that internals will participate more actively in efforts for social change, since they believe that their actions can have an effect. As we saw in Chapter V, their efforts at personal mastery have given them a potential for competence that not only makes them fit to resist the blandishments of other people or institutions. Rather than being the object of influence, their competencies enable them to become originators of social action, change, and help for others in society.

Discussion of the research on these two hypotheses occupies most of this chapter. We will look first at situations involving attempts by one individual to influence another. While a social psychologist (or sociologist) might study the factors affecting the function of the group as a unit (for this purpose, two people make a group), as personality psychologists we are most interested in the influenceability of one member of the group. Both psychologists study many of the same factors, such as the age, sex, reward power, and general attractiveness of the communicator(s), the content and style of the message, and other aspects of the situation. Of particular concern to the personality psychologist, in addition to these, is the way the target person's belief in an internal or external locus of control determines influenceability.

Susceptibility to Social Influence

CONFORMITY

Externals seem less confident and, indeed, less competent as compared to internals. If this is an accurate description, it should follow that externals will conform to judgments of others more readily than internals when in a social situation and that they will be less likely to depend upon their inner resources in formulating an independent judgment.

We might note that Riesman's (1954) typology of inner-directed and outer-directed persons bears a superficial relationship to locus of control, particularly in the sense of conformity. The inner-directed person is said to be controlled by internal goals and values while the outer-directed person is the conformist who looks to others for his standards. However, Riesman is talking more about the locus of values than about expectancies based on perceived locus of control. We are concerned here not with values but with the person's own efforts or characteristics as an agent in achieving reinforcements. Thus, in Riesman's terms, two persons, one directed by inner goals and the other conforming to social dictates, might both be internally controlled in the locus of control sense of the term. We must guard against reacting too literally to such words as internal, external, inner, and outer without understanding their theoretical connotations.

Crowne and Liverant (1963) designed an Asch-like conformity situation. That is, they placed each subject in a group and asked him to verbalize judgments that, if stated correctly, would run counter to the judgments verbalized by other group members. For one condition, the usual Asch procedures were followed. In the other condition, subjects were given money to bet on the correctness of their own judgments. In the first condition, internals and externals revealed similar patterns of yielding. But when money was being bet, internals were significantly less yielding than were externals. Further, when internals went against the majority, they bet more money than externals did when they were defying the majority. Finally, the internals showed no significant differences in their bets on conforming and yielding trials, whereas the externals bet significantly less on their independent trials than on their yielding trials.

This research suggests a greater resistance to group pressure on the part of internals and also a greater confidence level. Perhaps it is this greater confidence in self that enables internals to be more resistant. Many other data suggest that externals are generally more anxious (less confident in attaining valued goals?) and less proficient. Thus, it would not be a total surprise to find that a chronically insecure person with a history of less than successful attempts at attaining rewards from his or her environment would yield to pressure or become conforming.

In a related vein, Tolor (1971) found that when experimental conditions seemed to suggest that a stationary light was moving, externals were more prone to see that light as moving. In addition, those who reported movement received higher scores on separate measures of both alienation and anxiety. As Tolor suggests, such results imply greater susceptibility to persuasion on the part of alienated or externally oriented persons.

RESISTANCE TO SUBTLE INFLUENCE

Subtle influence is often regarded as a particularly virulent form of attempted control inasmuch as it almost seems to deprive individuals of the knowledge that they are being manipulated and, therefore, of the right of personal choice. It is as if they might say, "I don't mind someone coming right out and telling me he is going to work on me. What bugs me are those people who try to manipulate you without your even knowing it. That really makes me mad!" Perhaps this is akin to what Brehm (1966) labels reactance, a negative response to perceived loss of freedom.

Gore (1962) tried to confront this possibility by establishing conditions of overt influence, subtle influence, and no influence. More specifically, she asked subjects to examine TAT cards, ostensibly to determine which produced longer stories or had more stimulus "pull." In the overt influence conditions, she simply told subjects which card she thought was best. In the subtle influence situations, however, she would smile and ask, "Now let's see what you can do with *this* one." She was able to show that internals and externals did not differ under either the no-influence or the overt-influence conditions. However, under the subtle condition, internals produced significantly *shorter* stories than did externals as well as significantly shorter stories than did control subjects in the no-influence condition. Thus, the response of internals seemed to be one of negativism or active resistance in the face of subtle influence attempts. Indeed, it may be that given overt options to conform or not conform, internals will, under certain circumstances, conform, but not when they are being "deviously" pushed or influenced.

Biondo and MacDonald (1971), studied the responses of internal and external students to some proposed changes in university grading procedures in a pre- and post-influence design. They reported several things. Externals conformed to both high and low levels of influence by shifting in the direction of the influence. Internals, however, reacted against the high-influence attempt and moved in the opposite direction. Finally, the internals were not particularly responsive to the low-influence condition. These results obviously reflect the more conforming behavior of externals as compared to internals. However, the authors feel there is some question whether internals are more reactant (resistant) to subtle influence because of (1) certain flaws in the Gore design and analysis, (2) the failure of their own internals to respond with reactance to their low-influence condition (which seemed to involve issues of importance to students), and (3) an apparent "cue sensitivity" of externals in their responding to the low-influence attempts.

There is a real question whether the "subtle" influence condition of Gore's study and the "low" influence condition in Biondo and MacDonald's study are empirically equivalent. Certainly, the words "subtle" and "low" are quite different in their connotations. It would seem logical to argue that internals might not resist low influence but would resist subtle influence. In addition, the fact that internals showed reactance under high-influence conditions (as opposed to no difference between internals and externals in the Gore study) does not seem surprising given Biondo and MacDonald's communication: "Taking everything into consideration, it is obvious that this is a very good procedure; I don't see how you have any choice but to rate this procedure highly." This seems especially so in view of Pines and Julian's (1972) suggestion that externals are particularly attuned to what the experimenter wants while internals are concerned with the problem demands of the situation. The internals' concern with informational demands, coupled with their belief in their own control (and perhaps need for control), could easily lead the internal to show greater reactance in Biondo and MacDonald's high-influence condition while, at the same time, not responding one way or the other in their low-influence condition.

However, the link between locus of control and resistance to subtle influence is not composed solely of these two studies. Let us examine evidence based on the verbal conditioning paradigm (often regarded as a subtle-influence situation).

OPERANT CONDITIONING OF VERBAL RESPONSES

Operant conditioning of verbal responses generally refers to a process by which individuals' verbalizations are brought under the control of or are significantly influenced by rather unobtrusive behaviors of the experimenter. The original implication seemed to be that subjects' increase or decrease in verbalizations from a preexperimental baseline was "automatic or unconscious," a point that has been hotly debated. Regardless of this controversy, such operant conditioning does represent an example of behavioral influence. That is, the phenomenon does exist, although its mode of operation may not be completely clear. It does not seem likely, for example, that mere exposure to reinforcement will automatically ensure that response changes in the subject will occur. Nor does simple awareness of the reinforcement contingencies alone account for the behavior. Rather, such variables as need for conformity and the value of the reinforcements inherent in the situation would seem important also.

One could argue that internals, being highly aware of their surroundings and often better learners, should quickly adjust their behavior to the reinforcements in the situation and thereby show rapid conditioning. However, given the evidence for internals' apparently greater resistance to subtle influence, one could also argue that to the extent that verbal conditioning paradigms are essentially occasions for the exercise of subtle influence, internals will be resistant and perhaps will manifest less evidence of conditioning. Getter (1966) felt that the latter interpretation should hold. Using both acquisition and extinction trials, he identified four groups of subjects: (1) conditioners, those who reached a given criterion during both the acquisition and the extinction trials; (2) latent conditioners, those who did not reach the criterion during the acquisition trials but did so during the so-called extinction trials; (3) nonconditioners, those who failed to reach the criterion on either set of trials; and (4) conditioner extinguishers, those who reached the criterion only during the acquisition trials.

As expected, the "conditioners" showed the highest external scores on the I-E Scale. This supports the notion that the verbal conditioning situation is one in which the experimenter tries to exert influence and that the external, being more suggestible, conforming, or dependent on social cues, will manifest greater conditioning. But of special interest were the results of the "latent conditioners." These were subjects who showed no significant evidence of conditioning during the training trials but who, when no reinforcement was forthcoming during extinction, showed a significant increase in the reinforced response. These subjects were significantly more internal than either subjects who did not show such latent conditioning or who conditioned during the training trials.

Strickland (1970) also carried out a verbal operant conditioning study involving internals and externals. This study utilized a post-experimental interview to divide subjects into those who were aware of the reinforcement contingency and those who were not. Those who conditioned and those who did not were also separated. There was no overall relationship between I-E scores and ability to condition. However, there were substantial differences between subjects who were aware and did not condition and subjects who were aware and did condition: the former were significantly more internal than the latter.

Strickland's (1970) findings appear to be consistent with findings reported in the preceding section that suggested internals resist subtle influence. They also agree with Getter's findings concerning "latent conditioners." It might be noted that Baron (1969) found no difference in awareness between internals and externals following trials in a verbal conditioning experiment. However, he did not report differences between aware internals and aware externals regarding their conditioning behavior. Likewise, Lichtenstein and Craine (1969) could find no support for either Getter's or Strickland's results in a rather different study that included a success-praise, failure-criticism manipulation prior to the verbal conditioning procedures.

It was some of the aforementioned inconsistencies that led Jolley and Spielberger (1973) to investigate the relationship among awareness, locus of control, and anxiety as they relate to performance in a verbal conditioning situation. Their results are interesting in that they bring into focus the complexities in the relationship among the three variables. They found that only aware subjects showed an increase in performance on the verbal conditioning task. Neither locus of control nor trait anxiety affected the performance of unaware subjects. However, of particular interest was an interaction between locus of control and anxiety in aware subjects: high-anxiety externals were more responsive to social reinforcement than high-anxiety internals, but low-anxiety internals were more responsive to social reinforcement than low-anxiety externals.

One explanation offered by Jolley and Spielberger for these findings seems reasonable, but it must, of course, be validated by further research. Jolley and Spielberger speculate that people who obtain high scores on trait anxiety scales are rather candid in responding to personality inventories and more readily admit negative things about themselves. Subjects who score low on such scales may do so for two reasons: they rarely experience anxiety, or they are defensive, are reluctant to admit negative things about themselves, and are more prone to give socially desirable responses. Consequently, the low-anxiety groups may have included a substantial number of social-desirability internals (internals who responded on the I-E Scale in what they regard as a socially desirable fashion) and defensive externals (externals who respond on the I-E Scale in such a way as to provide an "excuse" for any future failures or who display suspiciousness toward authorities). These distinctions are elaborated in a subsequent section on defensive externals. At any rate, the superior performance of the low-anxious internals (social-desirability subjects) might be explained in terms of the desire of the subjects to create a good impression. By the same token, the relatively poor performance of the low-anxiety externals (defensive subjects) could be attributed to the fact that these subjects were less responsive to social reinforcement because of their suspiciousness of the experimental procedure.

A subsequent study by Doctor (1971) required subjects to construct sentences from stimulus cards that contained one of six randomly ordered pronouns (I, We, He, She, You, and They) and a past tense verb. After establishing a subject's base rate for the use of reinforced pronouns, the experimenter responded to each subject's sentence constructions by saying "Good" whenever that subject used the pronouns "I" or "We." As anticipated, externally oriented subjects, when selectively reinforced in the sentence construction activity, showed a significantly greater gain in the emission of I-We pronouns over their base rate than did similarly treated internal subjects. Doctor subdivided his subjects on the basis of their awareness of what was going on in the experiment. He found that aware externals accounted for the conditioning effect while aware internals, unaware subjects, and controls were essentially similar and showed no change in their rate of emission. Doctor interpreted his results as being a function of the internals' greater resistance to a subtle form of social influence and the externals' concomitant greater compliance, cooperation, or responsiveness.

In summarizing the foregoing set of studies on verbal conditioning, it seems safe to assert that externals are easier marks when it comes to inducing changes in verbal or related responses. In contrast, internals seem less easily influenced. Not all the evidence supports this conclusion—some indicates interactions of locus of control with other variables—but given the differences in methods, the evidence is generally supportive of the preceding interpretation.

Of course, saying that internals are more resistant to subtle influence is a somewhat inferential statement. There is little, if any, evidence that internals perceive verbal conditioning or other techniques as subtle or covert. That is, internals have not told us they are resisting such subtle forms of control. However, the fact remains that, by and large, when faced with what experimenters regard as relatively covert or subtle influence situations, internals (to a lesser degree than externals) do not do what it appears the experimenter wants them to do. Perhaps future research will reveal the phenomenological factors or antecedents that lead to this difference in behavior.

We might mention again the finding of Pines and Julian (1972) and Pines (1973), noted earlier, that internals respond to the informational demands of a task while externals are sensitive to the social demand parameters. Clearly, this could lead externals or other socially sensitive subjects to perform in a fashion they believe the experimenter demands. By the same token, internals might become annoyed at an experimenter who seemed to want them to relinquish their cognitive-searching prerogatives in favor of the experimenter's manipulation.

ATTITUDE CHANGE

Moving from the previous conformity and subtle-influence situations, we may also look at the differential persuasibility of externals and internals as reflected in the specific realm of attitude change.

Ritchie and Phares (1969) investigated the role of communicator status or prestige in producing differential changes in attitudes. They reasoned, based on some of the preceding subtle-influence data, that externals would exhibit greater changes in attitude following exposure to an argument emanating from a high-prestige source than one from a low-prestige source. Further, it was expected that externals would show more attitude change than internals following exposure to a high-prestige source. On the other hand, no differences were anticipated between groups of internals and externals presented with low-prestige communications. Finally, internals were expected to show about the same amount of change regardless of the status of the argument source. Subjects first filled out a survey regarding their attitudes toward national budget expenditures. Approximately two weeks later, subjects filled out the survey again. During the two-week period, half the subjects received arguments attributed to a prestigious national authority while the other half received arguments attributed to an obscure graduate student in a small college. The groups were matched for initial views. A similar (control) group received no influence attempts. The results can be seen in Table 1.

Table 1 *Mean attitude change scores*

| | Low Prestige | | High Prestige | |
	Internal	External	Internal	External
Mean	7.24	5.33	6.19	8.76
Standard Deviation	5.02	4.40	4.03	5.20

SOURCE: From E. Ritchie and E. J. Phares, Attitude change as a function of internal-external control and communicator status. *Journal of Personality,* 1969, 37: 438. Reprinted by permission.

As predicted, externals changed more in response to a high-prestige source than to a low-prestige source, and they also changed more than internals when both received a communication from a high-prestige source. Internals did not differ in attitudes toward communications from high- and low-prestige sources. Several conclusions can be drawn. First, externals are not uniformly susceptible to influence attempts in all situations; they are markedly affected by the prestige manipulation. Second, internals seem more responsive to the content of the communication in the light of their previously held opinions than to the prestige of the source. This idea is supported by the fact that the mean changes for both groups of internals fell between the two external groups and were not significantly different from each other, although the internal high-prestige group changed significantly less than the external high-prestige group. Finally, comparisons with the control group showed that none of the experimental groups showed any particular resistance to change.

Since both internals and externals showed evidence of change, perhaps the situation was not perceived as a subtle-influence situation. Rather, it may be that internals saw no need to resist influence. Also, externals could readily perceive the social demands of the situation and, in this case, probably "saw" the high-prestige source as a means of obtaining reinforcement (since they seem to lack confidence in their own ability).

Extending the above work, Ryckman, Rodda, and Sherman (1972) speculated that externals would tend to accept influence to the same degree from a high-prestige source whose expertise was irrelevant as they would from an expert whose knowledge was relevant to the issue under consideration. They expected internals to be more discriminating in their judgments about the abilities of a reputed expert and thus internals to be more willing to accept influence from the relevant prestige source than from the irrelevant one.

Ryckman, Rodda, and Sherman (1972) used undergraduates as subjects and selected attitudes about student activism as the content issue. The expertise of the source was manipulated by having present in an experimental setting a faculty member who was introduced either as a faculty advisor to the local chapter of Students for a Democratic Society (SDS) or as an expert on the history of China's Ming Dynasty. An attitude scale was administered before treatment, along with the I-E Scale, and again after treatment. As expected, externals tended to accept influence from a high-prestige source, regardless of its relevance or irrelevance. Internals did not yield more to a source with relevant as compared to irrelevant expertise. Such results may be consistent with those of Ritchie and Phares (1969), which indicated that internals respond to issues and not to the prestige or relevance of the source.

Following the general line of reasoning that externals are more persuasible than internals, Hjelle and Clouser (1970) predicted that external subjects would show more attitude change when exposed to standardized communications advocating a change in their preestablished positions than would internal subjects. Using a procedure similar to that of Phares (1965), the authors administered a scale measuring students' attitudes on several campus issues. About five weeks later, an experimenter presented arguments either for or against these issues in an attempt to influence the students' attitudes. Following this, subjects filled out the attitude scale again. Hjelle and Clouser selected for analysis only three items for each subject that reflected a moderate level of ego involvement. The results confirmed the hypothesis that externals would be more susceptible to attitude change than internals. Of some significance is the fact that differential attitude changes occurred in the context of at least moderately strong beliefs. The previous work of Ritchie and Phares (1969) purposely restricted its focus to rather nonengaging issues.

Not all studies of social influence attempts involve the techniques described so far. More recently, psychologists have been studying the effects of inducing people to behave in a fashion at odds with their beliefs and then observing the effects of such discrepant behavior on their beliefs. Sherman (1973), for example, had subjects either read a persuasive message about lowering the voting age or write an essay that was opposed to their stated views on the voting issue.

Sherman's results illustrate the complexity of the relationship between locus of control and social influence. Internals showed greater attitude change following the writing of counterattitudinal messages, while externals showed the greatest change after reading the persuasive message. In accounting for such results, at least one argument is possible. Internals generally take greater responsibility for their own behavior (especially for negative outcomes). Perhaps when induced to behave in a manner that produced cognitive dissonance, internals felt a greater responsibility for their behavior and thus exhibited greater attitude change as a way of reducing cognitive dissonance. Externals, however, attribute responsibility to outside forces when negative consequences flow from their behavior (Phares, Wilson, & Klyver, 1971). Hence little dissonance and little consequent attitude change should occur, since they believe their behavior was induced by forces outside themselves. This is consistent with Cooper's (1971) work suggesting that cognitive dissonance is not experienced by subjects when they are allowed to perceive the locus of causality for their behavior as being outside their control.

ACCEPTANCE OF INFORMATION

Another way of approaching the study of social influence is to examine factors underlying differential acceptance of information by internals and externals, a method that differs slightly from those discussed. An example would be the research, reported earlier in the context of mastery and control, carried out by James, Woodruff, and Werner (1965). They reported that following the Surgeon General's Report on the deleterious effects of smoking cigarettes, males who quit for a specific period of time achieved higher internal scores than males who believed the report but did not choose to quit. If nothing else, this research indicates that internals do not automatically resist every attempt at social influence. Rather, they seem to evaluate the cogency of the influence attempt and then respond accordingly. This is consistent with the attitude change data in the previous section, suggesting that internals will change attitudes but that the prestige and expertise of the source are not so influential as the content of the message. Such strategies would seem more serviceable if one is to maintain long-term control and influence over one's surroundings and life.

A study by Hamsher, Geller, and Rotter (1968) reports results that are consistent with the James, Woodruff, and Werner data but, at the same time, inconsistent with previous social influence data. The Hamsher, Geller, and Rotter study investigated the acceptance by college students of the Warren Commission Report on the assassination of former president John F. Kennedy. I-E Scale scores and scores on a measure of generalized interpersonal trust were obtained. For both males and females, low-trust scores were associated with relative disbelief of the commission's findings. For males alone, however, externality was also associated with disbelief of the report, which indicates resistance to information emanating from a presumed authority. Hamsher, Geller, and Rotter suggested that externals' feelings of being manipulated and dominated by powerful others or chance factors and their marked suspiciousness of authorities are consistent with what Rotter (1966) calls the "defensive external" (this topic is reviewed in greater detail in Chapter VIII). This defensive attitude is thought to be typical of competitive, achievement-oriented males who fear failure and thus project blame for their failures onto outside forces. They come to believe authorities are bent on undermining their efforts at control and achievement. The implication is that such defensive externals were responsible in large measure for the results of the Hamsher, Geller, and Rotter study.

What was the setting for the Warren Commission Report? It may be recalled that President Kennedy's assassination served as a catalyst for many strange, even paranoid theories. Thus, it is possible that this study generated different responses than did the communications used in the studies reported earlier, which involved more usual types of attitudes and beliefs. Also, subjects here were specifically asked whether they believed the Warren Commission Report. If the general population does contain a significant number of so-called defensive externals, then it is easy to see that this specific study, with the highly volatile, pathology-catalyzing issue involved, could jolt those individuals into responding in a fashion different from that of similar individuals in the earlier-reported studies of influence and attitude change.

A study by Snyder and Larson (1972) required subjects to take personality tests. All subjects were given identical interpretations of their general personality features. Then subjects (for whom I-E Scale scores were available) rated the degree to which they felt the interpretations described their personalities. In brief, the results showed that a higher external locus of control was associated with greater acceptance of the interpretations.

Jones and Shrauger (1968) set up an experimental situation in which internals and externals exchanged evaluations with two peers in a group testing situation. Each subject generally received positive evaluations from one peer and negative evaluations from the other peer. Half the subjects were told the test measured ability while the other half were told there were no right or wrong answers, only personal opinions. In essence, the results indicated that externals more frequently agreed with the negative and positive evaluators in the opinion condition than did internals. Jones and Shrauger interpreted this in terms of internals' greater desire to control social outcomes, but the results may also have implications in the realm of social influence.

Finally, Lefcourt (1972) noted that a series of studies from his laboratory, while not specifically designed to investigate differential responsiveness to influence by internals and externals, nonetheless is relevant to the issue. For example, in a level-of-aspiration paradigm, Lefcourt (1967) found that externals tended to perform in accordance with experimental instructions while internals did not. Similarly, again in a level-of-aspiration paradigm, Lefcourt, Lewis, and Silverman (1968) noted that internals less often than externals accepted instructions that emphasized chance determination of the task and more often accepted the skill instructions. Thus, internals resist accepting information that is at variance with their own perception of events.

As a conclusion to the foregoing research, one might assert that externals appear readily persuasible, conforming to what they believe is expected of them, and accepting of information or other sources of influence. This is not to say that internals never conform or never move their attitudes in the direction of the applied persuasion. But when they do, it appears to be on the basis of a considered analysis of the merits of the message. Majorities, peer influence, prestige of communicators, or the social reinforcements available in the situation all affect internals to a much lesser extent than they do externals. Indeed, the evidence suggests there may be an active resistance to influence, particularly subtle influence, on the part of internals.

What specific mechanisms may account for these differences between internals and externals? Social learning theory suggests at least three possibilities: expectancies, reinforcement values, or some combination of the two. For example, the resistance of internals may be based to a large extent on the idea of freedom from control of others and ability to act as one desires. That is, the internal places a high value on personal control and will work to achieve this valued goal by active resistance. The internal seems to be a generally more competent individual, with a longer string of past successes. This, of course, creates greater self-confidence, which would also lead the internal to eschew outside support and influence in favor of a reliance on self. We shall see later, however, that it may be difficult to determine whether internality leads to confidence—based on past success—or confidence leads to an internal belief system.

Externals may possess such a strong need for approval and reinforcement from social agents who have prestige, power, or other attractive qualities that they are easily led or induced to behave in a fashion they believe will attain those valued goals. Or, to focus on the expectancy side of the picture, perhaps the externals' general lack of belief in their own control determines conformity or nonresistant behavior. Still, it may not be so much the externals' generalized problem-solving expectancy for locus of control that is crucial as an associated low expectancy for the success of their own efforts (in part contributed to by the low generalized expectancy for control). Thus, the external may feel that success or the "right" behavior is possible only by paying attention to the cues of others. A lack of confidence breeds dependence on external sources.

By designing studies in the future that will separate the components of reinforcement value and the several aspects of expectancy, we may be better able to assess the antecedents of susceptibility to social influence. Identification of these factors may also allow us to predict the degree of pressure subjects will withstand and perhaps their emotional reactions. For example, if we experimentally lowered an internal's confidence or expectancy and he or she still persisted in resisting help or support, this might tell us something about his or her values. We now need research that will go beyond the sheer demonstration of differential conformity or persuasibility and will give us insight into the factors mediating such behavior.

The evidence reviewed so far in this chapter is entirely complementary to that dealing with mastery and control. Indeed, it would be surprising to find that internals are more active in their efforts at control and, at the same time, easily influenced or controlled themselves. The consistency is reassuring. Finally, the studies reported in this chapter seem to demonstrate that in addition to situational determinants of persuasibility and conformity, there are personality differences. Failure to include such personality variables in any systematic theory of social influence would be a serious omission.

Efforts for Social Change

To resist the manipulations of others, individuals must possess a belief in their own position and a confidence born of experience that they can make their own way. Such values and beliefs probably also characterize many of those who work for social change.

PARTICIPATION IN CIVIL RIGHTS ACTIVITIES

Some years ago, Gore and Rotter (1963) hypothesized that the greater effectiveness of internals would also be manifested in participation in civil rights activities. This was at a time when many of the social protest movements were at their height in the South. Gore and Rotter polled students in a southern black college regarding their willingness to participate in various kinds of social action behaviors. The students who agreed to be studied had earlier provided the investigators with

I-E scores. Subsequently, they were asked to answer the following questionnaire:

> I would be interested in
> (a) attending a rally for civil rights.
> (b) signing a petition to go to local government and/or news media calling for full and immediate integration of all facilities throughout Florida.
> (c) joining a silent march to the Capitol to demonstrate our plea for full and immediate integration of all facilities throughout Florida.
> (d) I would not be interested in any of the foregoing.
> (Gore and Rotter, 1963, p. 61)

It is apparent that (a) through (c) represent an increasing degree of personal commitment to social action. As anticipated, commitment toward a more active form of civil rights behavior was associated with higher internal scores in these black students. Of course, while this result supports the thesis that internals are more active and coping individuals, it is true that this evidence represents only a *stated* willingness to participate in civil rights activities; it does not demonstrate actual behavioral differences between internals and externals. Some subsequent research has affirmed the link between locus of control and actual participation in civil rights activities. For example, Strickland (1965) determined that blacks who were known to have been active in a variety of civil rights demonstrations achieved significantly higher internal scores on the I-E Scale than blacks who had no experience in such protest movements.

Other works (e.g., Blanchard and Scarboro [1972] and Evans and Alexander [1970]) do not corroborate this relationship between internality and activism. Indeed, Ransford (1968) and Sanger and Alker (1972) found that it was the externals who were the activists. There is apparently a strong tendency for externals to participate in certain forms of political action, as we shall see in the following discussion.

PARTICIPATION IN POLITICAL AND SOCIAL ACTION

Like Gore and Rotter (1963) and Strickland (1965), Rosen and Salling (1971) found that political action participation in their sample of 45 college males was positively correlated with internal locus of control. The 10-item scale they used to assess political activism made no distinction among liberal, conservative, or radical activities. However, differing but presumably related sociopolitical behaviors have not always shown the same relationship to an internal belief system. For example, Rotter (1966), in his original monograph, reported that

in Ohio State University students locus of control showed no relationship to willingness to sign petitions regarding (1) the admission of the
People's Republic of China to the United Nations, or (2) the advisability
of permitting postseason football bowl games. Geller and Howard
(1972), Hamsher, Geller, and Rotter (1968), Evans and Alexander
(1970), and Gootnick (1973) also failed to link locus of control to
sociopolitical activities.

This constitutes evidence that the I-E Scale is a multidimensional
instrument rather than a unidimensional one. Gurin, Gurin, Lao, and
Beattie (1969) raised the possibility that, in the case of black youth,
one should distinguish between how much control one believes most
people in society possess (control ideology) and how much control
one believes he or she personally possesses (personal control). These
researchers argue that personal-control items on the I-E Scale may
indeed be relevant for predicting such a phenomenon as occupational
aspiration while the ideological items may be hardly relevant at all.
Furthermore, they suggest that the ideological beliefs of black youth
pertaining to discrimination and prejudice may actually motivate the
behavior of those youths in a positve fashion.

Lao (1970), in studying black college students, distinguished
between locus of control beliefs at the *personal* and *ideological* levels.
To measure locus of control Lao used a three-part scale consisting
of (1) five first-person items from the I-E Scale (personal level),
(2) four items sampling beliefs about how discrimination works, and
(3) three items dealing with the extent to which discrimination can
be modified (the latter two parts representing the ideological level).
Lao found that belief in personal control (higher internal scores on
the first-person items) was related to competence defined as (1) academic
performance (entrance test scores, grade-point average, and scores on
an anagrams task), (2) self-confidence in one's grades for the coming
year, and (3) certainty of finishing college and pursuing further education. These are expected relationships between internality and mastery
or control. In addition, however, Lao found that students who blamed
"the system" for holding back the development of blacks were also
more likely to be what she termed "innovative." That is, "externals"
who blamed discrimination on the system tended to participate more in
civil rights activities and to be more personally involved. They also
tended to prefer social action strategies over individual action. Obviously,
these results are not consistent with the earlier results of either Gore
and Rotter (1963) or Strickland (1965). Of course, comparisons are
difficult because there are marked differences between the I-E Scale
and Lao's scale.

Another study that does not provide typical results is one by

Thomas (1970). Thomas felt that there may be a conservative bias built into the I-E Scale and that people's responses to the I-E Scale are determined at least in part by their political and social ideology. Both the correlation between internality and the Protestant Ethic reported by MacDonald (1972) and other evidence suggests externals are more oriented toward the New Left while internals are more conservative (Hjelle & Fink, 1972). Thomas selected parents with college-age children from upper-middle-class families. The parents (half liberal and half conservative in their political views) were quite visible in the community because of their political and social participation. Both parents and students completed a "shortened" version of the I-E Scale (10 items plus one filler). Thomas found that liberal parents and their student children scored lower on the internal control measure than did the conservative parents and their children (although a great deal of variability was apparent in the liberal group). Further, little if any evidence was found to support the notion that internal scores are associated with greater political participation.

Silvern and Nakamura (1971) reported that in males externality is positively associated with sociopolitical activity, particularly protest activity and activity in left-wing causes. It seems that the left-wing activists were particularly external while the non-left-wing activists were more internal. Such evidence is not incompatible with Thomas' (1970) results.

Abramowitz (1973) studied college students (primarily white Protestants) who were members of (1) groups acknowledged to have social action or political goals, and (2) groups whose goals were neither social-action oriented nor political in nature (this also included subjects from the subject pool derived mainly from psychology classes). He obtained three I-E Scale scores: one based on all 23 items, another based on the political or world-events items alone, and a third derived from the nonpolitical or personal items. The outcomes of this study suggest several things. First, only the I-E scores based on the political items are associated with subjects' sociopolitical action. Second, the two item clusters from the I-E Scale are unrelated. Thus, while neither the total I-E score nor the nonpolitical item score is related to sociopolitical behavior, there was a positive relationship between internality on the political items and action-oriented behavior.

Abramowitz' work with a white population is, therefore, both consistent and inconsistent with the results reported for black subjects by Strickland (1965) and Gore and Rotter (1963). It is consistent in that internality predicts social-action involvement but inconsistent in suggesting that the total I-E score does not predict while the political subscore does predict.

It is clear that the research on participation in sociopolitical action is much less consistent than previous work with locus of control. Some of these studies suggest that internals are more active and some do not. Some of these studies suggest externals are more socially and politically active, especially in the case of black subjects, whereas internals generally have been more active. Other work suggests that if you divide the Rotter I-E Scale items into subscales you may get results different from those based on total I-E scores.

What can we make of all this? Given the diversity of results and studies there is no way we can posit a single interpretation that will cleverly cover these diverse results. The studies are simply too variable in the populations they used (e.g., black-white, student-nonstudent, male-female), time frames (from 1960 to 1973), types of locus of control measures (e.g., scales developed for specific situations, shortened versions of the I-E Scale), procedures, and varieties of sociopolitical action (e.g., petition signing, voting, group membership). All we can do is suggest some possibilities and hope that they are relevant to at least some specific studies.

Gergen (1973) has discussed social psychology as history, and Manganyi (1972) has sketched the narrower events of psychotherapy and psychopathology as history. Since the culture changes over time, the data of psychology cannot reasonably be expected to remain stable. Our data are inextricably imbedded in the web of events of the time. As Gergen puts it:

> Variables that successfully predicted political activism during the early stages of the Vietnam War are dissimilar to those which predicted activism during later periods. The conclusion seems clear that the factors motivating activism changed over time. Thus, any theory of political activism built from early findings would be invalidated. (Gergen, 1973, p. 315)

It is possible that the historical perspective may be relevant to the inconsistencies between the early data of Gore and Rotter (1963) and Strickland (1965), and the later of data of Gurin, Gurin, Lao, and Beattie (1969) and Lao (1970), for example. It is possible that the very collection and dissemination of social science data regarding the impact of the social action of early participants may have a profound effect on subsequent participants, so that the latter are motivated differently or else have acquired a very different set of expectations.

Work by Evans and Alexander (1970) suggests that groups from different geographic regions may have been differentially effective in social action. Hence whether data was collected in the North or the

South might make a difference. Similarly, the work of Geller and Howard (1972) offers the possibility that political activity among white youth is essentially expressive in purpose while that among blacks is more instrumental. Therefore, the specific racial or socioeconomic composition of samples may be quite important in understanding the outcomes of various studies.

There seems to be a general consensus that the country has become much more politicized over the past few years. The rise of the civil rights movement and the consuming passions generated by the Vietnam conflict have served to make most people, especially the young, highly conscious in a political sense. The level of individual awareness is much higher now than it was 15 years ago. This makes it very risky to generalize from 1960 data to the present, as Gergen states. The whole meaning of social action was different in 1960 than it is now. Indeed, replicating 1960 data in 1975 becomes impossible—how could one equate political awareness then and now? Of course, some aspects of behavior, such as personal achievement and information seeking, are not nearly as affected by the swirl of events as more politicized events and activities.

It is interesting to speculate that changes in the factor composition of the I-E Scale may have occurred over time. Rotter (1966) reported that two factor analyses involving data from 1,400 subjects revealed only one general factor. More recent work (e.g., Collins [1974]; Gurin, Gurin, Lao and Beattie [1969]; and Mirels [1970]) strongly indicates the presence of several factors. Why? One possibility is simply that the I-E Scale items mean different things to people now than they did in the early 1960s. Finding a different factor structure does not imply a defect in the early work but rather an evolving culture. We saw earlier that I-E Scale mean scores have become more external over the past 10 years. It is not unlikely that the factor structure has undergone an analogous evolution.

Another possibility is that sociopolitical action behavior is not like other kinds of behavior. For example, the mastery behavior of Seeman and Evans' (1962) tuberculosis patients may be of a very different order than joining a political party. Or, the face-to-face altruism of Midlarsky's (1971) subjects may reflect an entirely different set of needs or motives than helping to mount an antipollution campaign. While it seems obvious to us that locus of control (or anything else) cannot be expected to predict every conceivable action-oriented behavior, some may be disturbed at this and may see it as a weakness.

Of course, it goes without saying that studies of action taking or mastery in the sociopolitical sphere must control for the nature of the goals toward which the activity is directed. As Ryckman, Rodda, and

Sherman (1972) discovered, locus of control is related to Women's Liberation activity in females but not in males. Likewise, before we assert that internality does not seem to predict the joining of anti-pollution groups, we should first make sure that our sample of internals *believes* in the necessity of conservation. And before we worry about internals' not signing a petition to fragment a giant corporation, let us first make sure that those internals believe that such fragmentation would be a good thing. In short, we must not confound action taking with the goals toward which the action is oriented. The goals will necessarily have a wider appeal than will any particular action proposed to implement them.

The previously discussed works of Thomas (1970), MacDonald (1972), Hjelle and Fink (1972), and Silvern and Nakamura (1971) were consistent with the view that there is a bias in the I-E Scale toward a conservative political and personal philosophy. Depending upon the nature of the sociopolitical activity under study, such a bias might represent externals as more active than they generally are. Certainly the liberal-conservative nature of the activity should be determined, if possible, before specific predictions are made.

As some of the foregoing studies imply, there may be so-called defensive externals. Such a possibility was raised by Rotter (1966) and will be discussed in much greater detail in Chapter VIII. In brief, however, it is thought that some externals may behave in a highly action-oriented way in very specific or highly structured situations while on the I-E Scale they respond as externals to cover themselves in the event they fail. (This enables them to say—if they fail—"I told you so," or to place blame for their failure on someone or something other than themselves.) Such maneuvers would limit the magnitude of the correlations between the I-E Scale and sociopolitical action (particularly in the case of certain populations or causes).

Finally, our discussion in Chapter IV regarding the multi-dimensionality and generality of the I-E Scale is relevant here also. While individuals may achieve an overall score on the I-E Scale that categorizes them as externals, their various subscale scores may reveal belief patterns that are inconsistent with their overall scores. Therefore, the behavior of individuals may be predominantly external but may be internal in some situations.

POWER TO THE POWERLESS

We discussed the relationship between internality and the potential for power in Chapter V, and the work analyzed there supported this relationship. Likewise, we mentioned Seeman's (1959, 1967) description of externality in terms of powerlessness or alienation. As Goodstadt and Hjelle (1973) pointed out in examining "psychologically powerless" externals, the manner in which internals and externals attempt to exercise interpersonal power in dealing with others has not been systematically examined. We have seen in some detail the differential manner in which internals and externals deal with their environment, but their interpersonal power activities have not been a major focus of study. Goodstadt and Hjelle raised the question, What happens when the powerless are given power?

In attempting to answer this question, the authors selected internals and externals based on their I-E Scale scores. These subjects were then given a range of options by which they could ostensibly supervise three ficitious workers (one of whom was a supervisory problem). As the "supervisors" tried to deal with the problem worker, the external or high-powerless supervisors used significantly more coercion. That is, they threatened the worker with a reduction in bonus points or with firing. The internal or low-powerless supervisors used coercion techniques less and tended to rely upon personal persuasive powers. Goodstadt and Hjelle's work suggests that the explanation of their results probably lies in a greater felt competency on the part of internals. Being both more persuasive than externals (Phares, 1965) and more confident in their own efficacy, internals can afford to be less coercive in their relations with others. A lack of confidence may lead one to resort sooner to punitive means.

Of course, not every manifestation of power is so obviously coercive as the foregoing. What about the "con artist's" subtle manipulations? He or she might be said to use a machiavellian approach, a notion Christie and Geis (1970) have discussed in some detail. Characteristic of a high "Mach" person would be belief in the following kinds of statements:

A white lie is a good thing.

Few people really know what is best for them.

Deceit in the conduct of war is both honorable and praiseworthy.

Whereas internals seek objective control of the environment, high Mach persons seek a form of power through manipulation of other people. One possible explanation for this is that the manipulations of others by high Mach persons result not from a belief in their own power or effectiveness but from a pervasive sense of powerlessness or lack of confidence, as noted in the work of Goodstadt and Hjelle (1973).

Solar and Bruehl (1971) correlated scores on Rotter's I-E Scale with Christie and Geis's (1970) Mach IV Scale and found a significant correlation of .44 between externality and machiavellianism. Two cross-validational replications also yielded significant correlations of .41 and .33. Thus, high Machs and internals are hardly cut from the same cloth. The high Mach person seems concerned with manipulating others to obtain intended effects, while the internal seems motivated by a belief in the efficacy, and perhaps the desirability, of hard work, planning ahead, etc.—in short, he or she appears committed to the Protestant Ethic (MacDonald, 1972). Yet machiavellianism and externality are not synonymous either, although externals may resort to coercive or manipulative strategies when placed in a situation requiring such action to obtain a valued goal. Internals might resort to coercion of others only after trying to achieve control by more acceptable means. Perhaps it boils down to internals and externals having different expectancies for success and for control over the outcomes of their efforts.

HELPING BEHAVIOR

Another facet of behavior in the social context that we might look at is helping behavior, or altruism. Certainly much social action behavior can be construed as helping. However, such behavior is often rather impersonal in the sense that the individual is supporting a movement or a cause. We have seen that internals evince a greater commitment to social action (Gore & Rotter, 1963; Ryckman, Rodda, & Sherman, 1972; Strickland, 1965) and that internals are generally more competent (Brown & Strickland, 1972; Hersch & Scheibe, 1967; Phares, 1965; Tseng, 1970). If one couples this evidence with Midlarsky's (1971) assertion that both the competence of the helper and the dependent status of the victim are significant contributors to aiding, then it seems logical to expect a relationship between internality and helping behavior.

Midlarsky (1971) told male subjects they were participating in an armed forces research project designed to develop tests of skilled behavior for potential pilots. Each subject worked in the presence of another person, who was actually an accomplice of the experimenter. They were instructed that due to the newness of the tasks, it was quite possible that one might finish before the other. In that event, either individual could help his partner if he wished. The task was one of motor coordination, in which subjects removed and replaced objects from a box in a prescribed manner. For each test item manipulated, the subject received an electric shock. Further, whenever a subject helped the partner, he received a shock just as if it were his own item. Midlarsky also utilized a 16-item true-false measure of fatalism, a measure presumably similar to the I-E Scale. (Of course, the utilization of such a scale poses problems in generalizing to other studies that have used the I-E Scale.)

Midlarsky found that subjects who were low in fatalism ("internals") were significantly more prone to help others in difficulty than were subjects high in fatalistic beliefs ("externals"). This study appears to extend the meaning of locus of control in two ways. First, it indicates that internality, or low-fatalism beliefs, is associated with aiding even when the aider can expect little material gain, and indeed, some discomfort. Second, while previous studies have related internality to social movements that may ultimately result in some help to distant or abstract people (Gore & Rotter, 1963; Strickland, 1965; Ryckman, Rodda, & Sherman, 1972), the present study addresses helping in a more immediate face-to-face context.

This study brings into focus another important consideration. While we have not stated the point explicitly, it may have been implied that the greater action taking, activity, achievement behavior, and accomplishments of internals were basically in the service of the internals' own interests. As Midlarsky points out, in both the Gore and Rotter and the Strickland studies, the subjects belonged to the group that stood to benefit from the action taking. The same could be said for the Women's Liberation activities in the Ryckman, Rodda, and Sherman study. However, in Midlarsky's study there is no apparent material gain (only an inner glow, perhaps) from helping. It may be, then, that the greater efficacy of internals serves not only themselves or their groups but also those in less favorable circumstances.

A more recent study by Midlarsky and Midlarsky (1973) also reveals that low-fatalism scores (or an internal locus of control) are associated with helping behavior. The authors speculated that a belief in people's capability to help, although a necessary precondition of helping, may not be a sufficient explanation. It may be that the internal is also motivated to help.

RESPONSIBILITY ATTRIBUTED TO OTHERS

Some years ago, Thibaut and Riecken (1955) observed that subjects perceive an internal locus of control for high-status persons and an external locus of control for persons of lower status. Further, deCharms, Carpenter, and Kuperman (1965) found that coerced individuals were seen as "pawns" rather than as "origins" of their behavior. They also noted that internal subjects tended to perceive heroes in stories as origins rather than pawns.

Such work, combined with the general nature of the locus of control construct, suggests that internally oriented people not only see themselves as responsible for events but they attribute self-control to the behavior of others and see them as responsible for their own be-havior as well. By the same token, externals tend to attribute less responsibility to others just as they do to themselves. Such a notion may have important implications for altruism, helping behavior, and a host of other interpersonal reactions.

Phares and Wilson (1972b) selected 40 internal and 40 external college students based on their I-E Scale scores. Each subject provided four ratings of the degree of responsibility that should be attributed to individuals involved in auto accidents that varied in terms of severity of outcome and the ambiguity inherent in the accident descriptions. Internals attributed more responsibility to the drivers than did externals. This finding certainly extends the construct validity of the I-E Scale. If the attribution to others of the responsibility for their behavior mediates such reactions as hostility, generosity, or acceptance, then locus of control may affect a wide range of interpersonal reactions. Holding another person responsible for an act may predetermine, to some extent, whether one likes that person, will assist him, or will be kind to him.

Building on this line of research, Phares and Lamiell (1975) asked internals and externals to read brief case histories of a welfare recipient, a Korean War veteran, and an ex-convict. The cases varied in the degree of self-responsibility for the individual's plight that was built into the descriptions. Each subject then rated cases in terms of worthiness of help, financial assistance, understanding, and sympathy. In general, internals sanctioned significantly less in the way of help, sympathy, and money than did externals. These results are consistent with the findings of Phares and Wilson (1972b) in suggesting that internals see not only themselves but also others as being responsible for their own circumstances. While it was expected that this effect would be more pronounced when case histories were somewhat ambig-uous with respect to locus of responsibility, such an interaction was not obtained. Thus, while locus of control may operate most clearly in am-biguous situations when the individual is trying to solve a problem or acquire information, it apparently does not do so when judgments are being made about the responsibility of others. Phares and Wilson (1972b) also failed to find the interaction.

The failure of two separate studies to obtain this interaction between locus of control and ambiguity suggests there is a qualitative difference between situations requiring attribution of responsibility for one's own behavior and those requiring attribution of responsibility for another's behavior. Perhaps the difference lies in the engagement of different expectancies regarding the consequences of attributional state-ments in the various types of situations. Attributions of responsibility to others are almost quasi-legal judgments, and people may be rather cautious in making them.

Of particular interest here is the suggestion by Phares and Wilson (1972b) and Phares and Lamiell (1975) that internals may be less helping or altruistic than externals. On the face of it, this would seem to contradict the work of Midlarsky (1971) and Midlarsky and Midlarsky (1973), which showed internals to be more helping in a face-to-face setting. Perhaps the differences lie in (1) the face-to-face nature of Midlarksy's situations as opposed to the impersonal judgmental situations used by Phares and his colleagues, or (2) the competence-achievement behavior that Midlarsky's helping situation probably engaged (aspects on which internals would normally be expected to be superior).

Further research is needed to explicate the relationship between locus of control and helping behavior. It certainly seems logical that if internals hold others responsible, they are likely to be less generous and altruistic toward them. At the same time, the greater competence and action orientation of internals should predispose them toward helping others. As usual, it is likely that the nature of the situation moderates the relationship.

Summary

In this chapter we have attempted to relate locus of control to behavior in interpersonal contexts. Several behavioral correlates of scores on the I-E Scale were noted. In general, internals appear more independent and more reliant upon their own judgment. They seem to be less susceptible to control and influence from others, as shown in attitude change studies. They particularly resist subtle forms of attempted influence, such as that which appears in verbal operant conditioning situations. Internals are more accepting of information when it has merit than when it does not. Internals are not as likely to respond on the basis of the prestige or expertise of the message's source as are externals. Some evidence did, however, imply a greater suspiciousness in externals (as exemplified in not accepting the findings of the Warren Commission Report). The possibility of a "defensive external" posture was noted.

In examining efforts for social change, the evidence is somewhat conflicting. In some instances, internals seem to be more active in seeking social change. This was observed especially in the early days of the civil rights movement in the South. Other, more recent work reveals that externals are more politically active. The reasons for such contradictions are probably complex. The increased politicization of the citizenry has probably resulted in a change in the characteristics of persons associated with various social action movements and possibly accentuated the multidimensional nature of the I-E Scale.

Finally, the relationship between helping behavior and locus of control was explored. What little research has been done suggests that internals are more likely to help other individuals, at least in face-to-face situations. However, the operation of many situation-specific factors is probably quite important here. Other research, in the area of responsibility attribution, indicates that internals tend to hold others responsible for their own predicments (as they do themselves) more than do externals, which would, of course, predispose internals to be less helping of those in trouble.

VII

Locus of Control and Achievement in Children

The development of several scales to measure locus of control orientations has led to the discovery of significant relationships between I-E scores and such behaviors as mastery, control, resistance to social influence, and efforts to induce social change. These results also provide ample evidence that personality differences in locus of control can greatly assist us in predicting important human activities. All of this represents further verification of the utility of the social learning view that regards behavior as the joint product of personality variables and specific situational influences.

However, the major portion of the mastery, social influence, and social change data we have reviewed was collected from adult populations. Such behaviors occupy significant portions of the lives of adults. Certainly in our culture the mastery-coping behaviors are exceedingly important and have almost become the standards by which we judge the worth or value of one another. This is why it is so important that we be able to understand the occurrence of these behaviors. The I-E Scale has demonstrated its value as a tool in this regard.

The development of children's I-E scales has enabled us to focus on the mastery-coping efforts of younger populations. The question is whether we can show relationships between I-E scores and specific behaviors similar to those of adults. A little reflection tells us that the adult activities that have been studied are probably not appropriate indexes of children's behavior. For example, we do not normally expect children to be oriented toward influencing others, resisting influence, or otherwise evincing adult coping. These are simply not significant aspects of the child's life in our culture. What, then, is the main focus of mastery in children? School is the business of childhood. This being so, the prediction of mastery behavior in children should reduce primarily to the prediction of school achievement and related activities. Therefore, the major realm in which we might study locus of control in children is academic achievement.

Academic Achievement

We shall examine a variety of evidence demonstrating relationships between several I-E measures and indexes of academic achievement performance. It is difficult to summarize the research briefly, since most of it is correlational and has used a variety of groups differing in race, socioeconomic status, age, sex, and educational level, and the achievement performance measures and I-E scales have been quite varied. It was probably the so-called Coleman Report (Coleman, Campbell, Hobson, McPartland, Mood, Weinfeld, & York, 1966) that most strikingly underlined the relationship between belief in personal control over academic rewards and academic achievement. The work emphasizes the crucial role of locus of control beliefs in understanding the academic achievement of children. Based on a large-scale study of United States school children, these authors conclude that

> A pupil attitude factor, which appears to have a stronger relationship
> to achievement than do all the "school" factors together, is the extent
> to which an individual feels that he has some control over his own
> destiny .... The responses ... show that minority pupils, except for
> Orientals, have far less conviction than whites that they can affect their
> own environment and futures. (Coleman, Campbell, Hobson, McPart-
> land, Mood, Weinfeld, & York, 1966, p. 23)

SOCIAL LEARNING THEORY AND ACHIEVEMENT

How shall we define achievement? It is possible, in keeping with social learning theory, to approach a definition by at least three routes. First, we can talk about achievement *behaviors* (e.g., grades in school, studying). Second, there is achievement viewed as a *need* or motiva-tional variable (e.g., desire to attain excellence, need to surpass others). Third, there is the *expectancy* component of achievement (the subjective probability held by the individual that achievement behaviors will lead to the attainment of an achievement-related goal). Unfortunately, in many objective and projective measures relating to achievement motivation, these three aspects are often confounded, leading to poor prediction and confusion (Rotter, 1960).

GRADES IN SCHOOL AND I-E SCORES

The Intellectual Achievement Responsibility Questionnaire (IAR), developed by Crandall, Katkovsky, and Crandall (1965) has been an important tool in studying the relationship between grades and locus of control in children. The IAR, it may be recalled, assesses children's beliefs in their own control of reinforcements in intellectual-academic achievement situations. The scale yields scores for success events (I+) and for failure events (I−). Crandall and colleagues found both report card grades and scores on the Iowa Test of Basic Skills to be positively related to total I scores for third-, fourth-, and fifth-grade children. However, I+ scores predicted grades for girls in the third and fourth grades while I− predicted scores for boys in the fifth grade. In the sixth, eighth, tenth, and twelfth grades, total I scores were related to grades. These data suggest that while internality on the IAR is related to report card grades, there is a tendency for I+ (self-responsibility for success) to predict young girls' grades and I− (self-responsibility for failures) to predict for young boys. For the upper grades, total I predicted significantly the report card grades of both sexes. Earlier, Crandall, Katkovsky, and Preston (1962) had found that total I scores (subscales were not used) were highly associated with the amount of time boys chose to spend in intellectual activities during free play and the intensity of their striving in these activities. Similar data for girls showed no such relationship.

McGhee and Crandall (1968) reported that internals on the IAR achieve higher school grades than do external subjects. However, again I− predicted differently for boys. In older boys I− predicted grades better than did I+. Solomon, Houlihan, and Parelius (1969) found that girls score higher than boys on the I+ and total I scores on the IAR. Messer (1972) also used the IAR with fourth-grade boys and girls. Internals achieved higher school grades. However, in contrast to the work by Crandall and colleagues, there was a tendency for I− to predict better for girls and I+ to predict for boys. This study also noted, as have others, that IAR predicts better to school grades than to standardized measures of school achievement. Messer suggests that perhaps in giving grades teachers are more likely to reflect subjective judgments about work, efforts, or attitude, aspects in which an internal is likely to excel. The failure to replicate the I− and I+ differential is difficult to explain. Perhaps it should be held in abeyance until more data become available.

A study by Chance (1965) reports relationships between IAR scores and several achievement indexes, including reading skills, arithmetic performance, spelling, and even IQ. There were no sex differences. Other studies that have demonstrated direct relationships between the IAR and achievement behaviors such as grades and achievement-test scores include Buck and Austrin (1970), Cellura (1963), and Solomon, Houlihan, Busse, and Parelius (1971). DuCette, Wolk, and Friedman (1972) tested lower-class males (ages 9 to 11 and evenly divided into blacks and whites). IAR scores correlated with a measure of creativity, an effect that was not related to race. Clifford and Cleary (1972) studied 99 grade school children and noted that vocabulary, spelling, and mathematics achievement were all related to scores on a test similar to the IAR. Katz (1967), however, did not find any substantial relationship between the IAR and achievement. Shaw and Uhl (1971), using the Bialer (1961) Locus of Control Scale, found that internality was related to reading achievement in white middle-class and lower-class second graders but not in black children.

Several studies have reported significant relationships in older children. Using a specially designed personal control scale, Lessing (1969) found internality in junior and senior high-school students to be related to grade-point average when IQ was controlled.

Brown and Strickland (1972) examined the cumulative grade-point averages (GPA) of college seniors and found a significant correlation of .47 between GPA and internality in males; a correlation of .16 for females was not significant. Warehime (1972) found negligible correlations between locus of control and grades at the end of the freshman year. Perhaps cumulative GPA over four years is a more sensitive and representative measure of academic achievement. Hjelle (1970) and Eisenman and Platt (1968) report no relationship between I-E Scale scores and GPA. However, their GPA measure involved students' recollections rather than actual GPA, and the class level of the students was uncertain as contrasted to the Brown and Strickland study.

One of the early studies of achievement behavior cited by Rotter (1966) was Franklin's (1963) nationally stratified sample of 1,000 high school students. In 15 out of 17 instances, Franklin found the predicted relationships between locus of control and achievement motivation, which included such things as intention of going to college, early attempts to investigate colleges, time spent doing homework.

Using a specially constructed scale designed to be similar to the I-E Scale, both Gurin, Gurin, Lao, and Beattie (1969) and Lao (1970) found that black college students with a strong sense of their own personal control (as contrasted to a belief in ideological system control) tended to achieve higher grades and test scores than did externals. They also displayed higher academic confidence, aspirations, and expectations.

Generally, then, the data support the basic hypothesis that internal beliefs are significantly related to academic achievement.

NEED FOR ACHIEVEMENT

Many people, when they hear the concept of internal versus external control mentioned for the first time, immediately think of the achievement motive (Atkinson, 1958; Atkinson & Feather, 1966; McClelland, 1961; McClelland, Atkinson, Clark & Lowell, 1953). However, the relationship between locus of control and need for achievement (n Ach) typically is modest. Although people high in n Ach usually show an internal control orientation, the reverse does not follow. A belief in an internal locus of control does *not* require that one be achievement-oriented. Indeed, many people may be internals but care very little how much they achieve. Likewise, a person may be high in n Ach but not high in internality (Rotter, 1966). Such a situation probably reflects a nonlinear relationship between locus of control and achievement motivation, hence the often modest empirical relationship.

As we move from performance measures of achievement to need for achievement, the relationship with locus of control becomes more complex. It was noted earlier that many measures of need for achievement do not systematically separate the expectancy component of achievement from the need value aspect, as would be encouraged by social learning theory. And some even include behavioral items. Therefore, a total need for achievement (n Ach) score may represent a conglomeration of needs, expectancies, and behaviors. As a result, one person may show a high need for achievement and low expectancy that he can attain such goals while another individual may show the reverse pattern. Their n Ach scores might well be similar and their achievement behavior quite different.

Rotter (1966) cited the following additional reasons why the relationships between I-E and various measures of achievement motivation may be limited: (1) some individuals may possess strong achievement needs and low expectations for success, thus leading them to verbalize external beliefs (so-called defensive externals, described more fully in Chapter VIII); (2) specific control over achievement-striving behavior (as in classroom situations) is exerted by situational cues (especially since I-E attitudes are not totally generalized). While there is some theoretical overlap between I-E and achievement motivation, the relationship is far from perfect.

Neither Lichtman and Julian (1964) nor Gold (1968) could establish significant correlations between the I-E Scale and the French Test of Insight, a well-known measure of need for achievement. While Odell (1959) reported a relationship between I-E scores and a TAT measure of need for achievement, the correlation was not large. More recently, Mehrabian (1968, 1969) has reported substantial correlations between internality and his semi-projective *n* Ach measure (.64 for males and .41 for females). Wolk and DuCette (1971) could not establish any clear relationships among I-E scores, the Mehrabian *n* Ach measure, and a TAT *n* Ach measure. Pedhazur and Wheeler (1971) found a small but significant correlation between Bialer's (1961) Locus of Control Scale and a Graphic Expression Scale, which is a measure of *n* Ach, in a sample of 44 sixth-grade minority group children. To further complicate matters, according to Chance (1965), internality in children is associated with significantly fewer achievement-related stories told by both boys and girls.

Internals tend to prefer skill activities while externals are more drawn to chance tasks (Schneider, 1968, 1972). To the extent that skill activities can be construed as opportunities for the demonstration of personal achievement, or need for achievement, then we have the possibility of an internal-achievement relationship here also.

In an interesting exploratory study, deCharms (1972) provided black elementary school teachers with "personal causation" training and then designed and carried out classroom exercises for sixth and seventh graders. DeCharms reports increased motivation for both teachers and students, and enhanced academic achievement on the part of students as well as heightened perceptions of being treated as "origins." The origin-pawn variable was found to mediate personal causation and academic achievement.

SOME CONCLUSIONS

In summarizing the results of research dealing with achievement performance and motivation, it seems fair to assert that locus of control generally relates to performance but does not relate so consistently to measures of motivation. Internals tend to show superior academic achievement. The relationship seems more substantial for younger children but also seems to be present in young adults, whose behavior is more likely to be determined by many more variables than is true for young children. But in the case of both objective and projective measures of achievement motivation, the results are quite inconsistent and even contradictory.

Wolk and DuCette (1973) suggested that the theory of achievement motivation, particularly as offered by Atkinson (1958, 1964) and Atkinson and Feather (1966), can best be utilized while considering locus of control as a moderator variable. Generally, achievement motivation theory predicts that high n Ach subjects will prefer intermediate risks and will perform in a test situation at a higher level than low n Ach subjects. Wolk and DuCette found this to be true only for internals; externals generally showed correlations that were not significantly different from zero. Also, as before, no relationship was obtained between I-E Scale and Mehrabian n Ach scores. Thus, only internal subjects produced data compatible with predictions derived from achievement motivation theory. Such a view supports Feather's (1967a) suggestion that a control-of-reinforcement factor may moderate the relationship between achievement-oriented personality variables and achievement-dependent variables.

How can we account for the discrepancy between studies that deal with achievement in terms of performance and those that deal with achievement as a test score? Three possibilities were suggested. First, there appear to be a significant number of so-called defensive externals (internals who have a fairly strong need for achievement but a low expectancy for the attainment of achievement goals and who, therefore, verbalize "external" beliefs as a protective device). What this may mean functionally, therefore, is that any single group of internals will be relatively homogeneous—that is, it will contain more high-expectancy, high-need achievement individuals. Such a select group would be more likely to attain excellence since they not only have a need for achievement but also have high expectancies. The external group, on the other hand, will not only include its normal complement of low-need, low-expectancy persons but also the aforementioned low-expectancy internals. The number of externals, then, may be overestimated by inclusion of internals with low expectancies. If this is true, it would be no surprise to find that internality is highly associated with achievement performance, whether it is measured as school grades, reading and arithmetic tests scores, or some other index.

The second point is that common motivational measures of need achievement are nowhere near so unidimensional as are grades or reading and arithmetic test scores. That is, such measures do not separate need value, expectancies, behaviors, and chronic or acute anxiety. High or low n Ach scores can be attained by so many different routes that it is no wonder locus of control does not consistently relate to such measures. Also, since some externals are really high n Ach internals trying to ward off responsibility for expected failure, any group of externals will be heterogeneous in n Ach. Parenthetically, n Ach measures have a long history of not correlating very highly among themselves.

Third, while it seems clear that successful achievers would almost have to be internally oriented, it is much less clear why internals should all be high in achievement motivation. While a person may have an internal locus of control, he or she may have little need to be successful in school or other achievement activities.

Attribution of Responsibility for Success and Failure

The manner in which people account for their successes and failures plays a significant role in the attainment of excellence. Consistent recourse to external explanations could hardly be expected to lead to the kind of striving and effort that is required to achieve excellence. The realistic employment of both internal and external explanations of performance by the individual is essential. Attributing all failures to luck or powerful others will not, in all likelihood, lead to the persistence necessary for achievement. On the other hand, always attributing outcomes to internal factors (even when unwarranted) might lead to a degree of guilt or self-abasement that could impair optimal performance. Granted that one person's realism is another's defense, it still seems that the most effective course is a realistic application of internal and external attributions of responsibility.

Internals seem to adjust their aspirations upward after success and downward after failure to a greater extent than do externals. Indeed, externals often adjust their expectancies upward after failure and down after success (Feather, 1968). Both Battle and Rotter (1963) and Lefcourt and Ladwig (1965) have also reported a greater incidence of atypical expectancy changes by external subjects. As in the early work of Phares (1957), this implies a failure on the part of externals to make systematic use of their prior experience in preparing for the future. Such behavior could only retard the development of realistic achieving behavior. Lefcourt (1972) and Ryckman, Gold, and Rodda (1971) reported similar results. A subsequent study by Ryckman and Rodda (1971) was not particularly supportive.

The work of DuCette and Wolk (1972) indicates that externals are characterized by a preference for extreme risks, low persistence, and atypical shifts in level of aspiration. Obviously, such reactions to success and failure are intimately related to various aspects of anxiety, defensiveness, and psychopathology in addition to their antiachievement character; we shall therefore return to these topics in Chapter VIII.

Garrett and Willoughby (1972) reported a study in which black children, classified as internal or external on the basis of the IAR, were either failed or allowed to succeed on an anagrams task. Externals performed better than internals following failure, while internals performed better following success. The authors felt that internals resembled high *n* Ach subjects in their responses to task feedback and that externals were more like failure-avoiders. The analysis by Wolk and DuCette (1973), noted earlier, with respect to achievement and locus of control appears relevant here also.

It seems quite reasonable, then, to assume that the manner in which one attributes responsibility for outcomes plays an important role in achievement-related behavior (Weiner, Frieze, Kukla, Reed, Rest, & Rosenbaum, 1971). An internal belief system should lead to reactions of pride following success or to a variety of negative emotions following failure. In either case, the effects on subsequent achievement behavior could well be positive. The belief system of externals, however, denies them either emotional experience and thus perhaps provides them little basis for the pursuit of excellence. After all, if one ascribes success to outside forces why should one either take pleasure in the attainment of success or make further efforts to achieve it?

Karabenick's (1972) work reinforces the relationship between locus of control and the satisfaction, or lack of it, experienced through success and failure. His results suggest that satisfaction experienced by internals following success on very difficult tasks is greater than it is for external subjects. On the other hand, the value of success on an easy task was rated as greater by externals than internals. However, failure on very easy tasks was more threatening for internals than it was for externals, although the reverse was true on very difficult tasks. These results clearly indicate that locus of control, through the mediation of both task difficulty and emotional reactions following success-failure, can significantly affect the occurrence of achievement behavior.

Phares, Wilson, and Klyver (1971) have noted that internals attribute less blame for their failure to the environment than do externals. Further, in a study involving both success and failure, Davis and Davis (1972) demonstrated that internals show a greater tendency to accept responsibility for their behaviors than do externals. More recently, Krovetz (1974) found that, as expected, subjects (either internal or external) form attributions to account for their successes and failures that are entirely congruent with their locus of control as determined by the I-E Scale. One can infer from these studies that in order to continue to pursue success one must, at least to some degree, attribute the locus of responsibility to internal factors. Otherwise, the pursuit of excellence becomes rather irrational, and the satisfaction that normally comes from success is impossible. That is, persistence in achievement behavior, the enjoyment of success, or the experience of disappointment in failure all seem necessary to attain competence, but they all seem inappropriate when the control over reinforcment is thought to reside in factors over which the individual has little control.

WILLINGNESS TO DELAY GRATIFICATION

To attain control over one's environment, to achieve competence, or to reach positions of power and influence generally all require that the individual eschew the lure of the present for the greater promise of the future. All of us are constantly assaulted by immediately present temptations that are more attractive than certain other activities that will lead to a larger goal in the future. The high-school student who drops out to work so he can buy a car may thereby mortgage his future. The young girl who marries because all her friends are doing it can easily cut herself off from a whole array of other potential rewards in the future.

Thus, the superior strategy would seem to be that of deferring immediate rewards, while being discriminating. Completely giving up *every* immediate gratification obviously might lead to a life that is rather barren. However, an internal locus of control ought to relate to a greater willingness to delay gratification in the service of long-term goals. As in the case of academic achievement, much of the delay of gratification research has been carried out with children. Partly this is because of the ready availability of children for this kind of research, but it probably is also due to the assumption that delay of gratification patterns are established in childhood. The actual methodologies and populations employed have limited the extent to which one can generalize. As Lefcourt has cogently observed:

> The most commonly employed technique has been to offer youngsters a small prize immediately or the option to wait for a larger gift to be delivered after some period of time. This method of testing delay capacity, reviewed in some detail by Mischel (1966), is clever in demonstrating the value of the immediate-delayed reinforcement dimension. However, it suffers in comparison to real decision making about valued goals. For instance, the reinforcements have more often been undeserved, fortuitous, and of only slight value so that the generalization from such choice activity to choices made about real life goals would seem tenuous at best. (Lefcourt, 1972, p. 15–16)

Bialer (1961) constructed a modified I-E scale based on questionnaires used earlier with college students (James, 1957; Phares, 1955). Using both normal and mentally retarded children, ranging in age from 6 to 14 years, Bialer reported a correlation of .47 between belief in internal control and the choice of delayed, more valuable rewards over an immediate but lesser reward.

Subsequently, Zytkoskee, Strickland, and Watson (1971) also employed Bialer's (1961) Locus of Control Scale. They tested groups of black and white ninth-grade students of low socioeconomic status. While they did find that black students were more external in their belief system than were whites and that blacks were also less likely to delay gratification as compared to whites, no relationship was found between locus of control and delay of gratification behavior.

In a follow-up study, Strickland (1972) speculated that a possible reason for Zytkoskee, Strickland, and Watson's failure to relate internality to delay behavior was their utilization of white experimenters. The black subjects may not have trusted the white experimenters to return later with the promised rewards. Using the familiar delay paradigm (Mischel, 1966) and the Nowicki-Strickland Locus of Control Scale for Children (Nowicki and Strickland, 1973), samples of black and white sixth-grade students were tested. Of the white students 80 percent chose the delayed, larger reward, regardless of race of the experimenter. Of the black students 33 percent chose the delayed reward from the white experimenter and 56 percent chose the delayed reward from the black experimenter. Also, black students showed higher external scores. Of specific import here, however, was the fact that while no relationship was found between locus of control and delay behavior in blacks, white internals chose more delayed rewards than did white externals.

In an attempt to extend the previous results while at the same time avoiding the factors of race or socioeconomic status, Strickland (1973) again attempted to relate belief in internal control to preference for delayed, larger rewards over immediate, smaller rewards. She used the Nowicki-Strickland Locus of Control Scale for Children. Her results rather clearly showed that for a sample of white, middle-class males and females 8 through 10 years old, internal control beliefs were substantially related to choices involving delayed, more valuable rewards.

Walls and Smith (1970) reported that internals are more likley to wait for a larger, delayed reinforcement than are externals. On the other hand, Walls and Miller (1970) could not find any significant relationships between I-E and delay behavior in a group of vocational rehabilitation and welfare clients.

In summarizing the foregoing studies, it seems fair to state that while there is a definite basis now laid for the relationship between an internal locus of control and a readiness to delay gratification in the service of larger rewards later, the magnitude of this relationship depends upon specific considerations, such as the population used, the nature of the experimenter, and the method utilized. Thus, a white experimenter testing black subjects can easily obscure the relationship, perhaps because of latent interpersonal trust factors involved in the situation.

As Lefcourt (1972) stated, better-educated, more achievement-oriented, or less deprived racial groups seem to be both more internal and more willing to delay gratifications. But unfortunately, the experimental paradigm employed has been quite restricted. Generally, it is on the order of simply asking subjects whether they want one piece of candy now or three pieces at some later date. Also, the subjects are usually grade-school children. Would the same results hold for older populations? In the most compelling comment on these procedures, Lefcourt states the following:

> Perhaps a major reason for the relatively weak findings reported thus far derives from the use of "empty time" in most delay of reinforcement studies. That is, subjects have more often been asked to simply wait rather than to persist in some effort directed toward a valued end. Such waiting for what are often undeserved rewards may be more related to the ability to restrain one's momentary impulses than to the willingness to commit oneself to long-term efforts directed at distant goals. (Lefcourt, 1972, p. 17)

Responding to such comments, Mischel, Zeiss, and Zeiss (1974) carried out a validity study with their Stanford Preschool Internal-External Scale. This is a forced-choice scale (described in Chapter IV) that attempts to elicit expectancies about locus of control separately for a positive $(I+)$ and negative $(I-)$ events. In some ways, it represents a downward extension of the scale developed by Crandall, Katkovsky, and Crandall (1965). Drawing upon data from several previously conducted studies at the Stanford laboratories, Mischel, Zeiss, and Zeiss were able to relate locus of control in preschool children to situations involving (1) waiting passively for reward, (2) engaging in instrumental activities designed to lead to the reward during the waiting period, or (3) signaling for an immediate reward. Their work seems generally supportive of an association between locus of control and delay behavior (or persistence), but only when the subject's delay behavior is designed to be instrumental in the attainment of desired but delayed contingent outcomes. Further, while $I+$ is related to instrumental delay behavior for positive outcomes, it is not related to such behavior when the outcomes are potentially negative. The converse is true for the $I-$ items. Mischel, Zeiss, and Zeiss argue that their results help clarify the reason previous research that investigated global relationships between locus of control and delay phenomena yielded ambiguous results; there had not been adequate specification of the moderating conditions.

Summary

In adults, power and personal efficacy are easily seen in efforts to control other people, to resist influence, and to maintain a more active posture regarding information acquisition, utilization, and processing. Children's lives however, revolve around the school and the achievement demands it makes upon them. Therefore, in investigating differential mastery and control in internal and external children, it is natural to study academic achievement.

In general, the achievements of internal children, as reflected in school grades and test scores, are more substantial than those of externals. The story with respect to various measures of achievement needs is not so clear-cut. Here, the relationships are often inconsistent and occasionally contradictory. A variety of potential contributors to this confusion were discussed.

Another characteristic that probably determines children's ultimate success or achievement orientation in adulthood is their capacity to delay gratification so as to attain larger rewards at a later date. Internals generally demonstrate a greater capacity to defer lesser rewards in the service of larger long-term goals. These findings are marred by the fact that the research in this area has been conducted in rather restricted or trivial experimental circumstances.

In both children and adults, internals' reactions to success and failure seem more realistic and more in keeping with their actual prior experience than is true for externals. The ways internals and externals attribute responsibility for the successes and failures generally seem closely related to the manner in which they respond to I- E scales. It appears that veridical characterization of prior experience is essential to the ultimate attainment of excellence and the maintenance of personal efficacy.

VIII

Anxiety,
Adjustment,
and Reaction to Threat

We saw in Chapter I that the development of the locus of control notion began in the therapy relationship with Karl S. With a clinical case providing the context, it is no accident that early conceptualizations of locus of control were at least loosely tied to considerations of adjustment, pathology, and defense mechanisms. Thus, in the early struggle to formulate the concept in a fashion that would assist in understanding and helping Karl S., locus of control assumed clinical overtones. These were overtones regarding the role of locus of control in the psychological economy and dynamics of an individual who was having enormous problems in living. The construction of the first crude I-E scale was guided by such considerations, along with some ideas gleaned from examination of the F Scale (authoritarianism) and others. Parenthetically, it might be noted that subsequent research has been equivocal regarding the relationship between locus of control and authoritarianism (Baron, 1968; Rotter, Seeman, & Liverant, 1962; Shumate, 1970).

Since these early activities, I-E work has increased in diversity and scope. While the borders between fields of study are inevitably blurred, much of the subsequent work has been in the realm of social psychology. This work has attempted to relate locus of control to

119

romantic love (Dion & Dion, 1973), to interpersonal attraction (Phares & Wilson, 1971) and to patterns of interest (Zytkowski, 1967). However, the role of locus of control in personal adjustment and psychopathology continues to hold great promise for increasing our understanding of human behavior. Shortly after publication of the I-E Scale in 1966, Hersch and Scheibe (1967) set out to enlarge the meaning of the I-E concept. They did so by relating I-E scores to scores on several personality measures (the California Psychological Inventory and the Adjective Checklist) along with several indexes of maladjustment. They found that externals were more maladjusted, were lower on defensiveness, achievement, dominance, endurance, and order, and were higher on succorance and abasement. Similarly, early work by Butterfield (1964) had indicated that internals tend to react to frustration in a constructive fashion and with less self-blame. On the other hand, the reactions of externals to frustration seem to be intropunitive and also less constructive. These results have been supported by Brissett and Nowicki (1973).

Anxiety and Adjustment

The work reviewed has described internals as active, striving individuals who exhibit greater resistance to influence and who seem to handle success and failure in a more realistic fashion than externals. These behavioral characteristics, coupled with a generalized belief in the efficacy of their own efforts, ought to provide a stronger basis for personal adjustment and reduced anxiety in internals. By contrast, externals should be more vulnerable and less capable of coping with their environment.

We shall see in the next chapter that there are a number of potential antecedents of external beliefs. Some of these involve family origins and may include parental attitudes such as rejection, hostile control, lack of warmth, withdrawal of relations with the child, or inconsistency and unpredictability of reinforcements. In addition, there may be a variety of social origins, particularly in those groups who are isolated from access to power and social mobility and who feel at the mercy of the social forces beyond their power. But regardless of whether the person's external beliefs emanate from social conditions, unfortunate parental-family conditions, or personal tragedies of one sort or another, it is easy to see that the outcome could be chronic anxiety. The early social, familial, and personal correlates of an external belief system would lead us to predict greater anxiety on the part of externals.

By now, a great deal of evidence supports this prediction. A brief sampling of this research (see Table 2) will confirm this conclusion. While not exhaustive, the list is representative and clearly supports a strong relationship between externality and a variety of measures of anxiety. Other research also supports this conclusion (Hountras & Scharf, 1970; Levenson, 1973c; Nelson & Phares, 1971; Platt & Eisenman, 1968), although a few investigators have failed to verify this conclusion (e.g., Berman and Hays [1973] and Gold [1968]).

Table 2   *Locus of Control and Anxiety Correlations*

Source	Anxiety Measure	Correlation with Externality
Butterfield (1964)	Alpert-Haber Facilitating-Debilitating Test Anxiety Questionnaire	.61 (debilitating anxiety) −.82 (facilitating anxiety)
Liberty, Burnstein, and Moulton (1966)	Mandler-Sarason Test Anxiety Questionnaire	.44
Watson (1967)	Taylor Manifest Anxiety	.36
	Alpert-Haber	.25 (debilitating anxiety) −.08 (facilitating anxiety)
Feather (1967b)	Alpert-Haber (Debilitating)	.36
Tolor and Reznikoff (1967)	Death Anxiety Scale	.32
Ray and Katahn (1968)	Mandler-Sarason	.22; .21
	Taylor	.40; .30
Berman and Hays (1973)	Death Anxiety Scale	.08
Strassberg (1973)	IPAT Anxiety Scale	.41

While any single study will surely manifest shortcomings that might dissuade us from accepting the relationship between anxiety and externality, the relationship has been found in so many different studies, with so many different anxiety measures, populations, and test conditions, that the conclusion now appears inescapable. Of course, one must be careful to emphasize that these studies are entirely correlational in nature. That being the case, it is difficult to separate cause from effect in any definitive way. Does anxiety lead to an external belief system or does externality lead to anxiety? Or do the same conditions (social and familial) that lead to external beliefs also lead to anxiety? These are important questions, but the research cited does not, by its nature, allow us to disentangle this web of cause and effect.

Within social learning theory, anxiety is often viewed as a series of responses indicative of a high expectancy for punishment or a low expectancy of success in a valued need area. The student who expects to fail, the suitor who expects to be rejected, or the employee who expects to be fired all would be regarded as possessing a high expectancy for punishment (and presumably all would value the avoidance of such punishment). A variety of anxious behaviors might flow from such a high expectancy, e.g., worrying, crying, withdrawing, and showing avoidant or inappropriate behaviors. One would expect external individuals to exhibit relatively high expectancies for punishment and therefore display greater anxiety than internals. Nelson and Phares (1971) predicted that locus of control would be associated with both anxiety and need values whose magnitude clearly outstripped their expectancies of satisfying those needs. As anticipated, externals rated themselves as being more anxious. At the same time, the difference between the value of their academic goals and their expectancy for achieving them was greater for externals than for internals. Also, the relationship between anxiety and the need value–expectancy discrepancy was clear and linear.

Strassberg (1973), using different measures, found essentially the same thing. A lower expectancy of achievement of valued goals was associated with both higher anxiety scores and more external scores. This supports the social learning theory analysis of the relationship between anxiety and expectancies. Whether it supports the idea that an external is anxious simply because he has a lower expectancy for success is not entirely clear. Strassberg carried out a regression analysis that revealed that adding locus of control doubled the amount of variability in anxiety scores predicted by valued goal expectancy scores alone. Thus, externals may not be more anxious than internals just because they tend to have a lower expectancy of achieving valued outcomes.

Of course, not all anxiety is to be regarded as undesirable. At least a reasonable degree of anxiety may motivate individuals to want to change, to better their lot, etc. Several studies, including those by Butterfield (1964) and Feather (1967b), suggest that externals manifest what might be termed debilitating anxiety while not exhibiting much in the way of facilitating anxiety.

Fitch (1970) has reported a low but significant positive rank-order correlation between locus of control and self-esteem. Specifically, low-self-esteem subjects tended to score as externals. In a related vein, Warehime and Foulds (1971) had male and female college students fill out both the I-E Scale and the Personal Orientation Inventory (a measure of self-actualization). They predicted a relationship between internality and self-actualization, since the latter is often construed as an indicator of personal adjustment. Interestingly, they found support for their hypothesis with females but not with males. Perhaps the generally different patterns of masculine and feminine interests (Zytkowski, 1967) require different adjustment criteria for males and females. That is, since traditionally defined femininity may imply greater concern with emotions and feelings, while masculinity is associated with greater overt activity and instrumental acts, the notion of self-actualization might make more sense as a criterion of adjustment for females than for males.

Most of the research in this area suggests a linear relationship between externality and anxiety or adjustment. Although there is little evidence to support the contention, it seems reasonable to suppose there might be a U-shape relationship, that is, both very external and very internal subjects might be maladjusted. Extremely internal individuals might be so overcome with a sense of personal responsibility over every little failure of their own or others that they would be inundated with anxiety-depressive reactions. Extreme externals might completely lose any initiative and become near vegetables because of total inability to see how they could exert any environmental effects. Failure to demonstrate a U-shape relationship could be due to the rather restricted samples that are usually used. College students, for example, do not offer many extreme scores, whereas a less elite group might. Or perhaps I-E scales are simply not as sensitive as they might be to such extremes. The nature of the adjustment-anxiety criterion may also be important. For example, according to one criterion, a highly motivated, aggressive, controlling internal might be regarded as the epitome of adjustment while another standard might regard him as overdriven and undesirable. Similarly, is the passive, fatalistic external person maladjusted or is he ultimately better off than most of us?

The preceding self-report, correlational evidence clearly suggests that externals are more anxious than internals. But "anxious" is a broad term that might better serve as a point of departure for our attempts at understanding than as the final word. Let us now try to be a bit more specific about the nature of the external's discomfort, adjustment, or problems.

Behavior Pathologies and Locus of Control

SCHIZOPHRENIA

While the nature and origin of schizophrenia may be obscure, most investigators have considered that patients so diagnosed ought to score in a more external direction than their normal counterparts. Sidestepping such issues as the reliability of diagnoses, homogeneity of membership in the schizophrenic class, and disease entity questions, it is possible to view schizophrenics simply as severely disturbed individuals. Therefore, extrapolating from previous discussions, greater externality would be predicted. The data certainly seem to support such a prediction. Cromwell, Rosenthal, Shakow, and Zahn (1961), using an early version of the I-E Scale, found that 15 white male schizophrenics were more external than 13 normal controls (white male conscientious objectors). Similar results were reported by Harrow and Ferrante (1969). Likewise, Shybut (1968) noted that long-term, severely disturbed patients were significantly more external than short-term, moderately disturbed individuals.

Lottman and DeWolfe (1972) attempted to relate process and reactive schizophrenia to locus of control. They hypothesized that the process schizophrenics, with their poorer premorbid adjustment patterns and longer history of social inadequacy and failure, would be more external than the reactive schizophrenics, whose maladaptive responses developed more recently. Their hypothesis was verified. Further, the process schizophrenics were more external than a control sample of nonschizophrenic psychiatric patients. No significant difference was found between the reactive and nonschizophrenic groups. Such results are consistent with the idea that within schizophrenic groups, greater externality can be viewed as a result of long-term social learning, beginning with premorbid adjustment levels, rather than as a simple aspect of typical schizophrenic symptomatology. Lottman and DeWolfe also feel that the reduced behavioral responsiveness of process schizophrenics may be related to externality, inasmuch as the environment poses a greater threat to them because of their perceived lack of control. With more felt control, the reactive schizophrenic does not find the world so threatening. Again, however, problems of cause and effect have not been disentangled.

In this process-reactive context it is also of interest to note that Fontana, Klein, Lewis, and Levine (1968) found that schizophrenic patients who wished to impress others that they were "healthy" were more internal than those who wanted to convince others that they were "sick."

Duke and Mullens (1973) have found that chronic schizophrenics prefer greater interpersonal distances than normals and that the degree of their withdrawal behavior from other human beings is not completely due to their hospitalization. As suggested by Harrow and Ferrante (1969), hospitalization is associated with greater preferred interpersonal distance and also with a more external belief system, but schizophrenics prefer even greater distances than do other psychiatric patients, and they are more external. While the nature of causal relationships is still obscure, it is possible that attempts to alter systematically the locus of control orientations of patients might result in reduced interpersonal distances and perhaps other benign interpersonal effects (Duke & Mullens, 1973; Lottman & DeWolfe, 1972).

Thus far, research has indicated that more extreme pathology is related to greater externality. However, such research can only be useful to the extent that each syndrome offers an explicit, reliable set of dynamics. For example, if it is known that schizophrenia refers to a certain constellation of problems, fears, or expectancies, then we are in a position to make intelligent predictions regarding the role of locus of control. However, as long as schizophrenia remains essentially a code word for extreme disturbance, any obtained relationships are going to be modest and probably not heuristic.

DEPRESSION

Clinically, depression often seems to be associated with anger, hostility, and self-destruction. Indeed, Williams and Nickels (1969) reported that externality is related to suicide-proneness, while Abramowitz (1969) found that externals report more feelings of anger and depression. Similarly, Williams and Vantress (1969) found a low but positive relationship in college students between externality and hostility.

The relationship between locus of control and depressive reactions appears to be complex. Phares (1972) has commented on the notion that depression may represent a situation in which the individual realizes not only that the achievement of valued goals is blocked but also that this blockage may be relatively permanent. If the blockage were recognized as temporary, the individual might react with anger or hostility. However, when the element of finality is present, the reaction is much more likely to be depression.

Miller and Seligman (1973) have offered an interesting analysis in their discussion of "learned helplessness." They argue that depression results from learning that reinforcement is independent of voluntary responses. Therefore, a depressive individual would perceive reinforcement or goal attainment as independent of any personal response. Miller and Seligman state that "depression in this model is a specific cognitive distortion of the perception of the ability of one's own responses to change the environment, rather than a general 'pessimism' " (p. 62). Based on this rationale, Miller and Seligman administered the I-E Scale and the Beck Depression Inventory to groups of undergraduates. Expectancy changes for success following reinforcement in skill and chance tasks were assessed in four groups—depressed high external, depressed low external, nondepressed high external, and nondepressed low external. As anticipated, the nondepressed subjects manifested greater expectancy changes than depressed subjects in skill tasks, while the changes of depressed and nondepressed subjects were similar in chance situations. External locus of control had no significant effect on expectancy changes in chance or skill tasks.

The hypothesis that depressed individuals tend to perceive reinforcement as more response-independent than do nondepressed subjects in situations where reinforcement is response-dependent seems supported. This can be placed in the context of previous evidence (reviewed in Chapter III) that clearly indicates greater expectancy changes by subjects when they view a task as skill-controlled than when they see it as chance-controlled. Thus, Miller and Seligman seem to feel that the smaller expectancy changes in their depressed groups in the skill task were due to their perceiving the reinforcement in the skill task as less response-contingent than the nondepressed subjects did.

Clearly, there ought to be a relationship between externality and depression, according to this view. Externals surely should be more susceptible to learned helplessness than internals. Abramowitz (1969) did find a small but significant relationship between externality on the I-E Scale and depression scores on the Guilford D Scale. But, this rather small correlation led Lamont (1972a, 1972b) to explain such correlations as due to the pessimistic wording of the external items and the optimistic wording of the internal alternatives on the I-E Scale.

Phares (1972) has offered a nearly opposite hypothesis, that perhaps depressions are found in people (1) who possess a strong generalized expectancy that outcomes are their own responsibility, and (2) who do not expect to attain valued goals or outcomes. Such a hypothesis is reminiscent of Rotter's (1966) speculation about a curvilinear relationship between pathology and locus of control: Both extremes tend to be maladjusted. Thus, one may find that a population of *extreme* internals and *extreme* externals, both of whom have very low generalized expectancies for success in attaining important goals, will show depression. The externals feel they cannot do anything about their plight and are sad. The internals are sad because of the guilt and responsibility they feel over incompetence or lack of ability.

It is important to remember that while there is a strong relationship between internality and mastery and competence, not every internal is so fortunate as to be competent. Some are surely very incompetent, with a history of failures. A strong internal locus of control could make internals very uncomfortable when they come face to face with actual or anticipated failure. It is also possible that extreme externals may learn to devalue important goals as a means of reducing anxiety and discomfort over their inability to achieve these goals. Thus, such externals might, over time, come to respond in a rather nonanxious fashion, their fatalism transformed into indifference. Phares (1971) has provided some preliminary evidence on this point (it is described later in this chapter).

The foregoing considerations illustrate the complexities in this area and suggest reasons for the failure of several investigators to find substantial correlations between locus of control and depression.

ALCOHOLISM AND OPIATE ADDICTION

Thus far, it seems clear that internal beliefs are associated with better adjustment, whether the criterion is anxiety or membership in a psychiatric category. Goss and Morosko (1970) therefore hypothesized that an alcoholic population would be characterized by relatively high external scores, on the supposition that alcoholics would have maintained, for a long time, a marginal social existence and would be passive and dependent. They administered the I-E Scale to 262 alcoholic outpatients (200 males and 62 females).

Interestingly, this alcoholic sample produced I-E scores that were significantly more internal than Rotter's (1966) general norms. This result is even more striking when we realize that the general norms have, since 1966, shifted increasingly in the external direction. Thus, the internal scores in Goss and Morosko's sample probably departed even more in the internal direction than it appears.

How shall we explain such apparently contradictory findings? Goss and Morosko argue that the answer lies in the behaviors available to various people to maintain their control in tense situations and to allay their fears and anxieties. In the case of alcoholics, they need only reach for a drink. Such an explanation is plausible and may be valid. However, most people are aware of alcohol as a means of altering feeling states, even though drinking may not have a high potential for occurrence.

Another possible explanation may lie in the nature of alcoholics. Many of them are quite glib and articulate and have a history of being attracted to group meetings and organizations, which reinforce the espousal of confidence, personal control, and optimism. Thus, many alcoholics may have learned over the years (both in clinical settings and in public situations) to express strong belief in self and in one's potential for self-improvement (the "I think I can" syndrome). The findings of Fontana, Klein, Lewis, and Levine (1968), noted earlier, are interesting in this regard. Schizophrenics who wished to impress others with their good adjustment tended to score more internally than did schizophrenics who wished to create a bad impression. Alcoholics may respond in a similar manner. It is frequently observed that alcoholics have an inordinate desire to impress others (even though they may be largely unsuccessful in their efforts). Further research may illuminate Goss and Morosko's contradictory finding.

Goss and Morosko (1970) also reported that the alcoholics whose scores were most internal also reported the least anxiety, depression, and clinical pathology as measured by the MMPI. Whether this means (as in other cases, such as the process and reactive schizophrenics) that better adjustment is associated with greater internal beliefs or whether the same hypothesized need to appear confident and in control that produces high internal responses also produces well-adjusted MMPI scores is uncertain at this point. However, it may be risky to generalize too far from pathological populations. For example, Burnes, Brown, and Keating (1971) report that certain MMPI patterns of pathological responses do not accompany external scores on the I-E Scale in a normal population.

Will opiate addicts show locus of control and behavior patterns similar to those of alcoholics? Berzins and Ross (1973) compared samples of 200 white males, 100 white females, 200 black males, and 100 black females (all from the Lexington, Kentucky Clinical Research Center) with samples of 400 males and 400 females (largely white) from introductory psychology classes at the University of Kentucky. Their results support the conclusions of Goss and Morosko (1970) in that the opiate users achieved significantly more internal I-E scores (especially on personal-control items) than the comparison group of college students. As in the explanation offered by Goss and Morosko, the results of Berzins and Ross could be predicted on the assumption that the use of drugs enables the users to exert control over such areas as their impulses, reactions, anxieties, and physical states. However, there are several differences between Berzins and Ross's addict and student samples—e.g., age, geographic origin, race, socioeconomic status, and recency of academic exposure—that might have been the reasons for the obtained differences rather than the presumed control over physical states gained through drug use.

Previous work by Berzins, Ross, and Monroe (1971) suggests that "comparable" groups of addicts obtained relatively low social-desirability scores on the Edwards Social Desirability Scale and appeared to be pathological based on MMPI profiles. Such findings, if they were also characteristic of Berzins and Ross's (1973) subjects, would increase our confidence that internal scores were not given merely as "socially desirable" responses (or else why not also "fake" healthy MMPI profiles?). However, we must await further research to determine whether the internality of addicts and alcoholics represents a special case of personal control achieved by chronic recourse to mind-altering substances or represents a socially desirable response designed to induce favorable responses from others. In the meantime, Berzins and Ross (1973) suggest the following:

> While most research with the internal-external control construct has focused on socially desirable correlates of internal control (e.g., mastery over the environment, achievement), the present study . . . suggests that internal control can additionally be conceptualized as a consequence or by-product of substance abuse. Perhaps a term such as "pseudo-internality" should be used to distinguish drug-engendered internality from its conventional, socially learned counterpart (Berzins & Ross, 1973, pp. 89–90).

Reaction to Threat

The preceding discussions point to a definite relationship between external beliefs and chronic anxiety, membership in various pathological groups, and other indices of maladjustment. However, clear cause-effect relationships have not been established. There is some basis for arguing that external beliefs lead to anxiety or maladjustment, but it also seems likely that in some instances maladjustment or anxiety could produce a sense of lack of control (externality). Let us now turn to an examination of how internals and externals handle threat or other stressful situations. Some of the coping behaviors may resemble what others might describe as defense mechanisms.

PERCEPTUAL DEFENSE AND DEFENSIVENESS OF INTERNALS AND EXTERNALS

Some years ago, Efran (1963) found that when high-school students experienced failure, they tended to forget such failure, and such forgetting was associated with high internal scores. As Rotter stated:

> It is possible that the functional value of a defensive tendency towards externality is indicated by these findings. The results suggest that the external has less need to "repress" his failures since he has already accepted external factors as determining his success and failure to a greater extent than those subjects scoring as more internal on the I-E control scale (Rotter, 1966, p. 22).

Subsequently, Lipp, Kolstoe, James, and Randall (1968) were interested in investigating some of the problems of physically disabled individuals, particularly their perceptions of being "different" from others. One defensive response to such threat is, of course, denial. The Lipp group felt that locus of control would determine, at least in part, the differential utilization of denial in disabled subjects. Therefore, they administered the James I-E Scale (James 1957) to a group of physically disabled subjects, which included persons suffering from amputations, paralysis, fractures, arthritis, and congenital deformities. Pictures of disabled and nondisabled people were presented tachistoscopically to these subjects and to a normal control group.

As anticipated, the disabled subjects showed higher recognition thresholds for the "threat" stimuli than did nondisabled subjects. At the same time, external disabled individuals had lower recognition thresholds and thus were significantly less denying of their disability than were either internal subjects or a middle group. Therefore, as in the case of Efran's (1963) results, an external belief system seems to allow a greater willingness to admit threatening stimuli to awareness or to report such awareness. Presumably, the greater anxiety level thought to characterize externals was dealt with by the simple expedient of denying the significance of the threat.

Building on the results of Lipp and colleagues, Phares, Ritchie, and Davis (1968) administered the I-E Scale and parts of several personality and intelligence tests to groups of college students. Later, they provided the students with what appeared to be individualized reports containing both positive and negative information about their personalities. It was expected that externals would have less need to deny unfavorable personal information and would, therefore, recall more of the unfavorable data. This was found to be the case. Further, externals' recall of all the information was better. This result is particularly interesting inasmuch as previous work relating locus of control to retention has uniformly indicated better retention on the part of internals (e.g., Phares [1968], Seeman [1963], and Seeman and Evans [1962]). The fact that the better retention found by Phares, Ritchie, and Davis and by Efran occurred in the context of threat while the other studies were much less personally threatening, suggests again the greater potential for defensiveness that an external locus of control affords.

Phares, Ritchie, and Davis were not able to show differences in anxiety between internals and externals in the experimental situation. It would have been expected that the externals would be less anxious, at least in this specific situation. The failure to find such differences may have been a function of the crude nature of the anxiety rating scales used. Another possibility is that anxiety dissipates at different rates in the two populations. That is, while they do not differ in their immediate anxiety reactions, after an unspecified period the external may become less anxious as his external locus of control denies the threat. At the same time, the greater anxiety level in the internal might have the effect of interfering with the recall of material associated with the threat.

Since emotional disorders imply a loss of inner control, Mac-Donald and Hall (1969) felt that internals would be more threatened by such a loss of control than would externals. Presumably, internals believe they possess such control and the threat of its loss would be especially disconcerting. Fifty graduate students rated the seriousness of four disability types in six personal-social areas as they would affect an adult male who was 28 years old, married, and had two preteen-age children. As expected, internal locus of control was significantly correlated with the more-serious ratings of emotional disorders. Similar results were found in a subsequent study (MacDonald & Hall 1971). However, it was noted that externals in the latter study rated physical disabilities as more debilitating than did the internal subjects. In view of earlier data suggesting a greater need on the part of externals to be dependent, to rely on others' opinions, etc., perhaps physical disabilities are more threatening to them because they feel such disabilities may lead to rejection or lack of support from others.

In some ways the greater willingness of externals to pay attention to threatening material seems to suggest less defensiveness. Indeed, our characterization of such behavior as defensive could be construed as an attempt to "have it both ways." However, the reader is invited to make a judgment regarding the utility of our characterization after he or she has reviewed all the research in this chapter relating to maladjustment and defensiveness.

Much of the foregoing work is reminiscent of the line of research beginning with perceptual defense and more recently embodied in the repression-sensitization work (Byrne, 1964). The evidence generally suggests that psychiatric populations achieve higher sensitization scores and that maladjustment is related to sensitization (tendency to respond to threatening stimuli). Thus, people who are open about their anxieties, fears, or pathologies (sensitizers) are more likely to show up in psychiatric populations or to be otherwise regarded as anxious or maladjusted. The use of a more denying approach seems to characterize the less anxious or better adjusted individuals. At the same time, externals have been observed to react to personal threat with what might be termed sensitization while internals are evasive, denying, or otherwise show evidence of disruption in cognitive processes. The works of Burnes, Brown, and Keating (1971) and Hersch and Scheibe (1967) both suggest that internals less often admit to difficulties or inadequacies.

All this suggests that, at least in some ways, externals are less disturbed. Put another way, they may be better able to handle immediately threatening material because their externality provides a convenient mode of anxiety reduction (denial). This is quite compatible with the observation of Byrne (1964), who reviewed evidence that suggests sensitizers show less evidence of physiological arousal to stress than repressors. Thus, repressors or internals may deny verbally what they fail to hide physiologically. In this connection, Houston (1972) instructed one group of subjects that they could avoid electric shock by not making mistakes on a task. Another group was told that shock was unavoidable. While internals and externals in that study did not differ in their reports of anxiety in stressful situations, the internals did show significantly greater physiological response than did externals. This finding parallels Byrne's observation with respect to differences between sensitizers and repressors. Houston observes the following:

> External-control subjects view forces outside themselves as being responsible for their fate and do not become very aroused when faced with threat because they resign themselves to the situation. Internal-control subjects become highly aroused when threatened but they are reluctant to report anxiety; hence a significant difference in heart rate change scores but no significant difference in AACL [Affect Adjective Check List] change scores was found between internal-control and external-control subjects across threat conditions. The interpretation that internal-control subjects are defensive about reporting anxiety is supported by ... research findings which indicate that internal-control subjects are more defensive and report less chronic anxiety than external-control subjects. (Houston, 1972, p. 254)

Thus, if we assume, as suggested by most of the correlational evidence reviewed earlier in this chapter, that externals are more maladjusted than internals, and that they also are sensitizers, then it seems to follow that they would react with less denial, as is indicated by most of the work described in this section. Of course, there is a circularity inherent in several aspects of this work. That is, what shall we use as the final, authoritative index of maladjustment or anxiety? By definition, repressors (and perhaps internals) respond to paper-and-pencil measures of adjustment in a defensive way. Unfortunately, most studies have used as their criterion of anxiety or adjustment the very same kinds of paper-and-pencil tests.

The greater defensiveness that seems to characterize internals on several paper-and-pencil measures also characterizes them in several different experimental situations as well. At first glance, such evidence seems to contradict the earlier statements or research indicating that internals are better adjusted than externals. However, we might recall that in the repression-sensitization literature at least, repression or denial is generally related to better adjustment. This would be consistent with better adjustment in internals.

It may turn out that the denial observed by Efran (1963) and

Phares, Ritchie, and Davis (1968)—expressed by forgetting—might ultimately be found to be a form of the facilitating anxiety noted by Butterfield (1964) and Watson (1967). Phares, Ritchie, and Davis noted that even though the behavior of internals was disrupted, internals more often than externals expressed a willingness to take overt steps to work on the problems posed by the negative personality interpretations. Therefore, even though some evidence suggests that externals are less disturbed, this immediate lack of disturbance may, in the long run, lead to a greater disability. Perhaps the internals respond with some anxiety in the immediate situation, but this has long-term benefits by goading them to greater activity calculated to resolve or cope with their problems.

REDUCTION IN THE VALUE OF THE GOAL

Failure usually leads to an experience of anxiety or other discomfort, which most people try to mitigate. There are obviously many different techniques for handling failure, some of them constructive and some not so constructive. The question here is whether knowledge of locus of control will assist us in furthering our understanding of how people cope with failure. Much of our previous discussions about mastery and control would lead us to expect that the reactions of internals are generally more constructive. That is, the greater disposition to action of internals seems to equip them in a variety of ways for superior coping over the long term.

There are several other ways to alleviate the feeling of failure or the inability to attain certain goals. From a social learning theory point of view, we are really describing a situation in which a person has either a low expectancy of attaining valued goals or a high expectancy of receiving punishment. In such situations, at least two possibilities offer themselves—following failure, individuals can raise their expectancy for success on the next occasion or they can reduce the value of the goal that was not achieved. Either alternative would reduce the discrepancy between expectancy and the value of the goal, and would thereby diminish the discomfort or anxiety arising from failure.

Of course, systematically raising expectancies after failure is possible, but doing so repeatedly over time is patently illogical and would usually appear to others to be obviously maladjusted. To avoid placing themselves in such a vulnerable position, individuals are perhaps more likely to opt for the strategy of reducing the value of the reinforcement. After all, the value one attaches to goals is a personal, idiosyncratic matter, not an actuarial one.

Such an analysis led Phares (1971) to predict that in skill or ability situations externals will evince a greater tendency than internals to devalue the reinforcement involved when they fail to achieve that reinforcement. An external locus of control seems to lend itself to the "sour grapes" approach of lowering the goal value following failure. It seems plausible that this technique may be used by externals to avoid unpleasant levels of anxiety. By lowering goal value, the external is saying, "I don't care whether I failed," or, "That goal was not important anyway!" Internals, being more achievement-oriented, would tend to value skill reinforcements—particularly those difficult to achieve—and thus would leave intact the value of such goals or even increase their value.

To test this hypothesis, Phares selected internal and external college students using the I-E Scale. Subjects were administered four tasks commonly associated with intelligence tests. The study was described to them as one designed to determine the effects on task performance of differential preferences for success on the tasks. Therefore, prior to performance, subjects indicated how much they wished to succeed on each of the tests. All subjects were then failed on the two tasks they ranked as most important. Following this, each subject provided preference ratings for the four tasks a second time. As predicted, externals, more than internals, devalued the tests on which they failed. As the author stated:

> . . . an external orientation may predispose one to reduce the value of reinforcements following failure. Internals are less likely to respond in such a fashion. Thus, a defensive function can plausibly be attributed to external expectancies. Whether the external expectancies represent a veridical perception of one's life or are developed themselves to rationalize low expectations for success, it seems probable nonetheless that S can turn to value reduction as a means of handling threat entailed by failure. (Phares, 1971, p. 389)

Of course, if certain externals come to expect failure on certain kinds of activities, they may learn to utilize strategies calculated to prevent failure in the first place. That is, a generalized expectancy for failure may prompt defensive activities in advance. Phares and Lamiell (1974) therefore predicted that, given an opportunity to state a preference regarding which tasks they most wished to succeed on, externals, more than internals, would choose subtests that provided them a kind of built-in rationalization for any subsequent failure. Thus, externals should prefer to perform on those tasks that would easily enable them to rationalize away any failure that might occur. In testing this proposition, Phares and Lamiell selected external and internal college students on the basis of I-E Scale scores and administered to them four tasks ostensibly designed to measure IQ. Two of the tests contained the built-in rationalizations designed to provide subjects with potential explanations for failure. As anticipated, externals demonstrated a significantly greater preference for the "rationalizable" tests than did internals. The actual nature of the tests was controlled so that this did not influence preferences.

To illustrate how the authors created the so-called built-in rationalizations, a symbol substitution test was described to subjects; to some of these subjects Phares and Lamiell added the following "rationalizable" description: "Unfortunately, some of the symbols or characters on this sheet did not print out very well—they are rather dim. It's too late to change them now, so we'll just have to make do. I hope that it won't affect your performance too much, but there is always that possibility." The stronger preference in externals for the rationalizable tasks would seem once more to illustrate the defensive potential that an external belief system offers.

ATTRIBUTION OF RESPONSIBILITY

Attribution of responsibility has been the object of more and more research in recent years. As individuals participate in activities, they may attribute the outcomes of these activities to any number of causal forces. Beginning with Heider's (1958) seminal ideas on the nature of phenomenological causality, much research has been directed to identifying the conditions that influence people to ascribe responsibility to personal forces (e.g., ability or effort) or to impersonal forces over which they exert little control (e.g., luck).

Obviously, the topic of attribution of responsibility is intimately related to locus of control. The latter is a personality variable that, by definition, deals with stable tendencies to attribute control or causality to either personal or extrapersonal forces. Since the research discussed thus far seems to allow us to speak of externality as serving a defensive function, it seems logical to suppose that the relationship between failure and the attribution of responsibility for that failure is mediated in part by locus of control. In Chapter VI we saw how the generalization of individuals' locus of control beliefs to others may influence interpersonal reactions, such as altruism and acceptance. Now we shall focus on attribution of responsibility as a reaction to personal success or failure.

Phares, Wilson, and Klyver (1971) proposed to test the hypothesis that internals are less prone than externals to blame forces outside themselves for task failure. In an effort to show also how the situation can interact with personality variables, blame attribution was measured under two conditions: (1) conditions that involved serious situational distractions that could logically interfere with subjects' performance, and (2) a situation that was relatively neutral in that no such obvious distractions were present. Phares, Wilson, and Klyver failed internal and external college students on two of the four tasks that had previously been described as measures of intellectual ability. Half the subjects were failed under the distracting conditions (experimenters conversed loudly with one another while subjects were trying to solve problems); and the other half, under the nondistracting conditions. Following this failure, subjects filled out a blame-attribution scale. In general, these items dealt with the adequacy of the experiment and its methods, the nature of the physical surroundings, and the current mental and physical state of the subject.

As predicted, under the nondistracting conditions, internals were significantly less prone than externals to place blame outside themselves following failure. Thus, we again have significant evidence for defensive behavior in externals. Belief in an external locus of control seems to provide one with the opportunity to reduce some of the negative consequences of failure by the simple expedient of blaming outside forces. It should be noted that under the distracting conditions, there were no differences in blame attribution between internals and externals. This once again demonstrates that when highly salient cues exist in the situation, they can neutralize the effects of personality differences.

Davis and Davis (1972), in a more comprehensive study, followed a similar line of reasoning. They expected that the relationship between locus of control and attribution of responsibility would be mediated by the nature of the outcome in an activity. Specifically, they argued that

> ... externals, following failure, would be more inclined than internals to rationalize this outcome by attributing it to forces beyond their control. In contrast, successful task performances would engender little or no threat and therefore differences between internals and externals in assigning responsibility to outside forces would be attenuated. (Davis & Davis, 1972, p. 124)

In two separate studies Davis and Davis (1972) demonstrated that internals did indeed show a stronger tendency to blame themselves for failure than did externals. However, the two groups did not differ in assuming personal credit for success. This, along with the results of Phares, Wilson, and Kylver (1971), provides clear evidence that externals have ready access to defensive attributional behaviors.

Another study has highlighted the great complexity involved in relationships among I-E, responsibility attribution, and maladjustment. DuCette, Wolk, and Soucar (1972) studied several groups of black and white subjects who were either residents in a metropolitan mental hospital or problem children in a middle-class suburban elementary school and had been referred to the resident school psychologist because of their disruptive behavior.

Neither internality nor externality per se seemed to be related to maladjustment. The nature of the situation determines the relationship. The results indicate that white problem children and high IQ children were both very internal with respect to negative outcomes—they assumed much responsibility for failure but very little for success. When they failed, they blamed their own inadequacy; when they succeeded, they attributed the success to luck. The black and low IQ subjects displayed the opposite pattern—they handled failure by blaming luck and regarded success as due to personal control.

DEFENSIVE VERSUS CONGRUENT EXTERNALS

Over the years, a number of investigators have suggested the possibility that there may be externals who verbalize an external orientation (e.g., Phares, Ritchie, and Davis [1968] and Rotter [1966]), but who, when placed in structured performance situations, behave more like internals. Their behavior often belies their verbalized external expectancies. As Hersch and Scheibe commented: "The data also suggest that the previously stated theoretical formulation of I-E may be too simplistic. Individuals scoring low on the I-E scale (internals) are more homogeneous on their test performances than are high scoring subjects. This may suggest a diversity in the psychological meaning of externality" (1967, p. 612).

Complementing this contention of Hersch and Scheibe was an informal survey of studies carried out by Phares and his colleagues during 1967 and 1968 at Kansas State University. Between 14 percent and 26 percent of the externals in those studies behaved more like internals as evidenced by nontest behavioral data or performances equal to or superior to the mean of internals. Furthermore, almost all I-E research, published and unpublished, reveals that externals, as a group, exhibit greater variability in test and nontest behavior than do internals.

Such observations led Davis (1970) to explore the possibility that individuals who verbalize external expectancies but otherwise behave much like internals in certain performance situations do so as a means of defending themselves against expected failure or negative reinforcement. These individuals Davis labeled "defensive externals." Externals whose I-E scores coincided with their behavior in certain other nontest situations she described as "congruent externals."

Her first problem in identifying such individuals was the selection of behavior that could be reasonably regarded as a typical kind of internal behavior. She decided on action taking since it had, in the past, reliably discriminated between internals and externals in a wide variety of studies (Gore & Rotter, 1963; Phares, Ritchie, & Davis, 1968; Strickland, 1965). Her operational definition of a defensive external was (1) an external score on the I-E Scale, and (2) a high score on an action-taking questionnaire designed to identify students who were willing to take action (of varying degrees of personal involvement) in an effort to improve their academic standing in college. Congruent externals, on the other hand, were those who received external scores on the I-E Scale and low scores on the academic action-taking questionnaire. The technique was analogous to that used by Gore and Rotter (1963) in their research on participation in civil rights activities.

Davis found support for several hypotheses. First, she found that defensive externals placed a high value on academic recognition goals and also showed a greater discrepancy between generalized expectancies for the attainment of academic recognition and the value ascribed to such goals. Such a result would suggest that in these subjects, verbalized external beliefs are defensively inspired to reduce the discomfort accompanying generalized expectancies for success that cannot keep pace with their needs.

During an experimental session, Davis also asked subjects to study excerpts drawn from several areas of academic psychology and later offered subjects the opportunity to ask questions, the answers to which could have, in the eyes of the subjects, increased their possibility of success. Interestingly, defensive externals and internals, as predicted, engaged in more of this information-seeking behavior than did congruent externals. This result is important, since it seems to demonstrate some consistency in the "internal" behavior of defensive externals.

While not all of Davis's results supported the distinction between defensive and congruent externals, the major findings did substantiate the hypothesis that defensive externals will behave more like internals in situations in which overt action by each individual might lead to reinforcement. Thus, the external I-E score may be seen as a defensive maneuver designed to protect the person from potential failure. One is tempted to assert that defensive externals are really internals hiding behind their I-E scores.

A somewhat different approach to the identification and study of of so-called defensive externals involves the use of an interpersonal trust dimension. Hamsher, Geller, and Rotter (1968) noted that externality in males correlates significantly with lack of trust. Similarly, Miller and Minton (1969) reported that externals show a proclivity for violating experimental instructions while internals do not. They also found a low but significant correlation between externality and machiavellianism. Taken together, these results may reflect a tendency for greater mistrust and suspiciousness on the part kof externals.

Hochreich (1968) construed trust as a moderator variable in studying the relationship between locus of control and defensive behavior. Briefly, scores on the Interpersonal Trust Scale (Rotter, 1967b) were taken to indicate a generalized expectancy that the promises of others cannot be relied upon. Generally speaking, externals did tend to be lower in trust, as suggested above; moreover, the correlations were usually more substantial for males than for females. Hochreich argued that subjects who score high in externality but low in trust may be espousing a characteristic verbal defense. These would be people who are ambitious but who habitually utilize blame projection to account for failure and in that sense can be regarded as defensive externals. Further, as anticipated by Davis (1970), such defensive externals can be expected to behave like internals, particularly in competitive achievement situations. Indeed, performance in these situations should differentiate so-called congruent externals (those who really believe in the external determination of events) from defensive externals.

Therefore, Hochreich (1968) predicted that an angle-matching task involving skill-competitive features would lead low-trust externals, as compared to high-trust externals, to behave in the same fashion as subjects operating under skill instructions in the early studies that manipulated instructions (skill versus chance). For males, her predictions were confirmed; low-trust externals exhibited expectancy or confidence statements that indicated greater responsiveness to feedback concerning their performance than did high-trust externals. The reverse obtained for female subjects.

Subsequently, Hochreich (1973) asked groups of subjects to read several stories. She predicted that defensive (or low-trust) externals and congruent (or high-trust) externals would differ in their attribution ratings of a series of stories that varied in achievement versus nonachievement tone and also in outcome (success or failure). More specifically, she expected that defensive externals would attribute less responsibility to story heroes under failure conditions than would congruent externals and internals and that this difference would be most pronounced when failure occurred in achievement situations. These hypotheses were strongly supported, again, for males but not for females. In addition, it was found (consistent with Hersch and Scheibe [1967]) that externals say more unfavorable things about themselves (based on Adjective Checklist scores) than do internals and that defensive externals represent an extreme subgroup within the larger group of externals. Again, these self-descriptive results applied to males but not females.

In commenting on the characteristically obtained sex differences,

Hochreich felt that the concept of the defensive external may simply be less meaningful for females. Since females are presumably not so subject to strong cultural pressures for achievement as are males in our society, they may not have the same need to resort to blame projection as a defense against anticipated failure, particularly when failure is either less important or less personally painful.

In an unpublished part of work by Phares and Lamiell (1974) an attempt was made to relate locus of control and interpersonal trust to preferences for tasks that had the so-called built-in potential for rationalization. The reader may recall from that study that externals preferred to perform the rationalizable tasks more often than internals. In addition, low-trust externals in that study clearly manifested the strongest preference for the rationalizable tasks. Thus, what was true for externals generally was especially true for the defensive externals, defined operationally here as low-trust externals.

It is also interesting to note in the Phares and Lamiell study that while no differences appeared among the trust and locus of control groups in stated expectancies for success on the rationalizable tasks, the defensive external group (high externality–low trust) stated significantly lower expectancies for success on the nonrationalizable tasks than did internals. There were no differences in expectancies between congruent externals and either of the other two groups. However, the location of the congruent externals' mean between those of defensive externals and internals replicates earlier findings by Davis (1970). Since Davis used different expectancy measures, this adds an encouraging element of stability to these results. In addition, Phares and Lamiell obtained no differences with respect to minimal goals for the rationalizable tasks. On the nonrationalizable tasks, however, both internals and defensive externals showed a tendency to set higher minimal goal levels than did congruent externals. No differences appeared between defensive externals and internals on this measure. Therefore, it is possible that defensive externals differ from congruent externals primarily with respect to the *value* attached to success in achievement-related activities, while defensive externals differ from internals primarily in terms of expectancies for achieving such success.

It seems entirely reasonable to expect that people will endorse external alternatives on the I-E Scale for different reasons. Some people (congruent externals) may believe in the statements, and, as a result, their behavior in nontesting situations will be consistent with their test-taking behavior. Other externals may not really believe in the external alternatives they have checked but may endorse such statements because they feel that by doing so they have, to some degree, defended themselves against anticipated failure. These are the defensive exter-

nals, whose nontest behavior often seems to belie their behavior on the
I-E Scale.

Yet, it often seems as if the internals are also being defensive,
but in a different manner. For example, internals typically deny the
common indicants of anxiety on most personality scales. In the case of
repressors (Byrne, 1964), internals verbally deny stress, but this denial
is belied by evidence of their greater concomitant physiological arousal
(Houston, 1972).

Perhaps the solution is to relinquish the search for evidence to
prove who is the more maladjusted and conclude that each group may
contain members who are threatened but that each handles this threat
in a characteristic fashion. The question then becomes not whether so-
called defensiveness is more maladjusted, or whether higher or lower
perceptual thresholds are the more maladjusted, or whether raising or
lowering reinforcement is more maladjusted, but whether these behaviors (such as perceptual thresholds, anxiety ratings, attribution of
blame, selection of rationalizable tasks on which to perform) offer a
greater or lesser potential for dealing adequately with certain problem
situations. The determination of this adequacy will be a value judgment,
as are all decisions involving questions of personal adjustment.

An overall external locus of control may, on many occasions, free
individuals from some anxiety. For these people, being able to escape
some of the blame for failure is surely not all bad! Indeed, such an
ability to avoid responsibility may allow one to admit more readily to
the common referents of anxiety or maladjustment and thus create a
more unfavorable impression of the external than is warranted. Thus,
it is conceivable that some of the differences between internals and externals are differences of style rather than substance. Similarly, there
may be some who might wish to argue that internals are really the maladjusted ones. After all, chronic denial of stress on questionnaires (assuming it is denial), disruption of memory processes after failure or
threat, and physiological evidence of anxiety arousal in the absence of
outward indications of anxiety do not add up to the epitome of adjustment either.

Perhaps the original hypothesis of a curvilinear relationship between adjustment and locus of control should be reexamined and will
turn out to be the ultimate explanation, if we can find ways to test that
hypothesis. In this view, it is both the extreme externals and extreme
internals who are disturbed. Since each is relatively removed from the
middle of the distribution, each is likely to respond in an inflexible way
after categorizing situations. The people nearer the middle should respond to situations in a more realistic fashion—that is, some situations, on a realistic basis, will seem largely within the individuals' con-

trol, while others will not. To be able to distinguish between these two classes of situations should turn out to be the most effective mode. We caution again that empirical evidence to date is not very supportive of the curvilinear notion, but it does not appear that the hypothesis has been adequately tested.

One's definition of maladjustment is a crucial thing. Outside the narrow confines of paper-and-pencil inventories, internals exhibit greater mastery and personal efficacy, are more resistant to control or influence from others, and are more achievement-oriented. This is evidence of superior adjustment in internals if your criteria of adjustment include such behaviors. But not everyone's criteria are the same. Some may regard achievement, mastery, and "insensitivity" to the influence of others as simply values foisted on them by those still enamored of the Protestant Ethic. Thus, perhaps externals are only marching to a different drummer. Science need go no further than determining which behaviors correlate with locus of control, and quantifying the relationships. Value judgments as to which group is better adjusted may make interesting party conversation, but they have no place in a scientific discipline.

Summary

The complexity of the locus of control construct is quite evident as we examine its relationship to anxiety, adjustment, and defensiveness. Not all the evidence we have reviewed hangs together in a coherent fashion. However, part of this lack of coherence probably lies in the use of terms such as maladjustment, schizophrenia, and depression. None of these terms is particularly precise, and all are capable of many interpretations or meanings.

The generally modest but significant correlations between anxiety and externality seem to indicate greater chronic distress, discomfort, or maladjustment on the part of externals. At the very least, they suggest a greater willingness for externals to admit to the more common aspects of personal difficulty. Conversely, internals frequently avoid endorsing statements on questionnaires that indicate anxiety or maladjustment.

In some ways, externals seem to react to threat in the same fashion they do to questionnaires; for example, the consequences of failure do not result in the disruption of memory processes to the same extent that they do for internals. In this sense, externals appear to be much less denying of threat than internals. A plausible interpretation is that at least one functional value of an external locus of control is its capacity to neutralize potentially threatening stimuli (i.e., failure or personal inadequacy). How can failure or inadequacy be threatening if forces outside the individual are regarded as ultimately responsible? Reducing the value of a goal after failure to achieve it, selecting tasks in advance that permit one easy access to excuses such as rationalization should failure occur, or attributing blame for failure to outside forces are all "defenses" available to the external individual.

IX

Antecedents
of Locus of Control
Beliefs

In the previous chapter we saw how external beliefs may arise because of individuals' needs to protect themselves from anticipated failure or other personal inadequacies. However, this is only one factor which contributes to the establishment of generalized I-E beliefs. What about social and family experience factors? Surely they must be important contributors to locus of control beliefs. This question provides the focus of the present chapter.

The general area of antecedents has been one of the more neglected facets of locus of control. The limited research most often is correlational in nature and frequently relies on retrospective data from both subjects and their parents. This contrasts sharply with the research that has focused on the consequences of locus of control beliefs, where the method has been more experimental in nature. Undoubtedly the sheer logistics of developmental research discourage many investigators. Unfortunately, this has created a situation where we know a great deal more about the consequences of locus of control beliefs in college freshmen and sophomores than in any other segment of the population.

While we can argue that the past does not cause the present (since the former no longer exists), knowledge of the origins of certain variables will enrich our understanding. Knowing the different ways people come by their locus of control beliefs should provide important clues as to how best to alter those orientations. In a sense, we are attempting to place a personality characteristic, locus of control, in an emipirical framework so we can predict differences in locus of control from knowledge of its antecedent conditions and then predict the effects of these differences on associated behaviors.

Family Antecedents

What is there in the parent-child relationship that will account for an internal or external locus of control? In the following pages we shall briefly review several categories of research that converge on such familial antecedents.

PARENTAL NURTURANCE

Using the IAR, Chance (1965) found that children's internality was associated with mothers' scores on the acceptance-rejection factor of the Parental Attitude Research Instrument (PARI). Permissive and flexible maternal attitudes and expectations for early independence seemed to be associated with internality. Similarly, Katkovsky, Crandall, and Good (1967), also using the IAR, reported that protective, nurturing, approving, and nonrejecting parental behavior is associated with the child's belief in internal control. As a methodological note, Katkovsky, Crandall, and Good cautioned against assuming any equivalence between self-report data and data based on actual observation by investigators of parent-child behavior. The self-report data obviously are likely to be influenced by a variety of factors, including social desirability, defensiveness, and the defective or self-serving facets of memory, upon which most of the retrospective, self-report data depend.

Studies by Shore (1967) and Davis and Phares (1969) have investigated some antecedents of children's generalized locus of control. While Shore used junior high school students and Davis and Phares used college subjects, both studies examined parental child-rearing attitudes, children's reports of parental behavior, and parents' own locus of control beliefs as determinants of the child's beliefs. Overall, the studies are similar enough that one can almost be viewed as a cross-validation of the other. As regards children's perceptions of parental behavior, both studies revealed significant differences between internals and externals on the warmth and acceptance-rejection dimensions. Davis and Phares found that internals report their parents showed less rejection, less hostile control, less withdrawal of relations, and more positive involvement. These results are similar to those of both Chance (1965) and Katkovsky, Crandall, and Good (1967) noted earlier. However, when parental child-rearing attitudes, such as control and rejection, were assessed in the parents themselves, there were no direct relationships between these attitudes and the child's locus of control beliefs. Also, no relationship was obtained between parents' locus of control and that of the child.

It is possible, however, that the relationship between a parent's locus of control (I-E score) and that of the child is attenuated by different parental child-rearing attitudes. Therefore, Davis and Phares divided families into several groups on the basis of the degree of parent–child I-E score similarity. Parents' child-rearing attitudes were then analyzed for each of the groups. Results strongly indicated that parents whose children have a locus of control similar to their own are less disciplinarian and more indulgent in their approach to child-rearing than are parents whose children have a locus of control different from their own. At this point we might also comment that Jessor, Graves, Hanson, and Jessor (1968), in a tri-ethnic study (using a specially devised locus of control measure) found that mother's teaching of internal control correlated significantly with the child's internal control score. This finding and the data of Shore (1967) and Davis and Phares (1969) indicate that children's perceptions of parental behavior, especially along the acceptance–rejection dimension, relate to the development of locus of control.

MacDonald (1971a) also carried out a retrospective study on the relationship between I-E Scale scores and parental behavior in a group of college students. He reports that internal females describe their mothers as more nurturant and as utilizing more achievement pressure. Fathers were described as more nurturant and as using more physical punishment with their sons. Subjects that reported their mothers were more protective and used affective punishment more (males only) were found to have higher external scores. A related result has been reported by Solomon, Hoolihan, Busse, and Parelius (1971), a study cited earlier. In a sample of black fifth graders, they found parental hostility to be associated with internality in sons. Tolor (1967) reported two conflicting results on the relationship between locus of control and indulgent parental attitudes.

Tolor and Jalowiec (1968) related college students' scores on the I-E Scale and responses to the PARI as they thought their mothers would have responded. It was found that external subjects perceived their mothers to be rather authoritarian and to have hostile-rejecting qualities. The implication is, of course, that mothers who have such tendencies contribute to an external belief system in the child.

Levenson (1973b) had undergraduates respond to a perceived

parenting questionnaire and the I-E Scale in three parts. She found that, in males, internality was related positively to perceived maternal instrumental companionship behavior, while in females internality was related negatively to maternal protectiveness. Subjects who described their parents as more punishing and controlling were found to have greater expectancies of control by powerful others.

Briefly summarizing the foregoing work, parental child-rearing practices that can be characterized as warm, protective, positive, and nurturant with only minor exceptions are linked to children who develop an internal locus of control. On the other side of the coin, many pathological populations (schizophrenics and others) are described as having sprung from cold, rejecting, negative parents. We probably will find that this is only a beginning, that other factors besides these broad attitudes are needed to produce an external or an internal locus of control in individuals.

CONSISTENCY OF EXPERIENCE

Extrapolating from the early research on skill-chance situations, it would seem to follow logically that inconsistency of reinforcement should be related to externality. It has been repeatedly demonstrated that situations that are unpredictable (i.e., that do not allow for generalization from the past) lead to relatively smaller increments in expectancy. While we are not implying that belief in chance determination of events is always the same as an external belief system (see Levenson [1973a,b]) there are some similarities. It seems reasonable to assume that a child who is subject to inconsistent, unpredictable environmental demands could easily develop an external orientation. Rotter (1966) hypothesized that the degree of consistency of discipline and treatment by the parents is *one* antecedent of an external orientation. When children are not able to anticipate parental discipline due to (1) inconsistency within the behavior of one parent, (2) inconsistencies between the parents, or (3) inability to fathom any consistency that may in fact exist, a foundation is laid for a belief that reinforcement is unpredictable and therefore is not subject to personal control.

The effects of parental consistency may depend on the degree of cognitive clarity provided the child by means of rules, information, or cues concerning the consequences of his behavior. As Davis argues:

> Lack of consistency in this regard would increase the likelihood that he will continually seek aid in an attempt to understand his environment, which would, in turn, lead to a belief that he is not the effective agent in controlling reinforcement. In contrast, a clearly structured system of family relationships in which regulations are consistently presented and enforced would allow the child to rely on his own judgments and

> interpretations of events and consequences. These circumstances would be expected to lead the child to develop a belief that he can, to some extent, predict and control the occurrence of reinforcement. However, while inconsistency may be a sufficient condition for the development of externality, the converse does not follow in regard to the development of internality. For example, parents who *consistently dominate decision making in the family would not be expected to produce an internal child.* (Emphasis added; Davis, 1969, p. 24)

Davis and Phares (1969) found that externals tended to report their parents as inconsistent in their discipline more often than did internals. To illustrate, externals were more likely to state that their parents would "punish me for doing something one day but ignore it the next." In a similar vein, Shore (1967) found a larger discrepancy in child-rearing attitudes between parents of externals than between parents of internals.

In a more experimental approach to these issues, Davis (1969) studied triads of mother, father, and their 11- or 12-year-old son (the son either internal or external). Each family group was asked to perform together on two tasks. Several questionnaires were also filled out privately by each family member. Later, the family was confronted with several problematic situations involved in family living, on which they had earlier disagreed as to the best way of handling. Some support was found for the hypothesis that externality in children is associated with inconsistent parental behavior resulting from a lack of consensus among family members regarding standards for behavior. There were also more discrepancies in child-rearing attitudes between mothers and fathers of externals than there were between the parents of internal children. Further, less agreement existed between external children and their parents regarding the solutions to various problems in family living.

It might be noted that Davis was not able to show, within the limits of his experimental situation, any association between locus of control in child and parental rejecting behavior, parental encouragement of participation in family decisions, or parental encouragement of self-reliance in children, as might have been expected from the data in the previous section.

MacDonald (1971a), in the study involving college students' retrospective reports of parental behavior mentioned earlier, found that an internal locus of control was more characteristic of subjects whose mothers were described as having more predictable standards for their children's behavior. This was true for male subjects, but there was also a marked trend in that direction for females. A highly similar set of results has also been reported by Reimanis (1971). In the same vein, Levenson (1973b) reported that subjects who viewed their parents as having unpredictable standards had stronger beliefs that events are controlled by chance factors.

Using a method that departs from the usual research procedures, Epstein and Komorita (1971) asked black children to respond to questions about the behavior of their parents. Those children who viewed their parents as being inconsistent in discipline also tended to attribute their own success on an experimental task to external kinds of causes. Also, in line with work discussed previously, children who described their parents as being very hostile also used external attributions to account for their successes on the task.

Considering the data available, then, it appears that there is the expected relationship between externality and inconsistency of reinforcement within the family. Whether this relationship holds in other situations outside the family, and with respect to different kinds of reinforcements, will have to be left to future investigations.

ORDINAL POSITION IN THE FAMILY

Chance (1965) found a weak tendency for both male and female first-born children to be more internal than their later-born counterparts. With total IAR scores, the same tendency was reported by Crandall, Katkovsky, and Crandall (1965). This held true for children in grades six through twelve but not for children in grades three through five. As Crandall, Katkovsky, and Crandall state:

> The fact that first-born children accept more self-responsibility than
> do those born later is predictable from most personality theories and
> from common observation. Not only are first-born children more often
> placed in positions of responsibility for household affairs and for their
> own conduct, but they are also often put in charge of younger siblings,
> as well. Thus, the eldest child comes to observe both the consequences
> of his actions upon his own successes and failures and also the effect
> of his actions upon the welfare of his younger siblings and of the total
> family unit .... Probably even more pertinent to the IAR, since it
> deals with intellectural-academic situations, is the fact that the eldest
> child must often use school success as his best pathway to parental
> approval. (Crandall, Katkovsky, & Crandall, 1965, pp. 105–106)

MacDonald (1971b) found also that later-borns from two-child families were more external than those later-borns from larger families. Later-borns from two-child families were more external than only children or first-borns from two-child families. In contrast, Eisenman and Platt (1968) noted that it was first-born males who were more external in their locus of control beliefs.

Marks (1973) studied some of the correlates of beliefs about personal power (a 48-item inventory). Birth-order provided a significant source of variance. Speculating on the processes underlying birth-order effects, Marks comments as follows:

> Parents of only female children, by being overly protective and setting rigid standards for the child, may induce an atmosphere in which many environmental encounters are perceived as harmful. In this case, external control beliefs can be viewed as a strategy for coping with threats to self-esteem. Parents of male only children, on the other hand, may encourage through their rearing practices exploration and mastery of the environment. Successful encounters would reinforce beliefs in internal locus of control. (Marks, 1973, p. 184)

Again, birth-order data are reasonably consistent in their correlation with locus of control. However, as with most birth-order studies, the effects are not large. Given the complex determinants of human behavior, large birth-order effects would not be expected. This complexity is implicit in the quotation from Marks. Nonetheless, most of the data seem generally consistent with commonsense notions and with the broad outlines of Alfred Adler's pioneering observations about the effects of birth order on human behavior (Ansbacher and Ansbacher, 1956).

SOME CONCLUSIONS ABOUT FAMILY RESEARCH ON LOCUS OF CONTROL

Perhaps the greatest deficiency of much of the preceding work on the familial determinants of locus of control is the marked correlational quality of the research. This entails heavy use of questionnaires, which often call for retrospective reports from both parents and children. Obviously, these kinds of reports are extremely sensitive to distortion. Indeed, very often what is being dealt with is perceptions of parent behavior rather than the behavior itself. More research relating parental behavior (as observed by trained technicians) to children's locus of control beliefs would be highly desirable and surely more heuristic in the long run.

As with so much child research, there often seems to be a search for rather simplistically construed early childhood experiences that will somehow leap over large amounts of intervening experience and relate directly to adult I-E scores. Much of this intervening experience serves as a moderator variable that significantly influences any direct effects of earlier childhood on adult behavior.

Drawing upon the work and comments of Katkovsky, Crandall, and Good (1967), Davis and Phares (1969), and Levenson (1973b), it would seem that additional work bearing on the following activities is specifically in order.

1. The effect of direct parental teaching of children about the origins of causation and the contingency between behavior and subsequent reinforcement.
2. Methods by which the parent reinforces the child's verbalization of locus of control beliefs.
3. The effect of the model the parents present (by their own behavior) on the child's locus of control.
4. The effects of consistency of reinforcement (through parental behavior and other environmental events) on children's locus of control beliefs.
5. An elaboration of the effects and importance of nurturance by the parents on locus of control in the child.
6. The role of sex differences in development of locus of control.
7. The differential role played by fathers and mothers.
8. The role of independence training and its effects on the child's locus of control.

It is hoped that future investigations of such topics will be more heavily represented by studies that involve both direct observations of parent-child behaviors and those that use experimental manipulations rather than correlations between the various paper-and-pencil devices.

Social Antecedents

Most of the work on social antecedents supports a relationship between locus of control and social class and ethnicity. For example, most evidence indicates that blacks are more external than whites and that lower social status is associated with external beliefs. The implication is that those social and ethnic groups that have relatively little access to significant power, social mobility, opportunity, or material advantages will manifest relatively higher external scores. While these statements seem reasonable, one should remember the nature of the data on which they are based. Once again, most of the work is correlational in nature and conveys little about the exact mechanisms that mediate such relationships. Such work may also encourage a kind of stereotyped approach to research that obscures rather than illuminates such mechanisms. We shall return to these points. In the meantime, let us review the evidence available in this area.

Battle and Rotter (1963) used Bialer's I-E measure along with a cartoon device for assessing locus of control. Lower-class black children were found to be significantly more external than middle-class blacks or whites. Generally, middle-class children were more internal than lower-class children, while lower-class blacks with high IQs were more external than middle-class whites with lower IQs. It is possible that the brighter lower-class blacks develop strongly external attitudes as a function of their greater awareness of the minimal opportunities for cultural or material rewards. However, as Battle and Rotter suggest, any interpretation must be tentative, since a triple interaction is involved and the number of subjects is small.

Lefcourt and Ladwig (1965, 1966) have reported that black prisoners are more external than comparable groups of white prisoners. However, Kiehlbauch (1967) was not able to show significant differences in I-E scores between black and white reformatory inmates, although there was a slight trend in the direction of greater externality among blacks.

Scott and Phelan (1969) studied a group of subjects who had spent years on the welfare rolls and who were essentially unemployable. The group contained whites, blacks, and Mexican-Americans. The unemployed whites were significantly more internal than either the blacks or the Mexican-Americans, and Mexican-Americans were slightly more external than blacks.

Previously reported work by Lessing (1969), Shaw and Uhl (1971), Strickland (1972), and Zytkoskee, Strickland, and Watson (1971) supports the greater externality of blacks relative to whites. In the case of the IAR, neither Solomon, Houlihan, and Parelius (1969) nor Katz (1967) could find racial differences in locus of control beliefs. Pedhazur and Wheeler (1971) compared black and Puerto Rican children with Jewish children of the same elementary school grade and from the same city. Both socioeconomic and ethnic differences characterized the groups. On the Bialer I-E measure, the black and Puerto Rican children scored more external than did the Jewish children.

Hsieh, Shybut, and Lotsof (1969) compared three groups of subjects: (1) Anglo-American high school students from a northern Illinois community; (2) American-born high school seniors from Chicago (at least one parent of each subject had been born in China); and (3) upper-grade students in a Baptist school in Hong Kong. Subjects were matched for age, and their socioeconomic status was checked. The Anglo-Americans were found to be the most internal. The Hong Kong group was the most external, while the American-born Chinese group was closer to the Anglo-American group. Hsieh, Shybut, and Lotsof expected these differences, based on the following assumptions.

> The "individual-centered" American personality is associated with a culture that emphasizes the uniqueness, independence, and self-reliance

of each individual .... It, among other things, places a high value on personal output of energy for solving all problems; pragmatic ingenuity; individualism, that is, self-reliance and status achieved through one's own efforts; power or ability to influence or control others ...., Life experiences appear to be largely a consequence of one's actions.
In contrast, the "situation-centered" Chinese personality is associated with a culture where kinship and emphasis on status quo are stressed .... Luck, chance, and fate are taken for granted in life, which is ... full of ambiguity, complexity, and unpredictability ....
Life situations may be viewed as being largely determined by circumstances outside one's control. (Hsieh, Shybut, & Lotsof, 1969, p. 122)

Gruen and Ottinger (1969) examined the effects of social class on children. Using a Bialer type locus of control scale, they found, in third-grade children, that greater internality was associated more often with middle-class than with lower-class background. Within both groups, wide differences occurred among individuals in the number of internal locus of control choices made. Gruen and Ottinger comment that neither social class group was highly internal, but, relatively speaking, middle-class subjects were more internal than their lower-class counterparts. However, it should be noted that locus of control and age are correlated in children—younger children are more external than older children or adults (Crandall, Katkovsky, & Crandall, 1965; Penk, 1969).

Jessor, Graves, Hanson, and Jessor (1968) used their own measure of locus of control in a tri-ethnic study of Anglo-Americans, Spanish-Americans, and American Indians. Among adults in these groups, Anglo-Americans exhibited the greatest internality; Spanish-Americans exhibited the greatest externality; and the American Indians were in between. Most of the significance of the obtained differences was contributed by the Spanish-American group, whose scores were significantly different from both the Anglo-American and Indian groups. These results must be accepted with caution, however. In a similar sample of tri-ethnic high school groups, no such ethnic differences in locus of control beliefs were found. Jessor and colleagues suggested that their I-E measure may not have been valid. It is possible, however, that a rise in externality occurs as one leaves high school. At this point in one's life, there is the first massive encounter with the dominant culture and all its implications as regards job discrimination, prejudice, etc. The child faces leaving the security of home and the institutionalized support of the school system and perhaps realizes that he or she now must adopt greater independence than ever before.

Parsons, Schneider, and Hansen (1970) could find no difference in the general level of internality manifested by Danish and American students. Thus, even though the two societies differ widely in degree of governmental control, and despite the fact that students might be expected to be more concerned about issues of alienation and power than most, no differences in locus of control were observed. However, while overall I-E scores did not differ, the patterns of scoring were quite different in the two populations.

SOME CONCLUSIONS ABOUT SOCIAL ANTECEDENTS RESEARCH

In general, the foregoing evidence is consistent with the view that those groups that cannot compete effectively for social status or power and that have little mobility or access to material wealth will be more likely to adopt an external belief system. As individuals accumulate a series of experiences that point up their relative inability to control their own destiny, an external generalized expectancy should ensue. What we lack here is knowledge of the exact conditions and mechanisms by which such an expectancy develops.

At least two possibilities emerge as potential reasons for the typically obtained external scores for blacks. One is direct teaching. The children's parents or older siblings and peers may coach them quite directly about the "true reality." When they make internal type statements based on their limited experiences, their older, "wiser" peers may laugh at them or flaunt their superior experience. This would quickly teach them not to verbalize such beliefs about internal control and might also lead to significant changes in locus of control beliefs. A second, equally plausible reason is the reality they face. Members of any ethnic minority quickly learn that they are restricted in terms of jobs, promotions, housing, etc. Such experiences teach them in vivid terms how little real power they possess.

In this connection, it is interesting to speculate about the development of locus of control orientations. The evidence suggests that as children become older and move out of the period of childhood helplessness and total reliance on the family, their locus of control becomes more internal. It seems unlikely that favored and deprived groups would show the same growth curve. One might hypothesize that for a deprived groups there would be an increase in internality up to a point at which individuals face the dominant culture on their own. This experience might result in an interruption in the growth of internality. Specifically, one might expect that black children, going to black schools with black teachers and tested in black settings, might well show the typical increase in internal scores over time (in the absence of any marked parental coaching to the contrary). But what will happen when those children transfer later to a large school with many white students and teachers?

Another point involves the nature of typical I-E scales. Most such scales probably relate mainly to the white culture. This being the case, I-E scores obtained from blacks may be somewhat misleading. For example, an individual could easily be external in the areas tapped by the I-E Scale or the IAR but internal in other life areas. The point is, we should not generalize too far beyond the specific nature of the scale as it interacts with the specific nature of the test population. As noted before, these scales, having some degree of generality, are subject to error when predicting to relatively narrow classes of situation.

To illustrate, a black student may respond in an external fashion to the following item: "Many times I feel that I have little influence over the things that happen to me." This student may well respond in an internal way to a hypothetical item on a more specific scale (Losing a basketball game is often a result of losing your cool at a crucial point). As stated by the author elsewhere, "In short, whether one is internal or external may depend upon what corner of one's life space is being examined. To the black student, getting a job in the white man's world may be largely a matter of luck, but winning a basketball game with his peers may be largely under his own control (Phares, 1973b, p. 19).

So far, very little evidence of a cross-cultural nature has been adduced. Studies of groups differing in national character or in religious or other cultural values would be of interest.

Potential Effects of the Classroom on Locus of Control

We have already seen that an internal locus of control relates to academic achievement. While the evidence was largely correlational in nature, most observers would probably make the interpretation that it is internality that leads to superior school achievement. On the other hand, is it not possible that a variety of factors may conspire to lead to school achievement and that following such reinforcement the child's sense of internal control is enhanced, leading in turn to greater accomplishments?

We briefly observed earlier that Jessor, Graves, Hanson, and Jessor (1968) found a relationship between maternal teaching of internality and subsequent internal locus of control beliefs in the child. In a study designed to assess the impact of two different approaches to enriched early childhood education for disadvantaged children, Stephens (1972) also attempted to examine their effects on locus of control. He commented that many different classroom techniques seem to specify growth in internal control (or related notions) as a basic target. Such techniques may encompass such seemingly different approaches as the "open classroom" and behavior modification programs. While his results are preliminary in nature, Stephens noted, "Despite the ... complexity of between-group differences, the differences are clear (and statistically significant) enough to assure that these experiences do have systematic effects on IE-type variables and that the test scores reflect not random processes but systematic variables" (p. 138).

Summary

The outlines of the story of how locus of control beliefs are developed in family and society are only beginning to take form. Such research is very difficult to carry out because it often involves work in the field with populations that are inaccessible or uncooperative. In some cases it must be longitudinal research—that is, the same population must be followed over a long time period—with all the pitfalls that entails.

Nonetheless, the research that has been done suggests that family environments that are characterized by warmth, protection, and nurturance seem to lead to belief in an internal locus of control. A history of consistent parental reinforcement also seems to be related to internality. These effects may depend upon the sex of the parent and the child. Of course, too much nurturance or too much consistency of reinforcement, if it implies control by "powerful others," could just as easily lead to an external locus of control. Some evidence suggests that ordinal position in the family affects locus of control. In general, firstborn and earlier-born children tend to be more internal. These effects are not large and may be affected by the sex of the child.

In the broader social context, there is a strong suggestion that persons in groups with restricted access to significant power or material advantages often develop external orientations. Blacks and other minority groups seem much more external than whites. Similarly, lower socioecomonic status is associated with externality. And, of course, minority groups typically occupy the lower socioeconomic levels.

However, one must interpret such findings carefully. Most of the I-E instruments that are utilized force the individual to compare himself to white, middle-class norms and values. It is conceivable that one could construct I-E measures that would reveal that a black person was internal in behavior within the black culture even though looking like an external in the wider social and political context.

It is certainly hoped that research on the antecedents of locus of control beliefs will be carried out vigorously. We cannot adequately understand the meaning of individuals' locus of control beliefs, and thereby be in a position to change such attitudes, until we have gained insight into the factors that give rise to their beliefs.

X

Changes in Beliefs about Locus of Control

We have documented in previous chapters the extensive influence that locus of control beliefs have on human behavior. It is important to understand the conditions that affect locus of control, since it is through alterations in such conditions that we can modify behavior. In this chapter, therefore, we address ourselves to questions of whether change in locus of control is possible, to what extent, and under what conditions. Our interest here is in locus of control beliefs as targets of influence rather than as sources of influence on behavior.

Any measure of a generalized personality variable must be both stable and at the same time sensitive enough to pick up real changes over time in the strength of that variable. What we mean is that a test should yield stable scores over time when there is no reason to believe that significant events have transpired in the life of the individual that could be expected to change the behavior being tested. Of course, the longer the time period between testing and retesting, the lower the reliability is likely to be because more events will have had an opportunity to affect the variable under study. For example, in a study of reformatory inmates (Kiehlbauch, 1967), test-retest reliabilities of .75, .39, and .26 were obtained at three-, six-, and nine-month intervals, respectively. The reason for this decline is thought to have been the nature of intervening events (discussed later in this chapter). Reliability variations are not to be eliminated or controlled so much as they are to be studied and understood. Aside from test construction considerations, what are the experience factors that produce changes in I-E scores?

Before we pursue the nature of those conditions that can alter beliefs about locus of control, however, let us briefly reiterate some points about the generality of I-E scores. The I-E Scale is designed to sample behavior from a wide range of situations. The IAR, by contrast, attempts to measure locus of control in both success and failure situations and thereby achieves a different predictive utility. The I-E Scale covers such a variety of situations, and is so brief, that the scores may be masking different components of locus of control and giving up specific predictive utility in the process. A suspicion that several factors probably contribute to locus of control as a generalized expectancy has given rise to several attempts to isolate factors in the I-E Scale. Although these efforts have been of mixed success, the suspicion persists. The approach of Gurin, Gurin, Lao, and Beattie (1969) and Lao (1970)—of separating personal and social aspects of control—appears to be fruitful and should be pursued further. It would surprise no one to find that a large number of people may believe in the efficacy of personal effort in individual achievement situations but not in reference to social institutions.

Thus, one general I-E score may not accurately depict the attitudes of the individual in every situation and, indeed, may lead to significant errors in prediction. We are also reminded that specific situations can be constructed with highly salient cues so that individuals will be induced to behave in ways that run counter to their generalized locus of control beliefs. Such highly structured situations evoke very strong specific expectancies rather than generalized locus of control expectancies.

Age Changes

Perhaps the simplest reason for changes in locus of control beliefs stems from age changes. Typically, internal control increases with the age of the child (Penk, 1969). Young children are relatively helpless and can effect little control over their own lives. They can be picked up, punished, hauled around, and generally controlled by all-powerful adults in their lives. It is not surprising, then, that as they become older, locus of control is increasingly internalized. It is not age alone that increases the strength of their internal beliefs but the accompanying growth in the capacity to care for themselves, independence, and real ability to influence their surroundings. Brecher and Denmark (1969) have reported greater verbal fluency on the part of internals than of externals. While such a relationship may simply indicate that reinforcement of verbal responses leads to a stronger internal locus of control, it is also possible that increasing verbal fluency leads to a greater capacity to influence one's environment. Again, it would be not age itself but the concomitants of age that produce the change.

The work of Crandall, Katkovsky, and Crandall (1965) on academic achievement provides evidence consistent with this general role of age. Although it was not the main focus of their study, Crandall, Katkovsky, and Crandall noted a trend for I-E scores to be relatively external at the third grade, with internality increasing to a maximum at the eighth and tenth grades. However, there was a reversion to a more external level in the twelfth grade, a trend more apparent for males than for females. Perhaps with the imminence of graduation and the potential for greater uncertainty in life stemming from the prospect of leaving the structured environment of school and family, the individual becomes temporarily more external in his and, to a lesser degree, her outlook as shown in I-E Scale scores.

There is little data on the relationship between age and locus of control beliefs. At best we can patch together a few relationships taken from a variety of populations in a variety of life circumstances. Ideally, we need longitudinal research here—a set of I-E Scale scores for the same population followed over a long period. Although purely speculative, it seems likely that life experiences or conditions that are fairly common among people may seriously affect locus of control and age relationships. For example, with advanced age, one may revert toward the helplessness of childhood. If so, we would expect the elderly, as a group, to exhibit more external beliefs.

Changes Observed in Reformatory Inmates

The preceding kinds of speculation encouraged Kielbauch (1967) to investigate some conditions that might induce changes in locus of control beliefs. Kiehlbauch tested several hypotheses using inmates of a reformatory, a setting that possesses a combination of structure and uncertainty that makes it ideal for such a study. He predicted that several clusters of events should significantly affect I-E Scale scores in ways that would be both logical and predictable. For a variety of practical reasons, he utilized a cross-sectional rather than a longitudinal approach.

Kiehlbauch found that both I-E scores and anxiety scores showed a curvilinear relationship with length of stay in the reformatory. When tested at the beginning and near the end of their sentences, inmates were relatively more external and more anxious than they were at a midpoint in their sentences. It seems reasonable to argue that as prisoners begin their sentences they are in a strange environment, without specific knowledge about the nature of the institution, and its values, unwritten rules, etc. This would lead to a heightened feeling of anxiety and helplessness. As time passes, the prisoners "learn the ropes" and become increasingly capable of predicting and controlling the rewards and punishments in their immediate (albeit narrow) institutional world. Accordingly, both externality and anxiety decline. As prisoners near the end of their sentences, the old uncertainties return. This time, however, they relate to the outside world: Will they find a job? Will people accept them? Has the world changed? All these considerations make them uncertain. Once again they are faced with the inability to predict and control and with the need to "learn the ropes" and again test their effectiveness in a now-strange world. While Kiehlbauch found no differences in the shape of curves for prisoners serving their first sentence and those having served time before, the latter were somewhat more internal (see Figure 1).

To support his interpretation of the curvilinear results, Kiehlbauch noted that he did not find the terminal rise in either I-E Scale scores or anxiety scores in a so-called work-release sample of prisoners. Individuals in this group (otherwise matched with those in the other samples), for a number of weeks prior to their final release, were allowed to work in the community during the day and return to the reformatory at night. Presumably this experience in the real world prepared them better for their subsequent release, so that fears and uncertainties normally associated with impending release did not occur to the same extent (see Figure 2).

These results strongly suggest that locus of control beliefs can be influenced in a predictable fashion by events in individuals' lives that relate to variations in uncertainty, lack of control, or unpredictability. Therefore, such variables presumably can be manipulated so as to alter locus of control beliefs and therefore behavior (to the extent that locus of control mediates a large number of behaviors). In other words, injecting greater stability and certainty into people's lives should be a way of increasing their internal beliefs; similarly, greater externality could be induced through increased uncertainty and felt lack of control.

Changes Observed in Student Populations

College students' scores on the I-E Scale have shifted in the direction of greater external control since publication of the scale by Rotter in 1966 (e.g., Schneider, 1971). This trend has been reported by several

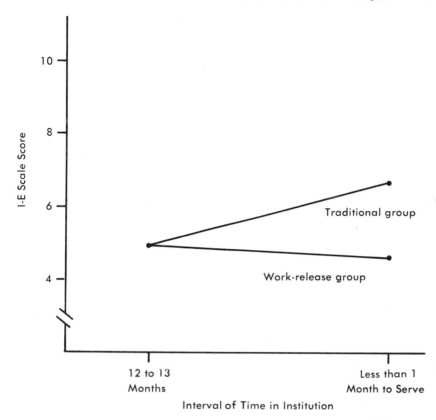

Figure 2. *Locus of Control in Reformatory Prisoners (After Kiehl-bauch [1967])*

laboratories across the country. Although the precise reasons for such a change is not known, it is interesting to speculate on its possible relationship to the general spirit of alienation that has prevailed in the country over the past ten years or so, a period that included events such as the Vietnam conflict and the Watergate scandal. Young people may be particularly sensitive to such events and may feel such events indicate they can no longer effectively control or influence what happens to them. It would not be surprising if I-E scores reflected that feeling. Figure 3 shows a series of I-E Scale scores of students (predominantly freshman) at Kansas State University from 1963 to 1974.

Transitory versus Stable Changes

Some changes in I-E orientations seem to be rather specific to the

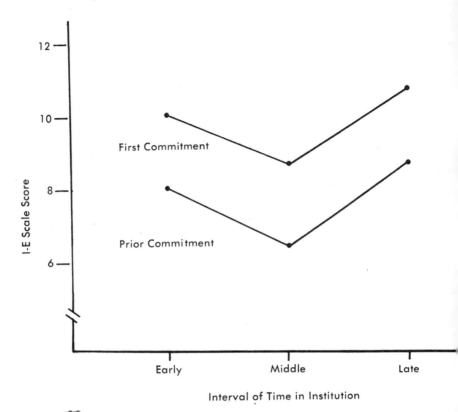

Figure 1 *Changes in Locus of Control as a Function of Release Status* (*After Kiehlbauch* [*1967*])

situation involved and transitory in nature. This is attributable to relatively brief, intense conditions. It is important to determine, through research, those conditions that affect perceived locus of control and the way in which they relate to specific (or transitory) versus general (or stable) changes.

Phares and Rotter (1956) demonstrated that the value of certain reinforcements could be altered by specific situational influences. The value of academic goals could be altered by having students make their value judgments in the presence of strong, explicit academic cues. Are such changes specific to those situations or do they transfer to other situations? The same question can be asked in the case of I-E scores. Do such changes always signify a basic change in generalized expectancies or do they signify a shift in situational expectancies (see also Gurin and Gurin [1970] and Lefcourt [1972])?

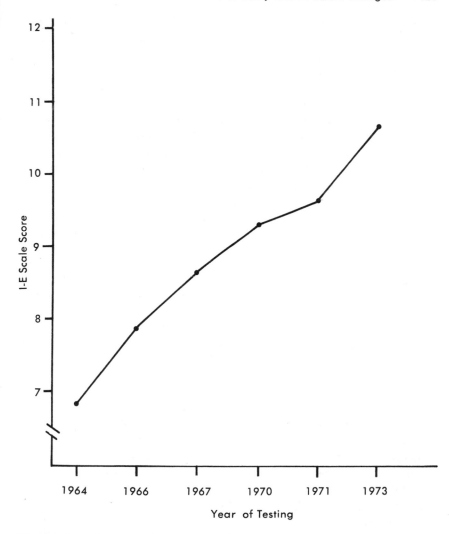

Figure 3   *Changes in I-E Scale Scores over Time at Kansas State University*

Several studies of changes in locus of control seem to invite such an inquiry. For example, Gorman (1968) studied a group of people who were predominantly supporters of Eugene McCarthy. After events at the 1968 Democratic National Convention had failed to go the way they wished, the group manifested I-E scores (one day later) that were more external than might have been predicted on the basis of existing norms. McArthur (1970) reported that students who became less susceptible to the draft by the operation of the lottery produced more external I-E scores than did students whose status was not much affected by the lottery. Eisenman (1972) has demonstrated that specific experience in experiments involving random guessing moved subjects' I-E scores significantly in the external direction, while experience in experiments in which they maintained control produced the opposite result. Brecher and Denmark (1972) found that a group of college students who were given very strong negative feedback about their performance on a course examination obtained I-E scores (administered immediately following the negative feedback) that were significantly more external than those of a comparable control group.

The issue raised by the foregoing studies is that of specific influences that are temporary versus those that have broader implications. Perhaps the issue can be clarified by recourse to a social learning theory analysis. Most likely, the effect depends on the time and specific situation to which one is predicting. That is, I-E changes that are obtained following brief, highly specific experiences probably are specific to that situation (and will be reflected only on an I-E Scale administered in that context) and are not relevant to a large number of situations. However, if one is predicting behavior in that specific situation, it is important to take such changes into consideration. If one is more concerned with behavior across many situations and over time, then such a change is probably not so important.

Perhaps an example drawn from another research area will provide further clarification. Several studies (e.g., Phares [1964] and Schwarz [1966]) offer strong evidence that a generalized expectancy for success has a declining influence on stated expectancies for success when trials are relatively massed. That is, under massed conditions, the overall level of confidence subjects bring to the situation exerts less and less influence as the trials go on; the specific experience in the situation is what really counts. However, when there are interpolated delay periods inserted among the trials, the generalized expectancy for success again exerts a strong influence immediately after each delay. That is, after a delay, subjects' stated expectancy for success tends to gravitate toward the generalized expectancy that existed before the trials.

Training Programs and Experience

Several years ago deCharms (1968) described the origin-pawn concept. He argued that a person's basic motivation is to become effective in producing desired outcomes in his or her enviornment—to have a feeling of personal causation. The origin-pawn dimension has been characterized by deCharms as follows:

When a person initiates intentional behavior, he experiences himself as having originated the intention and the behavior. He is the locus of causality of the behavior and he is said to be intrinsically motivated. Since he himself is the originator, we refer to the person as an *Origin* .... When something external to the person impels him to behavior, he experiences himself as the instrument of the outside source, and the outside source is the locus of causality. He is said to be extrinsically motivated. Since the person is impelled from without we refer to him as *Pawn*. (deCharms, 1972, p. 96)

In a direct application of this variable, deCharms attempted to foster the growth of personal causation in both black teachers and black children in an elementary school. He began the project with the assumption that treating people as origins would lead to their construing themselves as causal agents and that this restructured view of themselves would lead to more competent and satisfying behavior. No attempt was made directly to change behavior. The approach was largely that of showing teachers by example how to treat others as origins.

DeCharms discovered that while not "pushing people around" represents a start in treating people as origins, letting them do anything they wish is *not* treating them as origins. People must learn to take responsibility for their own behavior. Sometimes, when maturity and self-responsibility are defective, the teacher must impose restraints while helping the student to establish responsibility. This point is analogous to the one made by Davis (1969)—that while early experience of inconsistent reinforcement can lead to an external orientation, consistent but heavy-handed reinforcement can produce the same effect. In the present instance, total constraint as well as total freedom can lead to a pawn self-image.

The experimental treatment used by deCharms involved (1) requiring teachers to attend a week-long residential motivation training session (similar to that used by McClelland and Winter [1969] for achievement motivation), and (2) designing exercises for the teachers to use throughout the year in their classrooms. During the training session, teachers were (1) encouraged to engage in self-study and evaluation of personal motives, (2) acquainted with the thoughts and behaviors characteristic of people with various motives, such as affiliation, achievement, and power, (3) shown the value of planning and realistic goal setting relative to a motive, and (4) exposed generally to material designed to promote origin rather than pawn behavior. During the ensuing year, when these teachers were dealing with the experimental group of children, they met often with the research staff to design classroom exercises for the children. These exercises emphasized four major concepts: (1) self-concept, (2) achievement motivation, (3) realistic goal setting, and (4) the origin-pawn concept. The exercises were utilized in sixth- and seventh-grade classes. The reader is referred to deCharms' (1972) paper for a more elaborate description of the methods used.

A number of results support the efficacy of the training program. First, a follow-up analysis of 20 trained versus 20 untrained teachers revealed that significantly more of the former advanced within the school system (35 percent versus 5 percent). Second, a questionnaire administered later to the children showed that trained teachers were perceived by the children as significantly more encouraging of origin behavior than were similar teachers in a control group. Third, when children wrote imaginative stories that were then coded for the presence or absence of six origin-pawn categories, results showed that the origin score increased as a function of the child's training and did not increase in the absence of such training. While none of the children's training was oriented toward increased academic adhievement, one might expect that such achievement would increase as a function of training. Typically, children in the school district that was studied fell farther behind the national norms on the Iowa Test of Basic Skills as the years passed. In the children who received personal causation training, the observed decrements on this test were less than would have been expected. More detailed analysis revealed that the training had a greater effect on boys than on girls and that language skills were most affected, arithmetic skills less affected, and reading skills least affected by the training. The children who received training also showed better school attendance and tardiness records.

Overall, then, it appears that personal causation training had positive effects on the motivated behavior of both these children and their teachers and that certain aspects of the children's academic performance were related to their training experiences.

Even though the origin-pawn dimension is not the same as locus of control, there is considerable overlap, and this work seems to have obvious implications for locus of control. Further, while there are some design problems with the study, it represents a significant step toward the study of locus of control in natural settings. The study also provides us with significant insight into some potential antecedents of locus of control beliefs as well as some techniques by which we can hope to alter them.

Work similar to that of deCharms has been reported by Reimanis and Schaefer (1970). Nowicki and Barnes (1973), in a study with inner-city adolescents, showed that a highly structured summer camp experience that emphasized the relationship between behavior and reinforcement tended to enhance internal control expectancies. Levens (1968) suggested that welfare mothers can reduce their sense of powerlessness through participation in an organization that encourages political activism. Gottesfeld and Dozier (1966), studying deprived individuals in a ghetto who were trained in community organization in poverty areas, obtained scores suggesting that the experience of problem confrontation led to a heightened feeling of internal control. Tyre and Maisto (1974) administered an experimental treatment program designed to alter preadolescents' locus of control beliefs. Using experimental, control, and placebo groups, Tyre and Maisto were unable to show that their experimental program produced any immediate effects on subjects' IAR scores. Six weeks later, however, increased internal beliefs were noted for experimental subjects but not for control and placebo subjects.

MacDonald (1971c) discussed locus of control as a potentially important variable in rehabilitation work and attempted to show the contribution of an internal locus of control to an expectancy for success. He commented as follows on the nonmotivational properties of locus of control:

> Locus of control is not a motivational variable but rather an expectancy variable. Findings that persons do not *try* to improve their conditions because of negative expectancies do not indicate that those persons do not *want* to improve their conditions. A large number of the victims in our society are motivated to improve their living conditions, but they have low expectancies for success—often realistically. *Motivation coupled with positive expectancy equals optimism; motivation coupled with negative expectancy equals despair.* (McDonald, 1971c, p. 115)

Much of this work involving the promotion of an internal locus of control through the application of various techniques is preliminary in nature. It is clear that belief in an internal locus of control can provide individuals with a greater sense of control and thus a greater potential for power and efficacy. The next step is finding ways of inculcating such beliefs. The works cited provide some clues. This may prove to be the most important aspect of locus of control research in the years ahead. It is particularly important because it permits *groups* of people to be dealt with. The potential is much greater by virtue of the numbers involved and should encourage investigators to develop more and better training programs.

Therapeutic Intervention

Lefcourt (1966b) recognized quite early the importance of encouraging an internal locus of control as a goal in psychotherapy, "since an internal locus of control may be one prerequisite of competent behavior, and an external-control orientation seems common to many people who do not function in a competent, 'healthy' manner'' (p. 191). Again, not a great deal of research has been carried out in this area, particularly not systematic research. There are obvious difficulties in carrying out research on therapy. As a result, the findings in this area are still sketchy. However, what research has been accomplished and reported seems consistent with our previous conclusions.

Smith (1970) reported that patients who sought psychotherapy to resolve an immediate, acute life crisis showed a significant decrease in externality as they learned more effective coping techniques in therapy. On the other hand, patients who became involved in therapy without an immediate crisis state, and experienced about the same number of therapy sessions, showed little change in locus of control beliefs. Support for the notion that effectively coping with one's problems can raise internal beliefs is revealed in the work of Dua (1970). Both action-oriented and reeducative therapy led to increased internal scores in patients, particularly in the action-oriented group. Further, Gillis and Jessor (1970) noted that patients who showed improvement in psychotherapy also showed greater increases in internal beliefs than did an untreated group of patients.

Masters (1970), in presenting a clinical case study, argued that a useful therapeutic procedure ought to be discussions and behavior assignments designed to increase the extent to which the patients feel in control of their environment. In this particular case, an adolescent was encouraged to construe his behavior as an active, successful means of controlling the behavior of his parents rather than as a shrinking, meek submission to their demands. A variety of positive outcomes flowed from this treatment.

Foulds (1971) examined the effects of personal growth experiences on locus of control beliefs. Thirty undergraduates participated in 4 half-hour therapy-like sessions once a week for eight weeks. A control group of similar students did not participate. In a design involving before-and-after administrations of the I-E Scale, an increase in internal scores occurred for the experimental group, offering support for the hypothesis that experiences in an atmosphere of acceptance and unstructured group exploration and expression facilitate a sense of internal control.

The term psychotherapy covers a wide variety of often quite disparate techniques, ranging from Rogerian acceptance to the highly specific manipulations of behavior modification. In a general way, however, one can see how each could logically foster the growth of an internal locus of control. It will be helpful in the future if we can learn to specify exactly what it is in each of these techniques that seems to result in this increase in internality. Is it the consistency of reinforcement that is inherent in behavior modiication? On the surface, one might expect that such therapist control would foster a belief in *external* control—after all, it is the therapist who maintains control. However, patients may well perceive the inevitability of reinforcement following the appropriate behavior as the epitome of predictability. While behavior modifiers are reluctant to look into such "perceptions" on the part of the patient, it may be useful for others to do so. As in the family setting, perhaps the creation of a warm, nurturant, consistent environment in therapy may have positive outcomes while a cold, domineering, controlling environment may produce opposite outcomes. Thus, while the degree of consistency or predictability may be the same in either instance, patient perception of the nature of control might differ greatly.

Furthermore, the acceptance and warmth of a Rogerian approach may indeed result in patients' gaining a greater capacity to translate the regularities in their world into power that they can potentially exert. A problem-solving approach in therapy or a search for insight may also have similar effects. The point is that there may be many different bases for the development of locus of control beliefs, so there may be many different approaches to change in therapy.

One such approach is patient-therapist matching. For example, Helweg (1971) had both college students and psychiatric inpatients view sound films of Albert Ellis and Carl Rogers each conducting initial interviews with a patient in their characteristic styles. As Helweg predicted, students and patients who preferred the directive interview approach (Ellis) over the nondirective (Rogers) scored higher on a dogmatism scale and also were more external in their locus of control beliefs.

Jacobsen (1971) hypothesized that internals would prefer psychoanalytically oriented therapists while externals would prefer more behavioristically oriented therapists. Jacobsen asked several therapists of professed behavioristic and analytic orientations to write descriptions of themselves and their approaches to therapy. From these she constructed composite profiles. Five clinicians rated the behaviorist composite as more authoritarian, with a tendency to foster an external locus of control in their patients. Jacobsen administered a dependency measure, the F Scale, and the I-E Scale to subjects. They also were asked to imagine they were having psychological difficulties and to make selections of preferred therapists. As predicted, the internals chose the analytic therapist and the externals preferred the behavioristic therapist.

Wilson (1973) felt that Jacobsen's results were largely due to the manner in which the descriptions of therapists were presented. He constructed two descriptions each for a behavioristic and for a psycho-analytic therapist. Each therapist was described as either authoritarian and controlling or allowing patient participation and freedom. Procedures similar to those Jacobsen used were followed. In effect, Wilson concluded that there was no evidence that the particular school of therapy espoused by the therapist is important. Rather, it is the subject's *perception* of the therapist's standing on the participation-control dimension that is important. In short, internals will select either directive therapy or therapy that allows greater patient participation, depending upon whether they feel there is a likilhood that the particular therapy in question will provide them with personal control skills.

As is so often the case, the solution here is not to find *the right* therapeutic technique to enhance internal control beliefs. Many such techniques surely will have appropriate effects. Rather, the goal should be the systematic investigation of the effect of different techniques with various kinds of patients. Then we might be in a position to state that for patient X we should attempt to increase his or her internality by means of a "warm, accepting, listening" approach while for Patient Z, we should utilize active, manipulatory techniques. In short, the quest for techniques to increase internal beliefs in patients should articulate the technique with the patient's learning history. In this fashion we can eventually move away from a simple search for the "best" technique.

Summary

It seems apparent that I-E scores (reflecting the subject's locus of control) can be altered by a range of conditions. These conditions include, on the one hand, very specific influences whose effects may be transitory and narrow and, on the other hand, changes that have more pervasive, permanent effects on behavior.

Locus of control as a generalized expectancy can be altered by a variety of environmental forces. Some of these forces include factors that accompany age changes, conditions that affect a subject's certainty that control can be exerted, world or national events, special training programs, and a variety of therapeutic techniques.

Internal control can be construed as a very specific expectancy or as a very general one, but in either case it is important that we understand the conditions that will affect its strength. To enhance individuals' capacity to cope with the world successfully, one must influence their generalized expectancy for internal control. We are only beginning to focus on the investigation of techniques to bring about such influence.

XI

Conclusions and Implications for the Future

We have covered a wide range of research in our survey of the locus of control concept. This coverage has been representative (certainly not exhaustive) of the prodigious number of studies that have been done. The amount of effort expended and the number of investigators involved is impressive. But what accounts for the magnitude of such activity?

Perhaps our observations of Karl S. and our subsequent struggles to conceptualize his approach to life have uncovered many Karls "out there." They have been variously described as external, powerless, fatalistic, alienated, normless, experiencing anomie and loss of personal control, and as professing a belief in luck or chance occurrences. Regardless of the labels applied to them, they share the experience of living in a world characterized increasingly by overcrowding, overpopulation, pollution, unresponsive governments, generation gaps, authoritarianism, assassinations, campus disorders, ghetto riots, and fear of control by governments, specialists, or technocrats. Locus of control, although it started in the context of one clinical case, touches a series of social phenomena that were and are very much a part of our society. Such a concept has an intuitive appeal. More than that, it is a theoretically based concept that is significantly related to other concepts within the theory. It may be no accident that scientific interest has shifted from the achievement motive to locus of control just as many people in our society abandoned the achievement strivings of their parents and shifted to a form of alienated beliefs and attitudes.

Is Internal versus External Control a Useful Notion?

This question was raised in Chapter I. We are now in a position to answer it. Locus of control, viewed as either a situation-specific expectancy or a broad, generalized expectancy, is clearly a useful concept.

Our experience with Karl S. taught us that the effects of reinforcement on behavior vary depending on the way in which people construe the locus of control of that reinforcement, that is, whether individuals see it as dependent upon their own behavior or personality or as residing in factors over which they have little control. Subsequent research has taught us two additional things. First, Karl's tendency to attribute control to forces outside himself was not idiosyncratic. Rather, belief in predominantly external or internal control over the consequences of one's behavior is a concept that has wide application. The development of the I-E Scale and other measuring devices has allowed us to define an internal-external control dimension along which people can be ordered.

Second, locus of control operates both as a belief directed toward one specific situation and as a generalized expectancy covering many diverse situations (a personality characteristic, really). If the cues of the specific situation are strong enough, the behavior of most individuals will be similar, regardless of their generalized beliefs. On the other hand, when the situation is ambiguous, the behavior of individuals is much more likely to reflect their generalized locus of control beliefs.

By studying specific situations that differ in the extent to which they arouse specific expectancies about the internal or external locus of control we have observed several things. Learning and performance are influenced, expectancies for future success or failure are differentially stimulated, self-reported anxiety and autonomic arousal are affected, and even such phenomena as cognitive dissonance and reactance can be influenced. Most research in this area is clearly supportive of the contention that locus of control as a specific situational expectancy is helping to account for variations in behavior shown in highly structured situations.

As we shift to locus of control as a personality characteristic, the evidence for the utility of the concept is just as persuasive. Much research clearly identifies internals as superior in their efforts at coping with and gaining a measure of control over their environment. As compared to externals, internals acquire more information, retain and utilize it better, and are generally more effective in the broad realm of cognitive processing. In the case of children, their efforts at coping and mastery are most likely to be observed in the school setting. The academic success and achievement of internal children is superior to that of their external counterparts, and internal children show a greater capacity to delay gratification.

In social contexts, a similar theme emerges. Internals are more independent and more reliant upon their own judgments. They are less easily influenced. Most of the early research also suggests a greater tendency for internals to initiate efforts for social change, although more recent work suggests it may be externals who are more militant or more likely to seek social change. Nevertheless, the fact that locus of control is related to behavior in a systematic way gives us great hope.

Finally, the different manner in which internals and externals react to threatening situations is important. We have noted the various correlations between anxiety, adjustment, membership in pathological groups, and locus of control. All of the foregoing is more than just an abbreviated summary of research in locus of control. It is, at the same time, a supportive statement in behalf of the utility of the locus of control concept.

Locus of Control Research as a Demonstration of the Possible

The preceding paragraphs briefly summarized some of the correlates of locus of control. By conducting many studies with various experimental and statistical controls, we have achieved the right to assert the utility of the concept. Often, an individual piece of research may appear trivial. But when the pieces are woven together, they provide an example of what is possible in the way of human behavior.

We can now state that internal control will enhance coping efforts, resistance to influence, and achievement behavior. Furthermore, to the extent that such behaviors are deemed desirable, we have an added means for their attainment through the inculcation of internal beliefs. The importance of the locus of control concept, to a large extent, lies in what it signifies about us as human beings. It tells us, through the force of accumulated research, that belief in personal control can have widespread, important, and desirable outcomes. It demonstrates the possibility of altering our views of ourselves. No amount of armchair philosophizing can substitute for this evidence.

Utility Defined as Application

Certainly many problems exist in the world today. The great volume of published research on locus of control should give us increased confidence that the concept can be applied to the solution of many of these problems. We may hope that this will become an increasing focus for future research. Whether the problem is something as personal as weight loss or reduction in smoking, or as impersonal as helping a political candidate in a distant state, the previous research suggests knowledge of locus of control should be able to offer some guidance. Perhaps internals can be enrolled in more independent, self-regulated reduction programs while externals would profit most from programs that rely on prestige suggestion or support from others. These are examples of possible deductions from what we already know.

Utility Defined as Improved Technology

An important aspect of psychology is its technology. There are thousands of diagnostic tests of one sort or another, objective and projective, aptitude and achievement, personality and intelligence. This technology also embraces many different procedures for altering human behavior, e.g., psychoanalysis, conditioning, behavior modification, individual psychotherapy, group therapy, or encounter groups. We can now incorporate conceptions of locus of control into both diagnostic and therapeutic efforts. Careful evaluation of clients' or patients' locus of control beliefs in various life areas can be a real boon to understanding those persons and to planning a sensible, efficient program to bring about desired changes in their behavior. We can apply techniques that will enhance an internal locus of control (if the individuals lack sufficient self-confidence to mediate certain desired behaviors) or that will reduce an internal locus of control (if it causes undesirable quantities of guilt).

Existing data provide a very strong basis for the systematic incorporation of various means of evaluating locus of control beliefs into our diagnostic and therapeutic technology. This also argues, of course, for the development of even more sophisticated I-E instruments. The reader should not think that these suggestions apply only to the clinical realm; our remarks are meant to apply equally to school settings, social-industrial or organizational settings, and many more as well.

Is the I-E Concept as Useful as It Might Be?: Some Suggestions for Future Direction

The response here clearly must be no, since we obviously do not have a finished product. Numerous questions remain. While the broad outlines of the relationships between locus of control beliefs and behavior have been established, the details have not. Furthermore, much remains to be learned about the specific fashion in which such beliefs operate to produce certain outcomes. The following are representative of the many suggestions that can be offered for future endeavors.

1. Development of I-E scales of greater sophistication has begun and is accelerating with the advent of studies demonstrating the multi-dimensionality of the I-E Scale. More precise prediction will ultimately be achieved through subscale approaches that indicate the strength of an individual's locus of control beliefs in several different areas. This will be superior to the reliance on a single score to characterize the individual's beliefs.

   However, it might be noted that locus of control grew out of social learning theory. The serious employment of such a theory makes one less vulnerable to the weaknesses of any given I-E scale being employed. If one tries to predict behavior by means of an I-E scale alone, that scale will have to be potent and complex indeed to do the job. If, on the other hand, one simultaneously assesses needs, expectancies for success, and the nature of the situation with other instruments, the grossness of a single score on an I-E scale can partially be compensated for. The more the psychologists integrate their predictive efforts with such a theory of personality, the less will their predictions be dependent upon the idiosyncracies or inadequacies of one I-E scale. While this is no reason to rest in our efforts to develop better I-E scales, it does illustrate our belief in the vulnerability that one assumes when operating in the absence of an explicit theoretical framework.

2. We discussed the desirability of moving more in the direction of application. This is a direction the whole of psychology would do well to follow. Surely locus of control can be applied effectively to enhancing efforts of individuals to cope with many current problems. Knowledge of individuals' locus of control beliefs may tell us how best to reach them or convince them to initiate coping efforts.

3. Much more research is needed into the antecedents of locus of control beliefs. Our knowledge of the social and familial bases of locus of control is quite sketchy. If we are going to apply what we know about locus of control to bring about changes in people's behavior, precise knowledge of its origins is paramount. It is our assumption that knowledge of antecedents will lead to more efficient efforts at behavior change since no single score provides enough information about the role and function of locus of control in the psychological economy of individuals.

4. By the same token, we know little about how to induce changes in locus of control beliefs. Only the broadest outlines are visible now. Undoubtedly there are many ways of inducing either transient changes or relatively permanent changes. However, we must learn more specifically how to do this, with what kinds of people various changes are possible, under what conditions, etc. The possibilities for change include psychotherapy, the mechanical application of reinforcement schedules, and the teaching policies of institutions and schools, to name only a few.

5. Greater integration of research into a theoretical framework is required. More specifically, future research must incorporate an evaluation of subjects' expectancies for success, need value, and an analysis of how the particular situation relates to such variables. All this must then be related to locus of control in order to develop specific predictions. Studying behavior while assessing only I-E status leaves out at least 70 percent of the necessary predictive formula. This is analogous to swatting at tennis balls with only 4 strings in the racquet. Just as locus of control notions eventually forced a modification of a social learning theory predictive formula (Rotter, Chance, & Phares, 1972, pp. 39-41), so too can the integration of social learning theory into our efforts at applying I-E be highly useful.

6. Throughout much of this book and much of the research literature there seems to be a tacit assumption that an internal locus of control is desirable while an external one is not—clearly a value judgment. Perhaps more research should be devoted to the means of teaching individuals when one or the other locus of control belief is the more useful. Probably people would benefit from learning to discriminate among situations as regards an appropriate locus of control belief.

7. Many very specific research questions remain as well, for example: (1) the nature of the relationship between locus of control beliefs and willingness to help others in a variety of settings; and (2) the manner in which people project their own locus of control beliefs onto others or attribute responsibility to others. Such questions will tax the ingenuity of investigators. Perhaps the research summarized throughout this book will help to stimulate some of that ingenuity.

Some Final Ruminations on Power and Control

It certainly seems that one major component of power must be an internal locus of control. It is difficult to understand how individuals could consistently seek power or control over their environment without an accompanying belief in the efficacy of their own behavior.

The research presented in this book stands in marked contrast to the views of B. F. Skinner (1971), the most articulate and influential advocate of behaviorism in society today. His views have stimulated a tremendous amount of interest and criticism; his publications regarding control of human behavior have been attacked by many. Of course, behavior control did not begin with Skinner, nor is he its only exponent. Psychotherapy, counseling, behavior therapy, hypnosis, conditioning, drugs, shock treatments, and psychosurgery are only a few of the forms of control that have existed (London, 1964, 1969).

Skinner seems to regard the autonomy of man as a myth. He argues that we should not be talking about freedom or responsibility because behavior is determined by reinforcement, both in the laboratory and in real life. Although we talk about freedom and dignity, Skinner says, society is organized in a deterministic fashion exemplified by the law of effect. All of our institutions "shape" behavior; our schools do it through education, our economy through monetary rewards, our business structures through dispensing prestige, and our police through threat of punishment. At the same time, however, our legal and religious bureaucracies place the responsibility on the individual. By the Skinnerian view, all of behavior is a function of environmental forces applied to the individual. Yet, whenever the person deviates from accepted standards of behavior, society punishes that person as if he or she, rather than the environment, were responsible. To build a better society, Skinner would have us relinquish our mistaken notions of freedom and choice and turn to conditioning principles.

It is interesting to speculate whether Karl S. (as described in Chapter I) could be the prototype of the person who has no freedom or dignity. Certainly Karl did not believe he controlled events by his own behavior. One wonders whether the ultimate outcome of Skinner's beliefs is that we would all be Karls and whether such an outcome is at all desirable.

Skinner urged us to give up our myth of the autonomous man. But perhaps this so-called myth is the more useful reality after all. Throughout this book we have seen that effects of reinforcement vary depending upon how people relate reinforcement to their behavior. We cannot always prevent people from seeing their world in the way they do. Perhaps it is not only more *useful* but also *safer* for people to employ the belief of freedom, and with freedom, power. As London (1969) has remarked, "There is no antidote to power but power, nor has there ever been. But there are ethical uses of power. In order to exercise justice against lawlessness, it is necessary to array lawful power. ... In order to defend individual freedom, it is necessary to enhance the power of individuals" (p. 213).

Appendix A

The Rotter Internal-External Control Scale[1]

*1. a. Children get into trouble because their parents punish them too much.
   b. The trouble with most children nowadays is that their parents are too easy with them.
2. *a.* Many of the unhappy things in people's lives are partly due to bad luck.
   b. People's misfortunes result from the mistakes they make.
3. a. One of the major reasons why we have wars is because people don't take enough interest in politics.
   b. There will always be wars, no matter how hard people try to prevent them.
4. a. In the long run people get the respect they deserve in this world.
   b. Unfortunately, an individual's worth often passes unrecognized no matter how hard he tries.
5. a. The idea that teachers are unfair to students is nonsense.
   b. Most students don't realize the extent to which their grades are influenced by accidental happenings.
6. *a.* Without the right breaks one cannot be an effective leader.
   b. Capable people who fail to become leaders have not taken advantage of their opportunities.

7. *a.* No matter how hard you try some people just don't like you.
    b. People who can't get others to like them don't understand how to get along with others.
*8. a. Heredity plays the major role in determining one's personality.
    b. It is one's experiences in life which determine what they're like.
9. *a.* I have often found that what is going to happen will happen.
    b. Trusting to fate has never turned out as well for me as making a decision to take a definite course of action.
10. a. In the case of the well prepared student there is rarely if ever such a thing as an unfair test.
    b. Many times exam questions tend to be so unrelated to course work that studying is really useless.
11. a. Becoming a success is a matter of hard work, luck has little or nothing to do with it.
    b. Getting a good job depends mainly on being in the right place at the right time.
12. a. The average citizen can have an influence in government decisions.
    b. This world is run by the few people in power, and there is not much the little guy can do about it.
13. a. When I make plans, I am almost certain that I can make them work.
    b. It is not always wise to plan too far ahead because many things turn out to be a matter of good or bad fortune anyway.
*14. a. There are certain people who are just no good.
    b. There is some good in everybody.
15. a. In my case getting what I want has little or nothing to do with luck.
    b. Many times we might just as well decide what to do by flipping a coin.
16. *a.* Who gets to be the boss often depends on who was lucky enough to be in the right place first.
    b. Getting people to do the right thing depends upon ability; luck has little to do with it.
17. *a.* As far as world affairs are concerned, most of us are the victims of forces we can neither understand nor control.
    b. By taking an active part in political and social affairs the people can control world events.
18. *a.* Most people don't realize the extent to which their lives are controlled by accidental happenings.
    b. There really is no such thing as "luck."
*19. a. One should always be willing to admit mistakes.
    b. It is usually best to cover up one's mistakes.

20. *a.* It is hard to know whether or not a person really likes you.

     b. How many friends you have depends upon how nice a person you are.

21. *a.* In the long run the bad things that happen to us are balanced by the good ones.

     b. Most misfortuntes are the result of lack of ability, ignorance, laziness, or all three.

22. a. With enough effort we can wipe out political corruption.

     b. It is difficult for people to have much control over the things politicians do in office.

23. *a.* Sometimes I can't understand how teachers arrive at the grades they give.

     b. There is a direct connection between how hard I study and the grades I get.

*24. a. A good leader expects people to decide for themselves what they should do.

     b. A good leader makes it clear to everybody what their jobs are.

25. *a.* Many times I feel that I have little influence over the things that happen to me.

     b. It is impossible for me to believe that chance or luck plays an important role in my life.

26. a. People are lonely because they don't try to be friendly.

     b. There's not much use in trying too hard to please people, if they like you, they like you.

*27. a. There is too much emphasis on athletics in high school.

     b. Team sports are an excellent way to build character.

28. a. What happens to me is my own doing.

     b. Sometimes I feel that I don't have enough control over the direction my life is taking.

29. *a.* Most of the time I can't understand why politicians behave the way they do.

     b. In the long run the people are responsible for bad government on a national as well as on a local level.

Note: Items with an asterisk preceding them are filler items. Score is the number of italicized alternatives chosen.

¹ From J. B. Rotter. Generalized expectancies for internal versus external control of reinforcement. *Psychological Monographs,* 1966, *80*, No. 1 (Whole No. 609). Copyright by the American Psychological Association. Reprinted by permission of the author and publisher.

Appendix B
The IAR Scale[1]

1. If a teacher passes you to the next grade, would it probably be
   ____ a. because she liked you, or
   I + ____ b. because of the work you did?
2. When you do well on a test at school, is it more likely to be
   I + ____ a. because you studied for it, or
   ____ b. because the test was especially easy?
3. When you have trouble understanding something at school, is it usually
   ____ a. because the teacher didn't explain it clearly, or
   I − ____ b. because you didn't listen carefully?
4. When you read a story and can't remember much of it, is it usually
   ____ a. because the story wasn't well written, or
   I − ____ b. because you weren't interested in the story?
5. Suppose your parents say you are doing well in school. Is this likely to happen
   I + ____ a. because your school work is good, or
   ____ b. because they are in a good mood?
6. Suppose you did better than usual in a subject at school. Would it probably happen
   I + ____ a. because you tried harder, or
   ____ b. because someone helped you?

7. When you lose at a game of cards or checkers, does it usually happen
   _____ a. because the other player is good at the game, or
   I – _____ b. because you don't play well?

8. Suppose a person doesn't think you are very bright or clever
   I – _____ a. can you make him change his mind if you try to, or
   _____ b. are there some people who will think you're not very bright no matter what you do?

9. If you solve a puzzle quickly, is it
   _____ a. because it wasn't a very hard puzzle, or
   I + _____ b. because you worked on it carefully?

10. If a boy or girl tells you that you are dumb, is it more likely that they say that
    _____ a. because they are mad at you, or
    I – _____ b. because what you did really wasn't very bright?

11. Suppose you study to become a teacher, scientist, or doctor and you fail. Do you think this would happen
    I – _____ a. because you didn't work hard enough, or
    _____ b. because you needed some help, and other people didn't give it to you?

12. When you learn something quickly in school, is it usually
    I + _____ a. because you paid close attention, or
    _____ b. because the teacher explained it clearly?

13. If a teacher says to you, "Your work is fine," is it
    _____ a. something teachers usually say to encourage pupils, or
    I + _____ b. because you did a good job?

14. When you find it hard to work arithmetic or math problems at school, is it
    I – _____ a. because you didn't study well enough before you tried them, or
    _____ b. because the teacher gave problems that were too hard?

15. When you forget something you heard in class, is it
    _____ a. because the teacher didn't explain it very well, or
    I – _____ b. because you didn't try very hard to remember?

16. Suppose you weren't sure about the answer to a question your teacher asked you, but your answers turned out to be right. Is it likely to happen
    _____ a. because she wasn't as particular as usual, or
    I + _____ b. because you gave the best answer you could think of?

17. When you read a story and remember most of it, is it usually
    I + _____ a. because you were interested in the story, or
    _____ b. because the story was well written?

18. If your parents tell you you're acting silly and not thinking clearly, is it more likely to be

   I − _____ a. because of something you did, or

   _____ b. because they happen to be feeling cranky?

19. When you don't do well on a test at school, is it

   _____ a. because the test was especially hard, or

   I − _____ b. because you didn't study for it?

20. When you win at a game of cards or checkers, does it happen

   I + _____ a. because you play real well, or

   _____ b. because the other person doesn't play well?

21. If people think you're bright or clever, is it

   _____ a. because they happen to like you, or

   I + _____ b. because you usually act that way?

22. If a teacher didn't pass you to the next grade, would it probably be

   _____ a. because she "had it in for you," or

   I − _____ b. because your school work wasn't good enough?

23. Suppose you don't do as well as usual in a subject at school. Would this probably happen

   I − _____ a. because you weren't as careful as usual, or

   _____ b. because somebody bothered you and kept you from working?

24. If a boy or girl tells you that you are bright, is it usually

   I + _____ a. because you thought up a good idea, or

   _____ b. because they like you?

25. Suppose you became a famous teacher, scientist or doctor. Do you think this would happen

   _____ a. because other people helped you when you needed it, or

   I + _____ b. because you worked very hard?

26. Suppose your parents say you aren't doing well in your school work. Is this likely to happen more

   I − _____ a. because your work isn't very good, or

   _____ b. because they are feeling cranky?

27. Suppose you are showing a friend how to play a game and he has trouble with it. Would that happen

   _____ a. because he wasn't able to understand how to play, or

   I − _____ b. because you couldn't explain it well?

28. When you find it easy to work arithmetic or math problems at school, is it usually

   _____ a. because the teacher gave you especially easy problems, or

   I + _____ b. because you studied your book well before you tried them?

29. When you remember something you heard in class, is it usually
    I+ ____ a. because you tried hard to remember, or
    ____ b. because the teacher explained it well?
30. If you can't work a puzzle, is it more likely to happen
    I− ____ a. because you are not especially good at working puzzles, or
    ____ b. because the instructions weren't written clearly enough?
31. If your parents tell you that you are bright or clever, is it more likely
    ____ a. because they are feeling good, or
    I+ ____ b. because of something you did?
32. Suppose you are explaining how to play a game to a friend and he learns quickly. Would that happen more often
    I+ ____ a. because you explained it well, or
    ____ b. because he was able to understand it?
33. Suppose you're not sure about the answer to a question your teacher asks you and the answer you give turns out to be wrong. Is it likely to happen
    ____ a. because she was more particular than usual, or
    I− ____ b. because you answered too quickly?
34. If a teacher says to you, "Try to do better," would it be
    ____ a. because this is something she might say to get pupils to try harder, or
    I− ____ b. because your work wasn't as good as usual?

[1] From *Crandall, Katkovsky, & Crandall,* 1965, pp. 91–109. Copyright 1965 by The Society for Research in Child Development and reprinted by permission of the authors and the publisher.

Bibliography

Abrahamson, D., Schulderman, S., & Schulderman, E.   Replication of dimensions of locus of control. *Journal of Consulting and Clinical Psychology*, 1973, *41*, 320.

Abramowitz, S. I.   Locus of control and self-reported depression among college students. *Psychological Reports*, 1969, *25*, 149–150.

Abramowitz, S. I.   Internal-external control and social-political activism: A test of the dimensionality of Rotter's I-E Scale. *Journal of Consulting and Clinical Psychology,* 1973, *40*, 196–201.

Adams-Webber, J. R.   Generalized expectancies concerning the locus of control of reinforcements and the perception of moral sanctions. *British Journal of Clinical Psychology,* 1969, *8*, 340–343.

Adler, A.   *Understanding human nature.* New York: Garden City Publishing Co., 1927.

Altrocchi, J., Palmer, J., Hellman, R., & Davis, H.   The Marlowe-Crowne, repressor-sensitizer, and internal-external scales and attribution of unconscious hostile intent. *Psychological Reports*, 1968, *23*, 1229–1230.

Angyal, A.   *Foundations for a science of personality.* New York: Commonwealth Fund, 1941.

Ansbacher, H. L.   Anomie, the sociologist's conception of lack of social interest. *Journal of Individual Psychology,* 1959, *15*, 212–214.

Ansbacher, H., & Ansbacher, R.   *The Individual Psychology of Alfred Adler.* New York: Basic Books, 1956.

Atkinson, J. W. (Ed.) *Motives in fantasy, action, and society.* Princeton, N.J.: Van Nostrand, 1958.

Atkinson, J. W. *An introduction to motivation.* Princeton, N.J.: Van Nostrand, 1964.

Atkinson, J. W., & Feather, N. T. (Eds.) *A theory of achievement motivation.* New York: Wiley, 1966.

Averill, J. R. Personal control over aversive stimuli and its relationship to stress. *Psychological Bulletin,* 1973, *80,* 286–303.

Baron, R. A. Authoritarianism, locus of control and risk-taking. *Journal of Psychology,* 1968, *68,* 141–143.

Baron, R. A. The effects of intertrial activity and locus of control orientation on verbal operant conditioning. *Psychonomic Science,* 1969, *15,* 69–70.

Battle, E., & Rotter, J. B. Children's feelings of personal control as related to social class and ethnic groups. *Journal of Personality,* 1963, *31,* 482–490.

Bennion, R. C. Task, trial by trial score variability of internal versus external control of reinforcement. Unpublished doctoral dissertation, Ohio State University, 1961.

Berman, A. L., & Hays, J. E. Relation between death anxiety, belief in afterlife, and locus of control. *Journal of Consulting and Clinical Psychology,* 1973, *41,* 320.

Bernhardson, C. S. Relationship between individual social desirability ratings and Hand acquiescence and I-E scores. *Psychological Reports,* 1968, *22,* 773–776.

Bersoff, D. N. Silk purses into sow's ears: The decline of psychological testing and a suggestion for its redemption. *American Psychologist,* 1973, *28,* 892–899.

Berzins, J. I., & Ross, W. F. Locus of control among opiate addicts. *Journal of Consulting and Clinical Psychology,* 1973, *40,* 84–91.

Berzins, J., Ross, W. F., and Cohen, D. I. Skill versus chance activity preferences as alternative measures of locus of control: An attempted cross-validation. *Journal of Consulting and Clinical Psychology,* 1970, *35,* 18–20.

Berzins, J. I., Ross, W. F., & Monroe, J. J. A multivariate study of the personality characteristics of hospitalized narcotic addicts on the MMPI. *Journal of Clinical Psychology,* 1971, *27,* 174–181.

Bettelheim, B. *The Informed heart.* New York: Free Press, 1960.

Bialer, I. Conceptualization of success and failure in mentally retarded and normal children. *Journal of Personality,* 1961, *29,* 303–320.

Biondo, J., & MacDonald, A. P., Jr. Internal-external locus of control and response to influence attempts. *Journal of Personality,* 1971, *39,* 407–419.

Blackman, S. Some factors affecting the perception of events as chance determined. *Journal of Psychology,* 1962, *54,* 197–202.

Blanchard, E. B., & Scarboro, M. E. Locus of control, political attitudes, and voting behavior in a college age population. *Psychological Reports,* 1972, *30,* 529–530.

Block, J. Some reasons for the apparent inconsistency of personality. *Psychological Bulletin,* 1968, *70,* 210–212.

Brady, J. V., Porter, R. W., Conrad, D. G., & Mason, J. W.   Avoidance behavior and the development of gastroduodenal ulcers. *Journal of Experimental Analysis of Behavior,* 1958, *1,* 69–72.

Brecher, M., & Denmark, F. L.   Internal-external locus of control and verbal fluency. *Psychological Reports,* 1969, *25,* 707–710.

Brecher, M., & Denmark, F. L.   Locus of control: Effects of a serendipitous manipulation. *Psychological Reports,* 1972, 30, 461–462.

Brehm, J. W.   *A theory of psychological reactance.* New York: Academic Press, 1966.

Brissett, M., & Nowicki, S.   Internal versus external control of reinforcement and reaction to frustration. *Journal of Personality and Social Psychology,* 1973, *25,* 35–44.

Brown, J. C., & Strickland, B. R.   Belief in internal-external control of reinforcement and participation in college activities. *Journal of Consulting and Clinical Psychology,* 1972, *38,* 148.

Buck, M. R., & Austrin, H. R.   Factors affecting the socioeconomically disadvantaged child in an educational setting. Final report, Office of Education, Bureau of Research, July 1970, No. 9-5-034, Grant No. 6-9-009-034-0072 (010).

Burnes, K., Brown, W. A., & Keating, G. W.   Dimensions of control: Correlations between MMPI and I-E scores. *Journal of Consulting and Clinical Psychology,* 1971, *36,* 301.

Butterfield, E. C.   Locus of control, test anxiety, reaction to frustration, and achievement attitudes. *Journal of Personality,* 1964, *32,* 298–311.

Byrne, D.   The Repression-Sensitization Scale: Rationale, reliability and validity. In B. A. Maher (Ed.), *Progress in experimental personality research.* New York: Academic Press, 1964. Pp. 169–220.

Cellura, A. R.   Internality as a determinant of academic achievement in low SES adolescents. Unpublished manuscript, University of Rochester, 1963.

Champion, R. A.   Studies of experimentally induced disturbance. *Australian Journal of Psychology,* 1950, *2,* 90–99.

Chance, J. E.   Internal control of reinforcements and the school learning process. Paper presented at the biennial meeting of the Society for Research in Child Development, Minneapolis, March 1965.

Christie, R., & Geis, F. L.   *Studies in Machiavellianism.* New York: Academic Press, 1970.

Clifford, M. M., & Cleary, T. A.   The relationship between children's academic performance and achievement accountability. *Child Development,* 1972, *43,* 647–655.

Coleman, J. S., Campbell, E. Q., Hobson, C. J., McPartland, J., Mood, A. M., Weinfeld, F. D., & York, R. L. *Equality of educational opportunity.* Superintendent of Documents Catalog No. FS 5.238: 38001, U.S. Government Printing Office, Washington, D. C., 1966.

Collins, B. E.   Four separate components of the Rotter I-E Scale: Belief in a difficult world, a just world, a predictable world and a politically responsive world. *Journal of Personality and Social Psychology,* 1974, *29,* 381–391.

Cone J. D. Locus of control and social desirability. *Journal of Consulting and Clinical Psychology,* 1971, *36,* 499.

Cooper, J. Personal responsibility and dissonance: The role of foreseen consequences. *Journal of Personality and Social Psychology,* 1971, *18,* 354–363.

Corah, N. L., & Boffa, J. Perceived control, self-observation, and response to aversive stimulation. *Journal of Personality and Social Psychology,* 1970, 16, 1–4.

Crandall, V. C., Katkovsky, W., & Crandall, V. J. Children's beliefs in their own control of reinforcement in intellectual-academic situations. *Child Development,* 1965, *36,* 91–109.

Crandall, V. J., Katkovsky, W., & Preston, A. Motivational and ability determinants of young children's intellectual achievement behaviors. *Child Development,* 1962, *33,* 643–661.

Cromwell, R. L., Rosenthal, D., Shakow, D., & Zahn, T. P. Reaction time, locus of control, choice behavior, and descriptions of parental behavior in schizophrenic and normal subjects. *Journal of Personality,* 1961, 29, 363–379.

Crowne, D. P., & Liverant, S. Conformity under varying conditions of personal commitment. *Journal of Abnormal and Social Psychology,* 1963, *66,* 547–555.

D'Amato, M. E., & Gumenik, W. E. Some effects of immediate versus randomly delayed shock on an instrumental response and cognitive processes. *Journal of Abnormal and Social Psychology,* 1960, *60,* 64–67.

Davis, D. E. Internal-external control and defensiveness. Unpublished doctoral dissertation, Kansas State University, 1970.

Davis, W. L. Parental antecedents of children's locus of control. Unpublished doctoral dissertation, Kansas State University, 1969.

Davis, W. L., & Davis, D. E. Internal-external control and attribution of responsibility for success and failure. *Journal of Personality,* 1972, *35,* 547–561.

Davis, W. L., & Phares, E. J. Internal-external control as a determinant of information-seeking in a social influence situation. *Journal of Personality,* 1967, *35,* 547–561.

Davis, W. L., & Phares, E. J. Parental antecedents of internal-external control of reinforcement. *Psychological Reports,* 1969, *24,* 427–436.

Davol, S. H., & Reimanis, G. The role of anomie as a psychological concept. *Journal of Individual Psychology,* 1959, *15,* 215–225.

Dean, D. G. Alienation: Its meaning and measurement. *American Sociological Review,* 1961, *26,* 753–758.

deCharms, R. *Personal causation.* New York: Academic Press, 1968.

deCharms, R. Personal causation training in the schools. *Journal of Applied Social Psychology,* 1972, *2,* 95–113.

deCharms, R., Carpenter, V., & Kuperman, A. The "origin-pawn" variable in person perception. *Sociometry,* 1965, 28, 241-258.

Dies, R. R. Development of a projective measure of perceived locus of control. *Journal of Projective Techniques and Personality Assessment,* 1968, *32,* 487-490.

Dion, K. L., & Dion, K. K. Correlates of romantic love. *Journal of Consulting and Clinical Psychology,* 1973, *41,* 51-56.

Dissinger, J. K. Locus of control in achievement: Measurement and empirical assessment. Unpublished doctoral dissertation, Purdue University, 1968.

Doctor, R. M. Locus of control of reinforcement and responsiveness to social influence. *Journal of Personality,* 1971, *39,* 542-551.

Dua, P. S. Comparison of the effects of behaviorally oriented action and psychotherapy reeducation on introversion-extraversion, emotionality, and internal-external control. *Journal of Counseling Psychology,* 1970, *17,* 567-572.

DuCette, J., & Wolk, S. Locus of control and extreme behavior. *Journal of Consulting and Clinical Psychology,* 1972, *39,* 253-258.

DuCette, J., & Wolk, S. Cognitive and motivational correlates of generalized expectancies for control. *Journal of Personality and Social Psychology,* 1973, *26,* 420-426.

DuCette, J., Wolk, S., & Friedman, S. Locus of control and creativity in black and white children. *Journal of Social Psychology,* 1972, *88,* 297-298.

DuCette, J., Wolk, S., & Soucar, E. Atypical patterns in locus of control and nonadaptive behavior. *Journal of Personality,* 1972, *40,* 287-297.

Duke, M. P., & Mullens, M. C. Preferred interpersonal distance as a function of locus of control orientation in chronic schizophrenics, nonschizophrenic patients, and normals. *Journal of Consulting and Clinical Psychology,* 1973, *41,* 230-234.

Efran, J. Some personality determinants of memory for success and failure. Unpublished doctoral dissertation, Ohio State University, 1963.

Eisenman, R. Experience in experiments and change in internal-external control scores. *Journal of Consulting and Clinical Psychology,* 1972, *39,* 434-435.

Eisenman, R., & Platt, J. J. Birth order and sex differences in academic achievement and internal-external control. *Journal of General Psychology,* 1968, *78,* 270-285.

Epstein, R., & Komorita, S. S. Self-esteem, success-failure, and locus of control in Negro children. *Development Psychology,* 1971, *4,* 2-8.

Evans, D. A., & Alexander, S. Some psychological correlates of civil rights activity. *Psychological Reports,* 1970, *26,* 899-906.

Fazio, A. F., & Hendricks, D. E. Effects of chance versus skill instructional set and partial reinforcement on resistance to extinction. *Proceedings, 78th Annual Convention of the American Psychological Association.* Washington, D.C., 1970.

Feather, N. T. Valence of outcome and expectation of success in relation to task difficulty and perceived locus of control. *Journal of Personality and Social Psychology*, 1967, *7*, 372–386. (a)

Feather, N. T.   Some personality correlates of external control. *Australian Journal of Psychology*, 1967, *19*, 253–260. (b)

Feather, N. T.   Change in confidence following success or failure as a predictor of subsequent performance. *Journal of Personality and Social Psychology*, 1968, *9*, 38–46.

Felton, G. S.   The experimenter expectancy effect examined as a function of task ambiguity and internal-external control. *Journal of Experimental Research in Personality*, 1971, *5*, 286–294.

Festinger, L.   *A theory of cognitive dissonance*. Stanford, Calif.: Stanford University Press, 1957.

Fitch, G.   Effects of self-esteem, perceived performance, and choice on causal attributions. *Journal of Personality and Social Psychology*, 1970, *16*, 311–315.

Fontana, A. F., Klein, E. B., Lewis, E., & Levine, L.   Presentation of self in mental illness. *Journal of Consulting and Clinical Psychology*, 1968, *32*, 110–119.

Foulds, M. L.   Changes in locus of internal-external control: A growth experience. *Comparative Group Studies*, 1971, *2*, 293–300.

Franklin, R. D.   Youth's expectancies about internal versus external control of reinforcement related to *N* variables. Unpublished doctoral dissertation, Purdue University, 1963.

Frieze, I., & Weiner, B.   Cue utilization and attributional judgments for success and failure. *Journal of Personality*, 1971, *39*, 591–605.

Garrett, A. M., & Willoughby, R. H.   Personal orientation and reactions to success and failure in urban black children. *Developmental Psychology*, 1972, *7*, 92.

Geer, J. H., Davison, G. C., & Gatchel, R. I.   Reduction of stress in humans through nonviridical perceived control of aversive stimulation. *Journal of Personality and Social Psychology*, 1970, *16*, 731–738.

Geer, J. H., & Maisel, E.   Evaluating the effects of the prediction-control confound. *Journal of Personality and Social Psychology*, 1972, *23*, 314–319.

Geller, J. D., & Howard, G.   Some sociopolitical characteristics of student political activists. *Journal of Applied Social Psychology*, 1972, *2*, 114–137.

Gergen, K. J.   Social psychology as history. *Journal of Personality and Social Psychology*, 1973, *26*, 309–320.

Getter, H.   A personality determinant of verbal conditioning. *Journal of Personality*, 1966, *34*, 397–405.

Gillis, J. S., & Jessor, R.   Effects of brief psychotherapy on belief in internal control: An exploratory study. *Psychotherapy: Theory, Research and Practice*, 1970, *7*, 135–137.

Glass, D. C., & Singer, J. E.   *Urban stress: Experiments on noise and social stressors*. New York: Academic Press, 1972.

Gold, D.   Some correlation coefficients: Relationship among I-E scores and other personality variables. *Psychological Reports,* 1968, *22,* 983–984.

Goodstadt, B. E., & Hjelle, L. A.   Power to the powerless: Locus of control and the use of power. *Journal of Personality and Social Psychology,* 1973, *27,* 190–196.

Gootnick, A. T.   Locus of control and political participation of college students: A comparison of unidimensional and multidimensional approaches. Unpublished master's thesis, University of Arizona, 1973.

Gore, P. M.   Individual differences in the prediction of subject compliance to experimenter bias. Unpublished doctoral dissertation, Ohio State University, 1962.

Gore, P. M., & Rotter, J. B.   A personality correlate of social action. *Journal of Personality,* 1963, *31,* 58–64.

Gorman, B. S.   An observation of altered locus of control following political disappointment. *Psychological Reports,* 1968, *23,* 1094.

Goss, A., & Morosko, I. E.   Relations between a dimension of internal-external control and the MMPI with an alcoholic population. *Journal of Consulting and Clinical Psychology,* 1970, *34,* 189–192.

Gottesfeld, H., & Dozier, G.   Changes in feelings of powerlessness in a community action program. *Psychological Reports,* 1966, *19,* 978.

Gozali, J., & Bialer, I.   Children's locus of control scale: Independence from response set bias among retardates. *American Journal of Mental Deficiency,* 1968, *72,* 622–625.

Graves, T. D.   Time perspective and the deferred gratification pattern in a tri-ethnic community. University of Colorado, Tri-Ethnic Research Project, Research Report No. 5, 1961.

Gruen, G. E., & Ottinger, D. R.   Skill and chance orientations as determiners of problem-solving behavior in lower- and middle-class children. *Psychological Reports,* 1969, *24,* 207–214.

Gurin, G., & Gurin, P.   Expectancy theory in the study of poverty. *Journal of Social Issues,* 1970, *26,* 83–104.

Gurin, P., Gurin, G., Lao, R. C., & Beattie, M.   Internal-external control in the motivational dynamics of Negro youth. *Journal of Social Issues,* 1969, *25,* 29–53.

Haggard, E. S.   Experimental studies in affective processes: I. Some aspects of cognitive structure and active participation on certain autonomic reactions during and following experimentally induced stress. *Journal of Experimental Psychology,* 1943, *33,* 257–284.

Hammock, T., & Brehm, J. W.   The attractiveness of choice alternatives when freedom to choose is eliminated by a social agent. *Journal of Personality,* 1966, *34,* 546–554.

Hamsher, J. H., Geller, J. D., & Rotter, J. B.   Interpersonal trust, internal-external control, and the Warren Commission Report. *Journal of Personality and Social Psychology,* 1968, *9,* 210–215.

Harrison, F. I.   Relationship between home background, school success, and adolescent attitudes. *Merrill-Palmer Quarterly,* 1968, *14,* 331–344.

Harrow, M., & Ferrante, A.   Locus of control in psychiatric patients. *Journal of Consulting and Clinical Psychology,* 1969, *33,* 582–589.

Heider, F.   *The psychology of interpersonal relations.* New York: Wiley, 1958.

Helweg, G. C.   *The relationship between selected personality characteristics and perceptions of directive and non-directive psychotherapeutic approaches.* (Doctoral dissertation, University of Maryland) Ann Arbor, Mich.: University Microfilms, 1971. No. 71-26, 965.

Hersch, P. D., & Scheibe, K. E.   Reliability and validity of internal-external control as a personality dimension. *Journal of Consulting Psychology,* 1967, *31,* 609–613.

Hjelle, L. A.   Internal-external control as a determinant of academic achievement. *Psychological Reports,* 1970, *26,* 326.

Hjelle, L. A.   Social desirability as a variable in the Locus of Control Scale. *Psychological Reports,* 1971, *28,* 807–816.

Hjelle, L. A., & Clouser, R.   Susceptibility to attitude change as a function of internal-external control. *Psychological Record,* 1970, *20,* 305–310.

Hjelle, L. A., & Fink, H. C.   Ideological correlates of locus of control. Paper read at the Midwestern Psychological Association meetings, Cleveland, May 1972.

Hochreich, D. J.   Refined analysis of internal-external control and behavior in a laboratory situation. Unpublished doctoral dissertation, University of Connecticut, 1968.

Hochreich, D. J. Defensive externality and attribution of responsibility. Unpublished manuscript, University of Connecticut, 1973.

Holden, K. B., & Rotter, J. B.   A nonverbal measure of extinction in skill and chance situations. *Journal of Experimental Psychology,* 1962, *63,* 519–520.

Horney, K.   *Self-analysis.* New York: Norton, 1942.

Hountras, P. T., & Scharf, M. C.   Manifest anxiety and locus of control of low-achieving college males. *Journal of Psychology,* 1970, *74,* 95–100.

Houston, B. K.   Control over stress, locus of control, and response to stress. *Journal of Personality and Social Psychology,* 1972, *21,* 249–255.

Hsieh, T. T., Shybut, J., & Lotsof, E. J.   Internal versus external control and ethnic group membership. *Journal of Consulting and Clinical Psychology,* 1969, *33,* 122–124.

Jacobsen, R. A.   *Personality correlates of choice of therapist.* (Doctoral dissertation, Columbia University) Ann Arbor, Mich.: University Microfilms, 1971. No. 71-6193.

James, W. H.   Internal versus external control of reinforcement as a basic variable in learning theory. Unpublished doctoral dissertation, Ohio State University, 1957.

James, W. H., & Rotter, J. B. Partial and 100% reinforcement under chance and skill conditions. *Journal of Experimental Psychology,* 1958, *55,* 397–403.

James, W. H., Woodruff, A. B., & Werner, W.   Effect of internal and external control upon changes in smoking behavior. *Journal of Consulting Psychology,* 1965, *29,* 184–186.

Jessor, R., Graves, T. D., Hanson, R. C., & Jessor, S. L. *Society, personality, and deviant behavior.* New York: Holt, Rinehart & Winston, 1968.

Joe, V. C. Review of the internal-external control construct as a personality variable. *Psychological Reports,* 1971, *28,* 619–640.

Joe, V. C. Social desirability and the I-E Scale. *Psychological Reports,* 1972, *30,* 44–46.

Jolley, M. T., & Spielberger, C. D. The effects of locus of control and anxiety on verbal conditioning. *Journal of Personality,* 1973, *41,* 443–456.

Jones, S. C., & Shrauger, J. S. Locus of control and interpersonal evaluations. *Journal of Consulting and Clinical Psychology,* 1968, *32,* 664–668.

Julian, J. W., & Katz, S. B. Internal versus external control and the value of reinforcement. *Journal of Personality and Social Psychology,* 1968, *8,* 89–94.

Julian, J. W., Lichtman, C. M., & Ryckman, R. M. Internal-external control and need to control. *Journal of Social Psychology,* 1968, *76,* 43–48.

Karabenick, S. A. Valence of success and failure as a function of achievement motives and locus of control. *Journal of Personality and Social Psychology,* 1972, *21,* 101–110.

Katkovsky, W., Crandall, V. C., & Good, S. Parental antecedents of children's beliefs in internal-external control of reinforcements in intellectual achievement situations. *Child Development,* 1967, *38,* 765–776.

Katz, I. The socialization of academic motivation in minority group children. In D. Levine (Ed.), *Nebraska symposium on motivation.* Lincoln, Neb.: University of Nebraska Press, 1967. Pp. 133–191.

Keniston, K. *The uncommitted.* New York: Harcourt, Brace & World, 1965.

Kiehlbauch, J. B. Selected changes over time in internal-external control expectancies in a reformatory population. Unpublished doctoral dissertation, Kansas State University, 1967.

Kogan, N., & Wallach, M. A. *Risk taking: A study in cognition and personality.* New York: Holt, Rinehart & Winston, 1964.

Krovetz, M. L. Explaining success or failure as a function of one's locus of control. *Journal of Personality,* 1974, *42,* 175–189.

Lamont, J. Item mood-level as a determinant of I-E test response. *Journal of Clinical Psychology,* 1972, *28,* 190. (a)

Lamont, J. Depression, locus of control, and mood response set. *Journal of Clinical Psychology,* 1972, *28,* 342–345. (b)

Lao, R. C. Internal-external control and competent and innovative behavior among Negro college students. *Journal of Personality and Social Psychology,* 1970, *14,* 263–270.

Lasko, A. A. The development of expectancies under conditions of patterning and differential reinforcement. Unpublished doctoral dissertation, Ohio State University, 1952.

Lazarus, R. S. *Psychological stress and the coping process.* New York: McGraw-Hill, 1966.

Lazarus, R. S. Emotions and adaptation: Conceptual and empirical relations. In W. J. Arnold (Ed.), *Nebraska symposium on motivation.* Lincoln, Neb.: University of Nebraska Press, 1968. Pp. 175–270.

Lefcourt, H. M.   Risk-taking in Negro and white adults. *Journal of Personality and Social Psychology,* 1965, *2,* 765–770.

Lefcourt, H. M.   Internal versus external control of reinforcement: A review. *Psychological Bulletin,* 1966, *65,* 206–220. (a)

Lefcourt, H. M.   Belief in personal control: Research and implications. *Journal of Individual Psychology,* 1966, *22,* 185–195. (b)

Lefcourt, H. M.   Effects of cue explication upon persons maintaining external control expectancies. *Journal of Personality and Social Psychology,* 1967, *5,* 372–378.

Lefcourt, H. M.   Recent developments in the study of locus of control. In B. A. Maher (Ed.), *Progress in experimental personality research.* Vol. 6. New York: Academic Press, 1972. Pp. 1–39.

Lefcourt, H., & Ladwig, G. W.   The American Negro: A problem in expectancies. *Journal of Personality and Social Psychology,* 1965, *1,* 377–380.

Lefcourt, H. M., & Ladwig, G. W.   Alienation in Negro and white reformatory inmates. *Journal of Social Psychology,* 1966, *68,* 153–157.

Lefcourt, H. M., Lewis, L., & Silverman, I. W.   Internal versus external control of reinforcement and attention in a decision making task. *Journal of Personality,* 1968, *36,* 663–682.

Lefcourt, H. M., & Wine, J.   Internal versus external control of reinforcement and the deployment of attention in experimental situations. *Canadian Journal of Behavioral Science,* 1969, *1,* 167–181.

Lessing, E. E.   Racial differences in indices of ego functioning relevant to academic achievement. *Journal of Genetic Psychology,* 1969, *115,* 153–167.

Levens, H.   Organizational affiliation and powerlessness: A case study of the welfare poor. *Social Problems,* 1968, *16,* 18–32.

Levenson, H.   Reliability and validity of the I, P, and C Scales—A multidimensional view of locus of control. Paper read at the annual meeting of the American Psychological Association, Montreal, August 1973. (a)

Levenson, H.   Perceived parental antecedents of internal, powerful others, and chance locus of control orientations. *Developmental Psychology,* 1973, *9,* 268–274. (b)

Levenson, H.   Multidimensional locus of control in psychiatric patients. *Journal of Consulting and Clinical Psychology,* 1973, *41,* 397–404. (c)

Levy, L. H.   *Conceptions of personality: Theories and research.* New York: Random House, 1970.

Liberty, P. G., Jr., Burnstein, E., & Moulton, R. W.   Concern with mastery and occupational attraction. *Journal of Personality,* 1966, *34,* 105–117.

Lichtenstein, E., & Craine, W. H.   The importance of subjective evaluation of reinforcement in verbal conditioning. *Journal of Experimental Research in Personality,* 1969, *3,* 214–220.

Lichtenstein, E., & Keutzer, C. S.   Further normative and correlation data on the internal-external (I-E) control of reinforcement scale. *Psychological Reports,* 1967, *21,* 1014–1016.

Lichtman, C. M., & Julian, J. W.   Internal versus external control of reinforcements as a determinant of preferred strategy on a behavior task. Paper presented at the annual meeting of the Midwestern Psychological Association, St. Louis, May 1964.

Lipp, L., Kolstoe, R., James, W., & Randall, H.   Denial of disability and internal control of reinforcement: A study using a perceptual defense paradigm. *Journal of Consulting and Clinical Psychology,* 1968, *32,* 72–75.

Liverant, S.   The use of Rotter's social learning theory in developing a personality inventory. *Psychological Monographs,* 1958, *72,* (Whole No. 455).

Liverant, S., & Scodel, A.   Internal and external control as determinants of decision making under conditions of risk. *Psychological Reports,* 1960, *7,* 59–67.

London, P.   *The modes and morals of psychotherapy.* New York: Holt, Rinehart & Winston, 1964.

London, P.   *Behavior control.* New York: Harper & Row, 1969.

Lottman, T. J., & DeWolfe, A. S.   Internal versus external control in reactive and process schizophrenia. *Journal of Consulting and Clinical Psychology,* 1972, *39,* 344.

Lundy, J. R.   Some personality correlates of contraceptive use among unmarried female college students, *Journal of Psychology,* 1972, *80,* 9–14.

MacDonald, A. P., Jr.   Internal-external locus of control and the practice of birth control. *Psychological Reports,* 1970, *27,* 206.

MacDonald, A. P., Jr.   Internal-external locus of control: Parental antecedents. *Journal of Consulting and Clinical Psychology,* 1971, *37,* 141–147. (a)

MacDonald, A. P., Jr.   Birth order and personality. *Journal of Consulting and Clinical Psychology,* 1971, *36,* 171–176. (b)

MacDonald, A. P., Jr.   Internal-external locus of control: A promising rehabilitation variable. *Journal of Counseling Psychology,* 1971, *18,* 111–116. (c)

MacDonald, A. P., Jr.   More on the Protestant Ethic. *Journal of Consulting and Clinical Psychology,* 1972, *39,* 116–122.

MacDonald, A. P., Jr., and Hall, J.   Perception of disability by the non-disabled. *Journal of Consulting and Clinical Psychology,* 1969, *33,* 654–660.

MacDonald, A. P., Jr., & Hall, J.   Internal-external locus of control and perception of disability. *Journal of Consulting and Clinical Psychology,* 1971, *36,* 338–343.

Manganyi, N. C.   Psychotherapy and psycho-social relativity. *Journal of Behavioral Science,* 1972, *1,* 189–192.

Marks, E.   Sex, birth order, and beliefs about personal power. *Developmental Psychology,* 1973, *6,* 184.

Masters, J. C.   Treatment of "adolescent rebellion" by the reconstrual of stimuli. *Journal of Consulting and Clinical Psychology,* 1970, *35,* 213–216.

May, R.   *Power and innocence.* New York: Norton, 1972.

McArthur, L. A.   Luck is alive and well in New Haven. *Journal of Personality and Social Psychology,* 1970, *16,* 316–318.

McClelland, D. *The achieving society.* Princeton, N. J.: Van Nostrand, 1961.

McClelland, D., Atkinson, J. W., Clark, R. A., & Lowell, E. L. *The achievement motive.* New York: Appleton-Century-Crofts, 1953.

McClelland, D. C., Davis, W. N., Kalin, R., & Wanner, E. (Eds.) *The drinking man.* New York: Free Press, 1972.

McClelland, D. C., & Winter, D. G. *Motivating economic achievement.* New York: Free Press, 1969.

McFall, R. M. Unintentional communication: Expectancy effects as a function of subject and experimenter personalities, and subject's acceptance of interpersonal influence. Unpublished manuscript, University of Wisconsin, 1967.

McGhee, P. E., & Crandall, V. C. Beliefs in internal-external control of reinforcement and academic performance. *Child Development,* 1968, *39,* 91–102.

Mehrabian, A. Male and female scales of the tendency to achieve. *Educational and Psychological Measurement,* 1968, *28,* 493–502.

Mehrabian, A. Measures of achieving tendency. *Educational and Psychological Measurement,* 1969, *29,* 445–451.

Meier, D. L., & Bell, W. Anomie and differential access to the achievement of life goals. *American Sociological Review,* 1959, *24,* 189–202.

Merton, R. *Mass persuasion.* New York: Harper, 1946.

Messer, S. B. The relation of internal-external control to academic performance. *Child Development,* 1972, *43,* 1456–1462.

Midlarsky, E. Aiding under stress: The effects of competence, dependency, visibility, and fatalism. *Journal of Personality,* 1971, *39,* 132–149.

Midlarsky, E., & Midlarsky, M. Some determinants of aiding under experimentally induced stress. *Journal of Personality,* 1973, *41,* 305–327.

Miller, A. G., & Minton, H. L. Machiavellianism, internal-external control, and the violation of experimental instructions. *Psychological Record,* 1969, *19,* 369–380.

Miller, W. R., & Seligman, M. E. P. Depression and the perception of reinforcement. *Journal of Abnormal Psychology,* 1973, *82,* 62–73.

Minton, H. L. Power as a personality construct. In B. A. Maher (Ed.), *Progress in experimental personality research.* Vol. 4. New York: Academic Press, 1967. Pp. 229–267.

Mirels, H. L. Dimensions of internal versus external control. *Journal of Consulting and Clinical Psychology,* 1970, *34,* 226–228.

Mischel, W. Theory and research on the antecedents of self-imposed delay of reward. In B. A. Maher (Ed.), *Progress in experimental personality research.* Vol. 3. New York: Academic Press, 1966. Pp. 85–132.

Mischel, W. *Personality and assessment.* New York: Wiley, 1968.

Mischel, W. Continuity and change in personality. *American Psychologist,* 1969, *24,* 1012–1018.

Mischel, W., Zeiss, R., & Zeiss, A. Internal-external control and persistence: Validation and implications of the Stanford Preschool Internal-External Scale. *Journal of Personality and Social Psychology,* 1974, *29,* 265–278.

Moss, H. A. The influence of personality and situational cautiousness on conceptual behavior. *Journal of Abnormal and Social Psychology*, 1961, *63*, 629–635.

Mowrer, O. H., & Viek, P.   An experimental analogue of fear from a sense of helplessness. *Journal of Abnormal and Social Psychology*, 1948, *43*, 193–200.

Nelson, P. C., & Phares, E. J.   Anxiety, discrepancy between need value and expectancy, and internal-external control. *Psychological Reports*, 1971, *28*, 663–668.

Nettler, G.   A measure of alienation. *American Sociological Review*, 1957, *22*, 670–677.

Nowicki, S.   Factor structure of locus of control in children. Paper presented at the annual meeting of the American Psychological Association, Montreal, September 1973.

Nowicki, S., & Barnes, J.   Effects of a structured camp experience on locus of control orientation. *Journal of Genetic Psychology*, 1973, *122*, 247–252.

Nowicki, S., & Duke, M. P.   A locus of control scale for noncollege as well as college students. *Journal of Personality Assessment*, 1974, *38*, 136–137.

Nowicki, S., & Strickland, B. R.   A locus of control scale for children. *Journal of Consulting and Clinical Psychology*, 1973, *40*, 148–154.

Odell, M.   Personality correlates of independence and conformity. Unpublished master's thesis, Ohio State University, 1959.

Parsons, O. A., Schneider, J. M., & Hansen, A. S.   Internal-external locus of control and national stereotypes in Denmark and the United States. *Journal of Consulting and Clinical Psychology*, 1970, *35*, 30–37.

Pedhazur, L., & Wheeler, L.   Locus of perceived control and need achievement. *Perceptual and Motor Skills*, 1971, *33*, 1281–1282.

Penk, W. E.   Age changes and correlates of internal-external locus of control scale. *Psychological Reports*, 1969, *25*, 856.

Pervin, L. A.   The need to predict and control under conditions of threat. *Journal of Personality*, 1963, *31*, 570–587.

Phares, E. J.   Changes in expectancy in skill and chance situations. Unpublished doctoral dissertation, Ohio State University, 1955.

Phares, E. J.   Expectancy changes in skill and chance situations. *Journal of Abnormal and Social Psychology*, 1957, *54*, 339–342.

Phares, E. J.   Perceptual threshold decrements as a function of skill and chance expectancies. *Journal of Psychology*, 1962, *53*, 399–407.

Phares, E. J.   Delay as a variable in expectancy changes. *Journal of Psychology*, 1964, *57*, 391–402.

Phares, E. J.   Internal-external control as a determinant of amount of social influence exerted. *Journal of Personality and Social Psychology*, 1965, *2*, 642–647.

Phares, E. J.   The deviant personality. In H. Helson and W. Bevan (Eds.), *Contemporary approaches to psychology*. New York: Van Nostrand, 1967. Pp. 499–527.

Phares, E. J.   Differential utilization of information as a function of internal-external control. *Journal of Personality*, 1968, *36*, 649–662.

Phares, E. J.   Internal-external control and the reduction of reinforcement value after failure. *Journal of Consulting and Clinical Psychology,* 1971, *37,* 386–390.

Phares, E. J.   A social learning theory approach to psychopathology. In J. B. Rotter, J. Chance, & E. J. Phares (Eds.), *Applications of a social learning theory of personality.* New York: Holt, Rinehart & Winston, 1972. Pp. 436–469.

Phares, E. J.   Power, personality, and pathology. Unpublished manuscript, Kansas State University, 1973. (a)

Phares, E. J.   *Locus of control: A personality determinant of behavior.* Morristown, N. J.: General Learning Press, 1973. (b)

Phares, E. J., & Lamiell, J. T.   Relationship of internal-external control to defensive preferences. *Journal of Consulting and Clinical Psychology,* 1974, *42,* 872–878.

Phares, E. J., & Lamiell, J. T.   Internal-external control, interpersonal judgments of others in need, and attribution of responsibility. *Journal of Personality,* 1975, *43,* 23–38.

Phares, E. J., Ritchie, D. E., & Davis, W. L.   Internal-external control and reaction to threat. *Journal of Personality and Social Psychology,* 1968, *10,* 402–405.

Phares, E. J., & Rotter, J. B.   An effect of the situation on psychological testing. *Journal of Consulting Psychology,* 1956, *20,* 291–293.

Phares, E. J., & Wilson, K. G.   Internal-external control, interpersonal attraction, and empathy. *Psychological Reports,* 1971, *28,* 543–549.

Phares, E. J., & Wilson, K. G.   A note on attitudes and use of birth control techniques by three samples of females. Unpublished manuscript, Kansas State University, 1972. (a)

Phares, E. J., & Wilson, K. G.   Responsibility attribution: Role of outcome severity, situational ambiguity, and internal-external control. *Journal of Personality,* 1972, *40,* 392–406. (b)

Phares, E. J., Wilson, K. G., & Klyver, N. W.   Internal-external control and the attribution of blame under neutral and distractive conditions. *Journal of Personality and Social Psychology,* 1971, *18,* 285–288.

Pines, H. A.   An attributional analysis of locus of control orientation and source of informational dependence. *Journal of Personality and Social Psychology,* 1973, *26,* 262–272.

Pines, H. A., & Julian, J. W.   Effects of task and social demands on locus of control differences in information processing. *Journal of Personality,* 1972, *40,* 407–416.

Platt, J. J., & Eisenman, R.   Internal-external control of reinforcement, time perspective, adjustment, and anxiety. *Journal of General Psychology,* 1968, *79,* 121–128.

Platt, J. J., Pomeranz, D., Eisenman, R., & DeLisser, O.   Importance of considering sex differences in relationships between locus of control and other personality variables. *Proceedings, 78th Annual Convention of the American Psychological Association,* 1970, *5,* 463–464.

Powell, A., & Centa, D.   Adult locus of control and mental ability. *Psychological Reports,* 1972, *30,* 829–830.

Powell, A., & Vega, M.   Correlates of adult locus of control. *Psychological Reports*, 1972, *30*, 455–460.

Rank, O.   *Will therapy and truth and reality.* New York: Knopf, 1945.

Ransford, H. E.   Isolation, powerlessness and violence: A study of attitudes and participation in the Watts riot. *American Journal of Sociology*, 1968, *73*, 581–591.

Ray, W. J., & Katahn, M.   Relation of anxiety to locus of control. *Psychological Reports*, 1968, *23*, 1196.

Reid, D. W., & Ware, E. E.   Multidimensionality of internal versus external control: Addition of a third dimension and nondistinction of self versus others. Unpublished manuscript, University of Waterloo, 1973.

Reimanis, G.   Effects of experimental IE modification techniques and home environmental variables on IE. Paper presented at the annual meeting of the American Psychological Association, Washington, D.C., September 1971.

Reimanis, G., & Schaefer, M.   Effects of counseling and achievement motivation training on locus of reinforcement control. Paper presented at the annual meeting of the Eastern Psychological Association, Atlantic City, April 1970.

Richter, C. P.,   On the phenomenon of sudden death in animals and man. *Psychosomatic Medicine*, 1957, *19*, 191–198.

Riesman, D.   *Individualism reconsidered.* Glencoe, Ill.: Free Press, 1954.

Ritchie, E., & Phares, E. J.   Attitude change as a function of internal-external control and communicator status. *Journal of Personality*, 1969, *37*, 429–443.

Rogers, C. R., & Skinner, B. F.   Some issues concerning the control of human behavior: A symposium. *Science*, 1956, *124*, 1057–1066.

Rosen, B., & Salling, R.   Political participation as a function of internal-external locus of control. *Psychological Reports*, 1971, *29*, 880–882.

Rothschild, B. A., & Horowitz, I. A.   Effect of instructions and internal-external control of reinforcement on a conditioned finger-withdrawal response. *Psychological Reports*, 1970, *26*, 395–400.

Rotter, J. B.   *Social learning and clinical psychology.* Englewood Cliffs, N. J.: Prentice-Hall, 1954.

Rotter, J. B.   The role of psychological situation in determining the direction of human behavior. In M. R. Jones (Ed.), *Nebraska symposium on motivation.* Lincoln, Neb.: University of Nebraska Press, 1955, Pp. 245–269.

Rotter, J. B.   Some implications of a social learning theory for the prediction of goal directed behavior from testing procedures. *Psychological Review*, 1960, *67*, 301–316.

Rotter, J. B.   Generalized expectancies for internal versus external control of reinforcement. *Psychological Monographs*, 1966, *80*, (1, Whole No. 609).

Rotter, J. B.   Beliefs, attitudes, and behavior: A social learning analysis. In R. Jessor & S. Feshbach (Eds.), *Cognition, personality, and clinical psychology.* San Francisco: Jossey-Bass, 1967. Pp. 112–140. (a)

Rotter, J. B. A new scale for the measurement of interpersonal trust. *Journal of Personality,* 1967, *35,* 651–655. (b)

Rotter, J. B. External control and internal control. *Psychology Today,* 1971, *5,* 37–42, 58–59. (a)

Rotter, J. B. Generalized expectancies for interpersonal trust. *American Psychologist,* 1971, 26: 443–452. (b)

Rotter, J. B., Chance, J., & Phares, E. J. (Eds.) *Applications of a social learning theory of personality.* New York: Holt, Rinehart & Winston, 1972.

Rotter, J. B., Liverant, S., & Crowne, D. P. The growth and extinction of expectancies in chance controlled and skilled tasks. *Journal of Psychology,* 1961, *52,* 161–177.

Rotter, J. B., & Mulry, R. C. Internal versus external control of reinforcement and decision time. *Journal of Personality and Social Psychology,* 1965, *2,* 598–604.

Rotter, J. B., Seeman, M., & Liverant, S. Internal versus external control of reinforcement: A major variable in behavior theory. In N. F. Washburne (Ed.), *Decisions, values, and groups.* Vol. 2. New York: Pergamon Press, 1962. Pp. 473–516.

Ryckman, R. M., Gold, J. A., & Rodda, W. C. Confidence rating shifts and performance as a function of locus of control, self-esteem, and initial task experience. *Journal of Personality and Social Psychology,* 1971, *18,* 305–310.

Ryckman, R. M., Martens, J. L., Rodda, W. C., & Sherman, M. F. Locus of control and attitudes toward Women's Liberation in a college population. *Journal of Social Psychology,* 1972, *87,* 157–158.

Ryckman, R. M., & Rodda, W. C. Locus of control and initial task experience as determinants of confidence changes in a chance situation. *Journal of Personality and Social Psychology,* 1971, *18,* 116–119.

Ryckman, R. M., Rodda, W. C., & Sherman, M. F. Locus of control and expertise relevance as determinants of changes in opinion about student activism. *Journal of Social Psychology,* 1972, *88,* 107–114.

Ryckman, R. M., Rodda, W. C., & Stone, W. F. Performance time as a function of sex, locus of control, and task requirements. *Journal of Social Psychology,* 1971, *85,* 299–305.

Ryckman, R. M., Stone, W. F., & Elam, R. R. Emotional arousal as a function of perceived locus of control and task requirements. *Journal of Social Psychology,* 1971, *83,* 185–191.

Sanger, S. P., & Alker, H. A. Dimensions of internal-external locus of control and the Women's Liberation Movement. *Journal of Social Issues,* 1972, *28,* 115–129.

Schachter, S. The interaction of cognitive and physiological determinants of emotional state. In C. D. Spielberger (Ed.), *Anxiety and behavior.* New York: Academic Press, 1966, Pp. 193–224.

Schneider, J. M. Skill versus chance activity preferences and locus of control. *Journal of Consulting and Clinical Psychology,* 1968, *32,* 333–337.

Schneider, J. M.   College students' belief in personal control, 1966–1970. *Journal of Individual Psychology,* 1971, *27,* 188.

Schneider, J. M.   Relationship between locus of control and activity preferences: Effects of masculinity, activity, and skill. *Journal of Consulting and Clinical Psychology,* 1972, *38,* 225–230.

Schneider, J. M., & Parsons, O. A.   Categories on the Locus of Control Scale and cross-cultural comparisons in Denmark and the United States. *Journal of Cross-Cultural Psychology,* 1970, *1,* 131–138.

Schroder, H. M., & Rotter, J. B.   Rigidity as learned behavior. *Journal of Experimental Psychology,* 1952, *44,* 141–150.

Schwarz, J. C.   Influences upon expectancy during delay. *Journal of Experimental Research in Personality,* 1966, *1,* 211–220.

Scott, J. D., & Phelan, J. G.   Expectancies of unemployable males regarding source of control of reinforcement. *Psychological Reports,* 1969, *25,* 911–913.

Seeman, M.   On the meaning of alienation. *American Sociological Review,* 1959, *24,* 783–791.

Seeman, M.   Alienation and social learning in a reformatory. *American Journal of Sociology,* 1963, *69,* 270–284.

Seeman, M.   Alienation, membership and political knowledge: A comparative study. *Public Opinion Quarterly,* 1966, *30,* 359–367.

Seeman, M.   Powerlessness and knowledge: A comparative study of alienation and learning. *Sociometry,* 1967, *30,* 105–123.

Seeman, M., & Evans, J. W.   Alienation and learning in a hospital setting. *American Sociological Review,* 1962, *27,* 772–783.

Seligman, M. E. P., Maier, S. F., & Solomon, R. L.   Unpredictable and uncontrollable aversive events. In F. R. Brush (Ed.), *Aversive conditioning and learning.* New York: Academic Press, 1971. Pp. 347–400.

Shaw, R. L., & Uhl, N. P. Control of reinforcement and academic achievement. *Journal of Educational Research,* 1971, *64,* 226–228.

Sherman, S. J.   Internal-external control and its relationship to attitude change under different social influence techniques. *Journal of Personality and Social Psychology,* 1973, *23,* 23–29.

Shore, R. E.   Parental determinants of boys' internal-external control. Unpublished doctoral dissertation, Syracuse University, 1967.

Shumate, W. L., Jr.   The relation of authoritarianism and locus of control to ego development. *Dissertation Abstracts International,* 1970, 30 (7-B), 3395.

Shybut, J.   Time perspective, internal versus external control, and severity of psychological disturbance. *Journal of Clinical Psychology,* 1968, *24,* 312–315.

Silvern, L. E., & Nakamura, C. Y.   Powerlessness, social-political action, social-political views: Their interrelation among college students. *Journal of Social Issues,* 1971, *27,* 137–157.

Skinner, B. F.   *Beyond freedom and dignity.* New York: Knopf, 1971.

Sky, A. W.   An apparatus for a frustration task. *Australian Journal of Psychology,* 1950, *2,* 116–120.

Smith, R. E.   Changes in locus of control as a function of life crisis resolution. *Journal of Abnormal Psychology,* 1970, *75,* 329–332.

Snyder, C. R., & Larson, G. R. A further look at student acceptance of general personality interpretations. *Journal of Consulting and Clinical Psychology,* 1972, *38,* 384–388.

Solar, D., & Bruehl, D. Machiavellianism and locus of control: Two conceptions of interpersonal power. *Psychological Reports,* 1971, *29,* 1079–1082.

Solomon, D., Houlihan, K. A., Busse, T. V., & Parelius, R. J. Parent behavior and child academic achievement, achievement striving and related personality characteristics. *Genetic Psychology Monographs,* 1971, *83,* 173–273.

Solomon, D., Houlihan, R. D., & Parelius, R. J. Intellectual achievement responsibility in Negro and white children. *Psychological Reports,* 1969, *24,* 479–483.

Srole, L. Social integration and certain corollaries: An exploratory study. *American Sociological Review,* 1956, *21,* 709–716.

Stabler, J., & Johnson, E. E. Instrumental performance as a function of reinforcement schedule, luck versus skill instructions and sex of child. *Journal of Experimental Child Psychology,* 1970, *9,* 330–335.

Staub, E., Tursky, B., & Schwartz, G. E. Self-control and predictability: Their effects on reactions to aversive stimulation. *Journal of Personality and Social Psychology,* 1971, *18,* 157–162.

Stephens, M. W. Dimensions of locus of control: Impact of early educational experiences. *Proceedings, 80th Annual Convention, American Psychological Association,* 1972, *7,* (Part 1), 137–138.

Stephens, M. W., & Delys, P. A locus of control measure for preschool children. *Developmental Psychology,* 1973, *9,* 55–65.

Straits, B. C., & Sechrest, L. Further support of some findings about characteristics of smokers and non-smokers. *Journal of Consulting Psychology,* 1963, *27,* 282.

Strassberg, D. S. Relationships among locus of control, anxiety, and valued-goal expectations. *Journal of Consulting and Clinical Psychology,* 1973, *41,* 319.

Strickland, B. R. The prediction of social action from a dimension of internal-external control. *Journal of Social Psychology,* 1965, *66,* 353–358.

Strickland, B. R. Individual differences in verbal conditioning, extinction, and awareness. *Journal of Personality,* 1970, *38,* 364–378.

Strickland, B. R. Delay of gratification as a function of race of the experimenter. *Journal of Personality and Social Psychology,* 1972, *22,* 108–112.

Strickland, B. R. Delay of gratification and internal locus of control in children. *Journal of Consulting and Clinical Psychology,* 1973, *40,* 338.

Strickland, B. R., Lewicki, R. I., & Katz, A. M. Temporal orientations and perceived control as determinants of risk-taking. *Journal of Experimental Social Psychology,* 1966, *2,* 143–151.

Sullivan, H. S. *Conceptions of modern psychiatry.* Washington, D.C.: William Alanson White Foundation, 1947.

Thibaut, J., & Riecken, H. Some determinants and consequences of the perception of social causality. *Journal of Personality,* 1955, *24,* 113–133.

Thomas, L. E. The I-E Scale, ideological bias, and political participation. *Journal of Personality,* 1970, *38,* 273–286.

Throop, W. F., & MacDonald, A. P.   Internal-external locus of control: A bibliography. *Psychological Reports,* 1971, *28,* 175–190.

Tolor, A.   An evaluation of the Maryland Parent Attitude Survey. *Journal of Psychology,* 1967, *67,* 69–74.

Tolor, A.   Are the alienated more suggestible? *Journal of Clinical Psychology,* 1971, *27,* 441–442.

Tolor, A., & Jalowiec, J. E.   Body boundary, parental attitudes, and internal-external expectancy. *Journal of Consulting and Clinical Psychology,* 1968, *32,* 206–209.

Tolor, A., & Reznikoff, M.   Relation between insight, repression-sensitization, internal-external control and death anxiety. *Journal of Abnormal Psychology,* 1967, *72,* 426–430.

Tseng, M. S.   Locus of control as a determinant of job proficiency, employability, and training satisfaction of vocational rehabilitation clients. *Journal of Counseling Psychology,* 1970, *17,* 487–491.

Tyre, T. E., & Maisto, S. A.   The modification of external control perception in the pre-adolescent. Paper read at the annual meeting of the American Psychological Association, New Orleans, August 1974.

Ude, L. K. & Vogler, R. E.   Internal versus external control of reinforcement and awareness in a conditioning task. *Journal of Psychology,* 1969, *73,* 63–67.

Veblen, T.   *The theory of the leisure class.* New York: Macmillan, 1899 (Republished: Modern Library, 1934).

Veroff, J.   Development and validation of a projective measure of power motivation. *Journal of Abnormal and Social Psychology,* 1957, *54,* 1–8.

Veroff, J.   A scoring manual for the power motive. In J. Atkinson (Ed.), *Motives in fantasy, action, and society.* Princeton, N. J.: Van Nostrand, 1958. Pp. 219–233.

Veroff, J., & Veroff, J. B.   Reconsideration of a measure of power motivation. *Psychological Bulletin,* 1972, *78,* 279–291.

Walls, R. T., & Cox, J.   Expectancy of reinforcement in chance and skill tasks under motor handicap. *Journal of Clinical Psychology,* 1971, *27,* 436–438.

Walls, R. T., & Miller, J. J.   Delay of gratification in welfare and rehabilitation clients. *Journal of Counseling Psychology,* 1970, *4,* 383–384.

Walls, R. T., & Smith, T. S.   Development of preference for delayed reinforcement in disadvantaged children. *Journal of Educational Psychology,* 1970, *61,* 118–123.

Warehime, R. G.   Generalized expectancy for locus of control and academic performance. *Psychological Reports,* 1972, *30,* 314.

Warehime, R. G., and Foulds, M. F.   Perceived locus of control and personal adjustment. *Journal of Consulting and Clinical Psychology,* 1971, *37,* 250–252.

Watson, D.   Relationship between locus of control and anxiety. *Journal of Personality and Social Psychology,* 1967, *6,* 91–92.

Watson, D., & Baumal, E.   Effects of locus of control and expectation of future control upon present performance. *Journal of Personality and Social Psychology,* 1967, *6,* 212–215.

Weiner, B. *Theories of motivation.* Chicago: Markham, 1972.

Weiner, B., Frieze, I., Kukla, A., Reed, L., Rest, S., & Rosenbaum, R. *Perceiving the causes of success and failure.* Morristown, N. J.: General Learning Press, 1971.

Weiner, B., Heckhausen, H., Meyer, W. U., & Cook, R. E. Causal ascriptions and achievement motivation: A conceptual analysis of effort and reanalysis of locus of control. *Journal of Personality and Social Psychology,* 1972, *21,* 239–248.

Weitz, W. A. Experiencing the role of hospitalized psychiatric patient: A professional's view from the other side. *Professional Psychology,* 1972, *3,* 151–154.

Wesman, A. G. Intelligent testing. *American Psychologist,* 1968, *23,* 267–274.

White, R. W. Motivation reconsidered: The concept of competence. *Psychological Review,* 1959, *66,* 297–333.

Williams, C. B., & Nickels, J. B. Internal-external control dimension as related to accident and suicide proneness. *Journal of Consulting and Clinical Psychology,* 1969, *33,* 485–494.

Williams, C. B., & Vantress, F. E. Relation between internal-external control and aggression. *Journal of Psychology,* 1969, *71,* 59–61.

Williams, J. G., & Stack, J. J. Internal-external control as a situational variable in determining information seeking by Negro students. *Journal of Consulting and Clinical Psychology,* 1972, *39,* 187–193.

Wilson, J., Duke, M. P., & Nowicki, A. A pre-school and primary test of locus of control orientation. Paper presented at the annual meeting of the Southeastern Psychological Association, Atlanta, March 1972.

Wilson, K. G. Therapist choice as related to selected personality characteristics in a college sample. Unpublished doctoral dissertation, Kansas State University, 1973.

Winter, D. G. The need for power in college men: Action correlates and relationship to drinking. In D. McClelland, W. Davis, R. Kalin, and E. Wann (Eds.), *The drinking man.* New York: Free Press, 1972. Pp. 99–119.

Winter, D. G. *The power motive.* New York: Free Press, 1973.

Wolk, S., & DuCette, J. Locus of control and achievement motivation: Theoretical overlap and methodological divergence. *Psychological Reports,* 1971, *29,* 755–758.

Wolk, S., & DuCette, J. The moderating effect of locus of control in relation to achievement motivation variables. *Journal of Personality,* 1973, *41,* 59–70.

Wolk, S., & DuCette, J. Intentional performance and incidental learning as a function of personality and task dimensions. *Journal of Personality and Social Psychology,* 1974, *29,* 90–101.

Worell, L. The effect of goal value upon expectancy. *Journal of Abnormal and Social Psychology,* 1956, *53,* 48–53.

Zytkoskee, A., Strickland, B. R., & Watson, J. Delay of gratification and internal versus external control among adolescents of low socioeconomic status. *Developmental Psychology,* 1971, *4*, 93–98.

Zytkowski, D. G.   Internal-external control of reinforcement and the Strong Vocational Interest Blank. *Journal of Counseling Psychology,* 1967, *14*, 177–179.

Index